NORTH KOREA: 2005 AND BEYOND

Edited by
Philip W. Yun
and
Gi-Wook Shin

THE WALTER H. SHORENSTEIN
ASIA-PACIFIC RESEARCH CENTER

THE WALTER H. SHORENSTEIN ASIA-PACIFIC RESEARCH CENTER (Shorenstein APARC) is a unique Stanford University institution focused on the interdisciplinary study of contemporary Asia. Shorenstein APARC's mission is to produce and publish outstanding interdisciplinary, Asia-Pacific–focused research; educate students, scholars, and corporate and governmental affiliates; promote constructive interaction to influence U.S. policy toward the Asia-Pacific; and guide Asian nations on key issues of societal transition, development, U.S.-Asia relations, and regional cooperation.

The Walter H. Shorenstein Asia-Pacific Research Center
Freeman Spogli Institute for International Studies
Stanford University
Encina Hall
Stanford, CA 94305-6055
tel. 650-723-9741
fax. 650-723-6530
http://APARC.stanford.edu

North Korea: 2005 and Beyond may be ordered from:
Brookings Institution Press
Department 029, Washington, DC 20042-0029, USA
tel. 1-800-275-1447 or 202-797-6258
fax. 202-797-2960 Attn: Order Dept.
http://bookstore.brookings.edu

First printing, 2006.
10-digit ISBN 1-931368-08-2
13-digit ISBN 978-1-931368-08-7

NORTH KOREA: 2005 AND BEYOND

THE WALTER H. SHORENSTEIN
ASIA-PACIFIC RESEARCH CENTER

CONTENTS

ACKNOWLEDGMENTS

We are grateful for the support of Walter H. Shorenstein and Byeong Yop Park of Pantech Group, who generously sponsored the conference at which these papers were originally presented. Their continued support of Center activities, including the Korean Studies Program, is greatly appreciated.

We also acknowledge the contributions from other participants who made the conference stimulating and lively: Michael Armacost, Young Koo Cha, John Feffer, Eun Hye Kim, So Young Kwon, Stuart Nam, Daniel Okimoto, Sun Song Park, Won Soon Park, Barbara Slavin, Daniel Sneider, Curt Weldon, Hee Ryong Won, and Young-Kwan Yoon.

Finally we thank the staff of Shorenstein APARC, especially Neeley Main, Jasmin Ha, and Debbie Warren, who made the conference run so smoothly. Victoria Tomkinson, with the help of copy editor Richard Gunde, edited and typeset the papers into this final volume.

Introduction

Philip W. Yun
Gi-Wook Shin

History may show the year 2005 as a noteworthy one in East Asia. This is not because 2005 marks the 60th anniversary of the end of World War II, or because it is the first year of the traditional Chinese 60-year calendar cycle, symbolizing a new beginning. Instead, 2005 could be deemed significant because it may be a critical inflection point—the year the United States was able to establish a foundation to resolve, peacefully and once and for all, the intractable problem of North Korea's nuclear weapons activity. It could also be the year that North Korea (DPRK) committed itself to becoming a nuclear weapons state without compromise. Either way, 2005 may be remembered as a year with crucial implications for the Korean peninsula and beyond.

With the distraction of a contentious U.S. presidential election no longer a factor in decision making, there was an expectation that a second Bush administration would have no choice but to address the shortcomings of its first-term North Korea policy—a policy that has failed to prevent the following: an increased amount of fissile material in the possession of North Korea's Kim Jong-Il regime, the North's expulsion of international inspectors and removal of monitoring equipment from nuclear-related sites, the restarting and operation of the Yongbyon 5MW(e) research reactor, and Pyongyang's withdrawal from the Nuclear Nonproliferation Treaty (NPT). Indeed, as a new team at the U.S. Department of State— led by Secretary Condoleezza Rice and Assistant Secretary Christopher Hill—came on board, it was clear that reinvigorated diplomatic efforts to get the North Koreans back to the six-party talks were being shaped by a subtle shift in approach.

At the time of this writing, this new approach has produced measured progress. Following a 13-month hiatus, the North entered into another round of talks that lasted several weeks and at the end of that round accepted a statement of general principles to guide future discussions. In this statement, the DPRK again committed to abandoning all nuclear weapons and existing nuclear programs and to do so at an early, though undefined, date. Some greeted this outcome as a breakthrough, but many less sanguine observers argued that true success would depend on implementation. While the statement of general principles indicates the negotiating parties share assumptions as to what the pieces of an eventual implementation agreement would likely be (e.g., the removal of nuclear weapons from North Korea, security assurances, political normalization and economic assistance, among other things), it does little else. It fails to coherently link any of these stated elements to each other, and it fails to provide the operational framework needed to turn the general principles into a final deal. This will be the task of subsequent talks. It is a huge undertaking and will likely take years.

Notwithstanding questions about the sequencing of obligations and their definition and scope set forth in the general principles, more fundamental uncertainties appear to exist. For example, it is clear that the United States on one hand and South Korea and China on the other have divergent positions over the very nature of the North Korean nuclear problem. The United States sees the nuclear issue as a regional and global challenge (prevention of nuclear proliferation in the region is the priority, underpinned by a linkage of the North's nuclear program to international terrorism), while China and South Korea are more narrowly concerned with instability on the Korean peninsula. This gap makes it difficult to exact a price for North Korean intransigence. Another uncertainty relates to differing views of North Korea within the Bush administration—critics assert that the policy differences plaguing the formulation and execution of North Korea policy during President Bush's first term still remain, making long-term coordination with the other parties problematic at best.

Nonetheless, the United States' renewed focus on North Korea comes none too soon and is most welcome. In addition to the setbacks suffered by the United States during the past two years, concern is mounting about future North Korean activities. Justifiably, the United States continues to be wary of the North's Highly Enriched Uranium (HEU) program, though many in Asia question both the status of the program and the quality of U.S. intelligence analysis. More troublesome is the fact that the Yongbyon 5 MW(E) nuclear facility is currently producing weapons-grade plutonium at a rate of one weapon's worth of material per year. There is also the possibility, though farther into the future, that the North may seek to reconstruct its 50 MW(E) reactor at Yongbyon and its 200 MW(E) reactor at Taechon, which would significantly increase its plutonium production capability.

While the risk of a North Korean attack on South Korea, Japan, or the United States is remote, the greater U.S. worry in this post-9/11 world is that third parties come into possession of fissile material, which could eventually find its way to the United States in the form of a terrorist nuclear device. In addition, many observers of Korean affairs are concerned with obvious strains in the U.S.-ROK alliance.

They attribute the situation to divergent perceptions and policy toward the North. Clearly, the need to deal with North Korean nukes is an urgent one.

The Stanford Conference

Understanding that 2005 had the potential to be a watershed, the Walter H. Shorenstein Asia-Pacific Research Center (Shorenstein APARC) at Stanford's Freeman Spogli Institute for International Studies (FSI) hosted a conference on North Korea on May 26 and 27, 2005. The purpose of the conference was to take a snapshot of what is happening in North Korea now, to learn how Americans and South Koreans view these current developments, and to offer policy suggestions about what can and should be done. The papers presented at the conference or prepared in anticipation of this conference are contained in this volume.

This gathering of specialists adopted a decidedly different approach from past conferences held at Shorenstein APARC. First, we kept the number of participants small—around 25 in total—to encourage a more frank, in depth exchange of ideas. Formal presentations were kept to a minimum, with a number of hours devoted to comments and questions and debate. No media were present to cover the event.

Second, we invited "younger generation" academics and experts from South Korea. Given the generational change in Korean politics and especially the considerable political influence wielded by the so-called "386ers"—when the term was coined in the 1990s, it referred to Koreans who were in their thirties, attended college in the eighties, and born in the sixties—it was essential for U.S. counterparts to hear from this group of thinkers. The center of power in South Korea has been shifting over the years, but Americans are slow to recognize it. Any inquiry into circumstances and events on the Korean peninsula must reflect this new reality, which was one of the conference goals.

Finally, we brought together in one room people specializing in politics, economics, human rights, and security. While American policymakers tend to focus on security areas, the North Korean issue is multidimensional and thus demands a similar approach. For instance, despite the nuclear stand-off, inter-Korean relations, especially in the arena of economic affairs, have been moving along. Such a gathering of experts from different areas not only encourages a broad-based inquiry, but also facilitates a sharing of ideas among those who do not normally come into contact. In such an environment, potentially helpful connections often come into focus. Often, issues related to nonproliferation are binary—either one complies or one does not—which makes compromise difficult. However, in situations where solutions are seemingly nowhere to be found, it may help to widen the frame of reference. Indeed, this last point served as a touchstone for the discussions that took place.

Papers in This Volume

This volume includes ten articles of varying length and style; the articles were finalized at the end of October 2005. The volume's structure broadly reflects the format of the conference, which consisted of four substantive panels—two papers for each panel. U.S. participants wrote what is in essence a survey paper/thought piece, whose purpose was to give a "general lay of the land" in the areas of politics, economics, human rights, and security. Their South Korean counterparts contributed more research-oriented articles that delve into one area of current interest—the external and internal political pressures facing the North Korean regime, the status of the Kaesong Project, the problem of North Korean migrants in China, and an assessment of North Korean military capabilities. These pieces touch upon the nuclear issue, but do not focus on it exclusively. Still, recognizing that any book on North Korea, particularly now, would be of limited relevance if it ignored the current nuclear crisis, this volume ends with two papers that specifically address current U.S. efforts and their prospects for success. Again, the former in this final set of papers adopts the essay approach; the latter is a research piece.

Robert Carlin is the author of the volume's first paper, titled "Talk to Me, Later." Carlin is considered a leading authority on North Korean leadership and diplomatic issues. He has been an intelligence analyst and policy advisor to a number of U.S. negotiators and has visited North Korea countless times. Using the current nuclear stand-off as his reference point, Carlin begins his piece with general observations about the timing of diplomatic initiatives and the need to take advantage of opportunities when present. As a former U.S. State Department official, Carlin was intimately involved in virtually every significant U.S. negotiation with North Korea from 1993 to 2000. He is therefore well positioned to give insight into the political motivations, constraints, and miscalculations behind the policies and actions emanating from Pyongyang, Washington, Tokyo, Seoul, Beijing, and Moscow. To make his points, Carlin offers personal observations and anecdotes about behind-the-scenes events. He concludes with a final observation that the timing for the six-party talks is wrong, that the United States has lost ground—not gained it—and that, as a result, the prospects for success in the short term are slim.

The companion piece to Robert Carlin's essay is Haksoon Paik's thoughtful article titled "North Korea Today: Politics Overloaded." Where Carlin provides a sweeping political analysis of the six-party talks participants, Paik focuses on the internal and external motivations—and constraints—of the North Korean leadership. Currently the director of the Inter-Korean Relations Studies Program and the Center for North Korean Studies at the Sejong Institute in Korea, as well as a policy advisor to South Korea's Ministry of Unification, Paik describes the South Korean perspective on the Kim Jong-Il regime. Paik's paper begins with an analysis of Pyongyang's policy priorities and an explanation of the domestic and international political conditions that constrain the North Korean leadership's ability to achieve these priorities. Within this context, he points out that the attitudes of everyday North Koreans is changing as a result of recent economic reforms and observes that North Korea's ideology of self-reliance (*juche*) may soon be replaced by a focus on "making money." Paik later addresses the sustainability of the Kim Jong-Il regime, and touches upon issues related to Kim's succession. He moves on to a discussion about the state of inter-Korean relations and concludes with the observation that the North-South channel could be a source of crucial support for U.S. nonproliferation objectives.

In 2002, North Korea initiated a number of well-publicized reforms to get its ravaged economic system moving in the right direction. Many were initially skeptical that such reforms were in fact real. However, there is a consensus that something *is* happening in the North. To provide a better sense of these developments and their potential impact, William Brown's paper, "North Korea: How to Reform a Broken Economy," tackles key economics-related issues. Brown has considerable experience as an economist and economic analyst in the U.S. government, having worked as in the Chief Economist's Office of the Commerce Department, as Deputy National Intelligence Officer for Economics with the National Intelligence Council, and as an economic analyst in the CIA's Office of Economic Research. Drawing on this impressive background, he argues that significant changes in North Korea are under way, but that the force and motivation behind them are not clear. He believes that it is critical to understand whether the reforms result from a "top-down" decision or a "bottom-up" unleashing of market forces that the regime is unable to control. Brown discusses the implications of both possibilities and presents a list of potential winners and losers during this time of transition. In assessing the current state of affairs, Brown declares that North Korea "appears to be stuck, unable or unwilling to proceed further." Of great use to policymakers and North Korea watchers alike is a checklist of things to look for if economic reform is unfolding as it should. Brown has been a longtime critic of current efforts to engage with North Korea and lays out sensible alternatives from a distinctly economic perspective.

Balancing Brown's macro-level economic inquiry is Yong Sueng Dong's piece, "The Present and Future of the Kaesong Industrial Complex." As the title suggests, Dong takes a detailed, micro-level look at the Kaesong Inter-Korean Business Project, located in North Korea about 40 kilometers from the North-South border. Kaesong is not the first case of economic collaboration between North and South Korea. It is, however, the most recent example of increasing inter-Korean cooperation, and it received a great deal of attention in spring 2005, when the products manufactured there (pots, pans, and other kitchenware) found their way to market in Seoul for the first time. A senior researcher at the Samsung Economic Research Institute, a major private think tank in Korea, Dong has visited Kaesong a number of times and is thus well situated to describe what Kaesong is, and why. He recounts the history of the Kaesong project, lays out its objectives, and dissects the project's operational aspects. He explains the economic rationale for the North-South cooperation upon which the Kaesong project is based—a business model that combines the South's comparative advantage in capital and technology with the North's relatively cheap labor and land. Dong also analyzes what he sees as the project's problems and opportunities, including the always-present political and military constraints. These shortcomings notwithstanding, he concludes that the Kaesong project is moving forward, despite substantial hurdles, and asserts that the Kaesong environment will likely enhance the competitiveness of factories based there.

The next set of papers deals with the difficult matter of human rights in North Korea. David Hawk, a prominent human rights investigator and advocate, takes on the controversial subject in his piece, "Human Rights Issues and the Crisis in North Korea." In light of the Bush administration's clarion call for greater freedom and democracy throughout the world, a better grasp of the human rights issues in North Korea—and how the human rights community views the DPRK—is appropriate and necessary. Hawk uses his extensive experiences in Latin America, Southeast Asia, and Africa and relates it to what is occurring in North Korea. In so doing, he furnishes a frame of reference for confronting this problem. When discussing human rights, Hawk acknowledges that having a clear understanding of the standards by which actions are judged must be the starting point—and his paper begins with an analysis of the relevant standards. Hawk is quick to point out that North Korea has been an exceptionally problematic country for human rights watchers because of the lack of information. This past barrier notwithstanding, he argues that evidence of abuse in North Korea, predominantly testimonial in nature, is abundant. After identifying the nature of the abuses, Hawk devotes the remainder of his essay to the policies of South Korea, the

United States, and the international community. Hawk questions the approaches of the South Korean government and of nongovernmental groups (NGOs) in the South, while commenting on the recently enacted U.S. Human Rights Act. He concludes his piece with a perspective on the policy implications that human rights have on the nuclear issue. U.S. government officials recently linked human rights in North Korea to security assurances in the context of a nuclear deal, a clear indication that Hawk's consideration of this issue is both timely and urgent.

Complementing David Hawk's paper is an article by Ki-Sik Kim, titled "Perspectives on North Korean 'Displaced Persons.'" Kim analyzes the plight of North Korean refugees, but for reasons explained in his paper, he terms them "displaced persons." Kim begins his analysis by attempting to gauge the number of refugees, with the bulk recognized to be in China. He makes the case that the majority of displaced persons leave North Korea not to escape persecution from North Korean authorities, but for economic reasons. Kim disapproves of U.S. policies toward North Korean refugees, which he believes are too political. He scorns the U.S. Humans Rights Act and argues that, despite its good intentions, it has actually made conditions worse for those whom it seeks to help. In this regard, Kim criticizes as exploitive groups that organize "planned border crossings"—the systematic gathering of refugees for entry into foreign diplomatic offices, often to gain publicity for the activities of the organizing group. In this regard, he cautions the South Korean government to make sure its policies do not encourage this activity. In terms of policy prescriptions, Kim calls on China to grant "displaced persons" temporary residence and to end its current policy of forced repatriation. Kim is the Secretary General of the People's Solidarity for Participatory Democracy (PSPD), South Korea's leading NGO, which exerts considerable influence on policy issues. His perspective represents the new generation of South Koreans coming into power.

The two security-related papers in this volume address critical issues—the U.S.-South Korea alliance and North Korea's military capability. Great attention has been paid to perceived differences in North Korea policy between the United States and South Korea and to the challenges such differences pose for the alliance. In "A Comparison of U.S. and South Korean National Security Strategies: Implications for Alliance Coordination toward North Korea," Scott Snyder takes an unconventional approach to analyzing the problem. Snyder, a senior associate at the Asia Foundation/Pacific Forum CSIS, compares and contrasts the National Security Strategies (NSS) of the United States and the ROK: the United States markedly revised its NSS in 2002, while the ROK issued its first NSS last year. Because an NSS document distills a country's basic approach and philosophy to foreign affairs worldwide,

Snyder believes the exercise is a way to pinpoint areas of potential friction. Using this method of inquiry, he concludes that the U.S.-ROK alliance will be subject to extensive, and possibly irreparable, stresses and strains due to 1) a shift in North Korea military doctrine from a reliance on conventional forces to nuclear threat; 2) emerging political and philosophical differences between South Korea and the United States; and 3) uncertainty over the regional security environment once the North Korean nuclear crisis is resolved. More troublesome to Snyder is the existence of fissures in how each country views existing threats and the method of dealing with them. The United States sees North Korea as a weapon to be neutralized, while South Korea focuses on the North's gradual transformation and integration with the outside world.

Completing the general security section is Taik-young Hamm's piece, "North Korea: Economic Foundations of Military Capability and the Inter-Korean Balance." Hamm is a professor at Korea's Kyungnam University and a recognized authority on North Korean military issues. His information-rich paper presents an excellent assessment of the current North Korean military. Overall, Hamm maintains that North Korea's military prowess is overrated and that the South's capability far outstrips the North. Hamm regards "bean-counts" or firepower scores as inadequate; rather, he views the use of military capital stock as most representative. Hamm concludes that an arms race on the Korean peninsula will not buy more security for either North or South; he observes that there is a "'balance of threat' or asymmetric balance'" between North and South. Despite what he sees as the ROK's vast superiority, he believes North Korea's conventional weapons and purported WMD capability are enough to hold Seoul hostage.

The last two papers of this volume specifically discuss the North Korean nuclear issue and the prospects for resolving it. Henry S. Rowen, director-emeritus of Shorenstein APARC and former Assistant Secretary of Defense for International Security Affairs from 1989–91, wrote the first paper on this subject, "On Dealing with a Hard Case: North Korea." Rowen argues that there is little chance North Korea will give up its nuclear weapons or accept extensive inspection rights. Because the United States is constrained from initiating a preventive attack and because South Korea (and probably China) are likely to continue supporting Kim Jong-Il's regime, Rowen asserts that the United States is forced to accept the status quo. However, he cautions that the United States must remain vigilant and guard against the danger that North Korea might sell nuclear weapons or critical components. Most interestingly, Rowen—once an outspoken critic of engagement with North Korea—concludes that the "best worst approach" is to foster conditions for political change in North Korea through "pro-commerce" policies, rather than following an agenda that pressures eventual collapse, or that extends unconditional economic aid.

Philip W. Yun is the author of the final paper of this volume. In 2004–05, he was Pantech Scholar in Korean Studies at Shorenstein APARC. Previously, he served in the U.S. Department of State, and participated in all major negotiations with North Korea from 1998 to 2000. In his research piece, Yun argues that any Bush policy with regime change as its objective and the threat of force as the means is highly unlikely to succeed. The implication of such an unchanging Bush policy, Yun concludes, is that the United States will then be faced with the grim choice of either accepting North Korea as a permanent nuclear weapons state that regularly produces fissile material, or risking a terrible war to prevent this from occurring. Unlike other works that reach the same conclusion, Yun's paper is one of the few that attempts to analyze the U.S. policy on the North Korean nuclear problem using—in a predictive manner—an established theoretical framework on international conflict, namely the pioneering work of Alexander George on coercive diplomacy. Utilizing 15 case studies of past U.S. confrontations, done by George andf others, Yun identifies the salient factors needed for coercive diplomacy to succeed and applies them to the North Korean situation.

A Window of Opportunity

In his opening paper, Robert Carlin talks about timing—"Timing may not be everything in diplomacy, but it is surely something." He adds that "Good timing is important and rare. Something is always out of kilter."

In his policy review of United States policy toward North Korea, dated October 12, 1999, former U.S. Secretary of Defense William J. Perry offered his own thoughts on timing:

> [A] confluence of events this past year has opened what we strongly feel is a unique window of opportunity for the U.S. with respect to North Korea. There is a clear and common understanding among Seoul, Tokyo, and Washington on how to deal with Pyongyang. The PRC's strategic goals—especially on the issue of North Korean nuclear weapons and related missile delivery systems—overlap with those of the U.S. Pyongyang appears ... convinced of the value of improving relations with the U.S. However, there are always pressures on these positive elements. Underlying tensions and suspicions have led to intermittent armed clashes and incidents and affect the political environment.... Nevertheless, the year 1999 may represent historically, one of our best opportunities to deal with key U.S. security concerns on the Korean peninsula for some time to come."[1]

Indeed, the pressure of time, or the need for favorable timing, provides a constant backdrop in this book. Negotiating a final agreement to implement the general principles produced at the last round of the talks might take a few years under the six-party format; but it is unclear whether the governments of the key parties will be able to maintain and coordinate polices necessary to permit a final accord. In the case of the United States, events tied to the calendar—such as the 2006 Congressional elections and soon thereafter the U.S. Presidential sweepstakes leading to 2008—are certain to constrain the Bush administration's ability to sustain major initiatives without incurring significant domestic political costs. Yet, if bold actions are not taken soon and—just as critical—given time to build momentum, the result will be a U.S. policy toward North Korea ensnared in partisan and ideological strife. Meanwhile, North Korea will remain content with the status quo. It will do just enough to keep other parties hopeful, but will nonetheless continue to steadily increase its stockpile of fissile material each year. The problem of North Korea's nuclear weapons will become progressively harder, and more costly, to solve. In this context, the U.S.-ROK alliance will remain strained, and growing tensions will persist throughout the Northeast Asian region.

This volume offers a variety of perspectives, even as it aims to rectify misconceptions and increase collective understanding about North Korea. It is intended to be a "snapshot" of what is going on now, in 2005, in North Korea. This was the rationale for addressing so many topics—that it might prove useful to policymakers now and scholars later. Many who contributed to this volume believe that the Bush administration's first-term policies toward North Korea have been less than effective, yet these authors were not charged to advance an overall solution. To be sure, one overarching theme connects these pieces: there is much we still do not know. Yet another, more hopeful *policy* element also emerges from the many viewpoints in this book. To some extent, Henry Rowen speaks for all of the authors collected here when he observes that economics and commerce can be a powerful, positive force for change.

Hope therefore remains. Let us hope that 2005 will indeed mark a rebirth and a new beginning for East Asia.

Notes

[1] William Perry (U.S. North Korea Policy Coordinator and Special Advisor to the President and the Secretary of State), "Review of the United States Policy toward North Korea: Findings and Recommendations," unclassified report, Washington, DC, p. 17.

TALK TO ME, LATER

Robert Carlin

Timing may not be everything in diplomacy, but it is surely something. The bleached bones of countless failed diplomatic efforts bear the unmistakable tooth marks of bad timing. Epitaphs for failures are depressingly similar: "Good concept, fair execution. Alas, too late (or, perhaps, too soon)."

To be sure, the need for close attention to timing—put another way, the imperative of correctly gauging windows of opportunity—is not a central consideration for all negotiations, all the time. It may be less important, for instance, when the broad foundations for diplomatic movement are already in place. A network of relations developed in a more propitious period is like money in the bank during rainy diplomatic weather.

Timing is also of less concern when the means to sustain forward motion, or at least to preserve minimal stability, already exist. If the two sides are lucky enough to have an already-negotiated agreement being implemented, they are liable to find it easier to reach additional agreements, even if the circumstances for any particular set of negotiations may not otherwise seem favorable. Positive performance on existing agreements provides traction for additional negotiations. Success in one set of negotiations can keep windows of opportunity open for others. With a process already en train, failure at one point may not be fatal all along the line.

But timing is crucial if the process is moving from a standing start or sliding backwards. In that case, a single failure can weigh heavily; one reversal can close many windows.

By any standard, precious few (closer to none, actually) of the right circumstances exist now, or have for the past several years, for serious, sustained multilateral negotiations dealing with the DPRK nuclear issue. This should not be a shocking observation. That Washington has spoken forcefully and often on the need for multilateral talks does not mean conditions exist for those talks to succeed. Endless repetition of the mantra could not make it so, especially when all of the previous agreements and ongoing sets of talks that had been put in place between the United States and the DPRK from 1994 to 2000 had fallen by the wayside. With nothing left in place, and worse, with the previous foundation discredited and rejected by one of the parties, it would have been difficult even in the best of circumstances to restart the negotiating process. In this case, timing became vital to understand whether or how new talks on the nuclear issue might begin.

Bear in mind that timing is frequently not a question of volition or even foresight. Sometimes it can depend more on the stars being in alignment, and a diplomat can do little about the stars. Countries must deal with the situation that exists, even if they helped to create it in the first place. But if you cannot always pick your environment, it helps to know where you are, in relative terms, in time and space. In this sense, diplomacy and working on a trapeze have much in common. If the trapeze is moving toward you, you can calculate when to leap from your perch to catch it. If it is moving away, you might want to consider another option.

To be sure, one major difference between working on a trapeze and diplomacy (other than trapeze artists generally work with a safety net) is that diplomacy should be seen as a dynamic process rather than simply a question of physics. In the diplomatic arena, what seemed impossible yesterday might become attainable tomorrow, depending on what you do today. Successful diplomacy often changes reality as it moves. Thus, when it comes to diplomacy, timing is not just a matter of waiting (though waiting can have its advantages) but rather of assessing and then, to the extent possible, affecting the environment.

In situations where, say, Tokyo, Seoul, and Washington have not really agreed on a common course (like now, for instance), good timing for diplomacy with North Korea will end up being episodic, tactical, and usually out of synch. Diplomacy will be driven by external events and be almost wholly dependent on luck. For example, election periods will be more than usually disruptive to diplomacy. As a rule, election periods are never a good time to try to engage North Korea, and that will be doubly so as long as current circumstances hold. In a period of diplomatic stalemate, few politicians in Tokyo or Washington will imagine that much can be gained from seeming "soft" on North Korea. In Japan, there can actually be real danger in doing so.

What is more, bureaucracies become especially chary during elections, and will be even more inclined that way if the policy direction is not clearly defined. In an election period, the decision-making apparatus of government seizes up. Few bureaucrats are willing to risk taking a step before elections that, in the immediate aftermath, might end up being undone—along with their careers. To take one example, despite Pyongyang's autumn 1992 pleas for a positive gesture from the United States in order to sustain whatever gains had been made from the high-level U.S.-DPRK meeting of January 1992, Washington was unable to respond—the presidential election was looming.

Curiously, if election periods tend to be a bad time for diplomacy, the post-election period may be better. Pyongyang has a pattern of seeking to take advantage of such periods to signal that it might be able to start with a clean slate. That was in the case in late 1971, following the end of the government of Prime Minister Sato Eisaku, and in 1976, after Jimmy Carter's election. The latter election year was especially interesting. In August 1976, the links between Washington's exceptionally tough public response to North Korean soldiers' slaying of two American army officers in Panmunjom and the Republican Party's national convention, which was being held at the same time, are worth contemplating.

A Crack in Time vs. the Picture Window

Timing is not simply the clock or the calendar. In a diplomatic sense, timing has a range of characteristics and components—operational, political, strategic, tactical. This essay does not deal with tactical or operational timing, of the "strike when the iron is hot" variety. Much of that depends on the personal chemistry between skilled negotiators on the scene. Even North Korean diplomats appear to have enough leeway to close a deal, at least on an ad ref basis, when they sense the time is right—or to balk if it is not.

Rather than tactical timing, this essay deals with something broader. This may not be exactly cosmic or epochal, but it is still on a fairly grand scale. For example, the timing was crucial, and crucially wrong, when Pyongyang tried to scramble ahead at the end of the Clinton administration, after a delay of nearly 17 months, to reciprocate the May 1999 visit by Presidential Special Envoy William Perry. Some of that delay was understandable, not least because in early 2000 the North was focused on the possibility of summit talks with Seoul. But a key part of that delay remains inexplicable, at least to outsiders. It turned out to be fatal. No matter how much Washington cajoled, probed, and parried during that period, DPRK diplomats could do no more than promise that the issue was being considered seriously and at a high level in Pyongyang. A meeting between Secretary of State Madeleine Albright and DPRK Foreign Minister Paek Nam Sun in Hanoi at an APEC foreign minister's meeting in summer 2000 was a positive exchange that further solidified the foundation but led to no immediate progress. An effort to break through by utilizing a visit by DPRK Supreme People's Assembly (SPA) Presidium President Kim Yong Nam to the UN General Assembly came to naught when airport authorities ordered Kim's delegation to submit to body searches when they changed planes in Germany. Instead, they went home.

In the end, the process was literally squeezed into a few weeks of exhausting activity, starting with a September meeting in New York, at which the DPRK revealed it was prepared to send a high-level envoy to Washington; followed a few weeks later by Vice Marshal Cho Myong Rok's visit; and then capped by Secretary Albright's trip to Pyongyang less than two weeks after that. Washington and Pyongyang's inability to engage at a high level in summer 2000 meant that when major progress was finally achieved a few months later, in October of that year, it had no time to take root before the U.S. presidential elections and their unanticipated aftermath. There was too much left to do and not enough time to do it. U.S. efforts to hurry the process along in talks in Kuala Lumpur in early November went nowhere—and actually set the process back—because of a mismatch in the two delegation's instructions and tactics.

When it comes to engaging North Korea, current problems of timing are, of course, two-edged, or more accurately these days, multi-edged. Not only must "both sides" be ready to move, all six parties involved in the talks must be able to move ahead, more or less in synch. Yet, a simple rule of thumb needs to be applied here: the more parties involved, the more difficult to bring the necessary stars into alignment. That is not just true for the six-party process. It was true as well for the multiple parties involved in the Agreed Framework negotiations a decade earlier. In late 1993, Washington attempted to put the pieces in place for a deal that would result in exquisitely choreographed movement by the United States, North Korea, South Korea, and the International Atomic Energy Agency (IAEA). It could not be achieved—and probably was impossible from the start. That failure provided a useful lesson: when dealing with North Korea, too many moving parts, involving too many parties, could only gum up the diplomatic machinery. As a result, Washington tried to strip the process down to two manageable negotiating elements—the United States and the DPRK. The ROK and IAEA remained key components, but mainly in terms of implementation rather than as part of the direct bargaining process.

To state this lesson in more general terms, although one might hope that when multiple parties are involved, the most advanced will pull along the laggards, the process usually works the other way around. The lowest common denominator—the party least prepared to move—sets the pace. In a multiparty setting, if someone is not ready, then no one is ready. If the time is wrong for one party, then it is wrong for all. Strong, effective leadership might temporarily deal with the problem, but it rarely fixes it for long.

Circumstances can—and do—change. But for the past four years, diplomacy concerning North Korea has been only a slogan, not a reality. The question, of course, is why. One way of understanding the answer is to examine, in the current setting, who is ready and who isn't.

The sad, short answer is that none of the parties was really ready for multilateral talks when they began in 2003. That would not have been so bad—the players, after all, might learn their parts with enough practice and coaching. A deeper problem was that the key players were not prepared for the sort of long-term effort necessary to fashion the circumstances that have to be in place to begin successful diplomacy with Pyongyang. In dealing with North Korea, the window for getting into talks is as important as constructing the passageway that leads to a successful outcome.

The North Koreans themselves were probably the only party even halfway ready to discuss the problem, though from the beginning they balked at a multilateral setting and were never committed to it. Neither Japan nor the United States was prepared, the ROK was ill-equipped, and China was thrown into a role as organizer and mediator that it never wanted. Finally, Moscow wanted to be seen as sitting at the table but was largely uninterested in the process—and has played seemingly a minor role—because of more pressing problems.

Pyongyang

Among the first questions to ask when preparing to deal with North Korea should always be, is the situation in Pyongyang—that is, the state of play in the leadership, the personalities involved, the options being considered, the trends in domestic policies—propitious for diplomatic engagement? The answer will never be simply yes or no. In fact, most of the details will be obscure. But trends in policy reflecting answers to such questions can be observed, and these are crucial.

Beginning in 1991, the DPRK was ready to engage the United States in a way not seen before. "Ready" meant not simply dueling diplomatically with the United States but moving toward a fundamental improvement in relations. There was nothing easy about recognizing this massive shift in policy, draped as it was in difficult-to-parse propaganda and official statements. Nevertheless, Pyongyang slowly let it be known that this new—and very large—window had opened because Kim Il-Sung had decided it was critical for North Korea's survival to have the United States remain on the Korean peninsula. In short, the North's position was that U.S. troops could stay, and indeed should stay, and that U.S. influence must remain dominant in the region, most of all against China. This was not tactical maneuvering. Rather, it represented a strategic decision at the highest level, a decision that worked its way into nearly every step the North took over the next decade. Reinforcing this strategic decision, and apparently closely linked with it, has been a nearly constant, if not always well focused impulse on Pyongyang's part to improve its economy by undertaking a reform program.

Along the diplomatic way, of course, the North Koreans could not help wading into tactical swamps. But the strategic course they had set permitted them to return to dry ground—if only someone would throw them a rope. It is difficult to judge the relative weight of economic, diplomatic, and security calculations in Pyongyang's formation of policy, but these three elements were at least well enough aligned from 1993 to 2001 to provide DPRK diplomacy, and most especially the foreign ministry, with unusual traction. In short, the timing was right to engage the DPRK.

The North Koreans made a number of decisions during this period designed to keep the window open with the United States, even when it meant taking part in negotiations they did not otherwise see as useful or necessary. The four-party talks and bilateral missile negotiations with the United States are prime examples. After a great show of reluctance, the North agreed to participate in both, not to make progress in either but because it believed that the improved atmosphere with Washington would suffer if it continued to say "no." For several years, neither of those sets of talks got very far. The missile talks, in particular, were almost a pro forma exercise on both sides until summer 2000, when Kim Jong-Il signaled substantial, positive changes in the North's position. The key was that neither the four-party nor the missile talks stood in isolation, and the inability to move them beyond a certain point did not bring down the entire diplomatic process.

In fact, there was so much momentum behind that process that even in the first two years of the Bush administration, Pyongyang was prepared—even eager—to pick up the diplomacy where it left off on January 20, 2001, as the new administration took office. From North Korea's perspective, the window was still open for diplomacy, and throughout 2001 there were numerous signs of DPRK frustration that the process was not continuing. By this time, the links between the North's diplomacy and its economic policy had become increasingly obvious, with economic considerations rising in priority. The imperative to launch the economic reforms seems to have been a driving factor behind a noticeably active phase in DPRK diplomacy, from late 2001 through October 2002. It is hard to believe that Kim Jong-Il would have publicly launched his economic reform program in July 2002 if he had anticipated a showdown with the United States only three months later.

With the North's pullout from the Nuclear Nonproliferation Treaty (NPT) in January 2003, and its formal declaration, in February 2005, that it possesses nuclear weapons, the question arises whether the window of opportunity has closed for diplomacy—at least diplomacy designed to bring the DPRK back into the NPT as a member in good standing. The situation would look darker but for signs that Pyongyang continues to explore and expand changes that appear, to any serious observer, to be initial steps in a process of economic reform. And this impulse toward economic reform has seemingly propped open a window for diplomacy. The logic is straightforward, and precedent suggests it is more than simply theory. Economic reform appears to be very high on Kim Jong-Il's list of priorities. How, then, does Pyongyang currently perceive the relationship between a successful economic reform path and an improved external security situation?

As noted above, for the past 15 years, there has been a link between the North's efforts at economic reform and its diplomacy aimed at achieving an improved—less threatening—external security environment. In practical terms, that translated into DPRK efforts to normalize relations with the United States, leading to a wide range of contacts between the two sides. Between 1993 and 2000, Washington and Pyongyang engaged in more than 20 different sets of talks, most of which led to operational agreements that went beyond paper declarations. The momentum of the diplomacy, though it did not seem steady at the time to those engaged in the process, was such that success in one area improved the chances for success in another.

Momentum grew with experience, as the negotiating teams refined patterns of progress and learned to limit—though never completely eliminate—setbacks. In this sense, the Agreed Framework was not a culmination but a starting point, a platform supporting multiple interactions and the exploration of new channels that broadened beyond U.S.-DPRK bilateral talks to include truly multilateral diplomacy— something that has been attempted but not replicated in recent years.

Washington

In at least one crucial respect, the United States was ready for the Agreed Framework negotiations in 1993. A long, slow dance toward engagement had begun late in the Reagan administration, in 1988, when contacts between the United States and the DPRK began at the level of political counselors of the two respective embassies in Beijing. The process continued during the first Bush administration, with a series of carefully plotted, lower level contacts that culminated with a January 1992 meeting between Undersecretary of State Arnold Kanter and Korean Workers Party Secretary Kim Yong Sun.

That is not to say that at this stage all the pieces were in place for sustained forward movement. They were not. The tenor of the times was reflected in the hilarious disagreement in Washington over whether Kanter should be allowed to have lunch with Kim. He finally was, and while dining with the North Koreans at a Manhattan restaurant did not undermine U.S. national security interests, neither was it enough to punch through years of hostility. It was a good beginning but, as noted above, going into the presidential elections later in 1992, Washington found it impossible to respond positively to North Korean requests to keep up the dialogue.

The Agreed Framework negotiations (1993–94) created the basis for sustained engagement on a range of issues, but not until several high hurdles were overcome. In the immediate post-Agreed Framework period, the diplomatic process was kept alive not by dint of senior level policy acumen on either side but because of a lucky confluence of personalities and skills in both negotiating teams. Still, that was barely sufficient to keep the entire edifice standing. The Perry process in 1999 created a new operational reality in Washington and gave the diplomacy an extra 12 months. Almost enough, but not quite.

Events of the past ten years are a textbook case (yet to be written) of timing gone wrong. The Agreed Framework created the platform, improved the environment, and put in place a process that began to alter the conditions, but that was all wasted. The Congress, for one, has never understood very well the need for diplomacy toward North Korea. The issue was quickly—almost instantly—politicized at the time of the Agreed Framework, and over the years few in the Congress were prepared to stand up to those who fought to limit, and where possible gut, the agreement. As a consequence, funding for the U.S. portion of implementation was severely restricted from the beginning; that only got worse over time. Lack of money led directly to the inability of the United States to fulfill its obligations, primarily on deliveries of heavy fuel oil, in a timely fashion. The U.S. failure to participate at all in funding the most visibly important symbol—the light-water reactors—of the Agreed Framework ensured that the Korean Peninsula Energy Development Organization (KEDO), which was formed to implement the project, would sooner or later face serious strains. Inability to move ahead on U.S. obligations caused the Agreed Framework to wobble until, by summer 1998, it threatened to collapse completely.

Meanwhile, discussion in American media on the North Korean nuclear issue has been, in a word, pathetic. Public discourse has been dominated by intellectual laziness. The press has become a primary proponent of the idea that North Korea is an information black hole—an approach much favored because, in essence, it lets most reporters and editors off the hook for doing much beyond cut and paste. More space is taken up by explaining that DPRK stands for the Democratic People's Republic of Korea than in serious treatment of the problem. Stories about Kim Jong-Il's hairstyle have substituted for the hard work of learning the facts.

The speed with which the diplomatic achievements of 1994–2000 unraveled in 2001 and then were completely reversed in late 2002 demonstrated how weak the foundations had been to begin with in the United States. Lessons learned from more than a decade of dealing with the North were tossed overboard without a second thought, with the result that the few subsequent forays into diplomacy were doomed. The timing for the October 2002 talks in Pyongyang was especially unpropitious. Neither side was prepared for the meeting that took place. The North Koreans, having just begun a long-planned economic reform process, were looking to get back on a diplomatic track that would create a new, improved security environment to support the reforms. The United States was looking for a confrontation over the highly enriched uranium (HEU) issue, but when that came to pass, it was unprepared for the crisis that ensued. The American effort, seemingly the result of poor planning, badly executed, caused the situation to deteriorate rapidly, undermining rather than bolstering the prospects for diplomacy.

Particular policies aside, over the past several years the pieces have not been in place for the United States to pursue the sort of patient, concerted approach with the DPRK that had yielded results in the past. From late 1988 though 2000, three presidents had employed policies that were broadly consistent, giving both Washington and Pyongyang a chance to build on experience, moving slowly but surely up a series of diplomatic plateaus. It is illustrative that in 1993, when plans were in place for opening U.S.-DPRK talks, the first thing that was done was to reach for the briefing books prepared for the previous administration's meeting with the DPRK (January 1992).

After October 1994, even if they grumbled over details, Asian observers looked at the Agreed Framework as a demonstration of U.S. ability not simply to identify a dangerous problem but to resolve it. Surely, none thought the Agreed Framework was the perfect nonproliferation tool. But it was important for another reason. It demonstrated continuing U.S. leadership by showing that Washington could confront a problem and successfully address it in a way that increased stability in the region.

By contrast, U.S. policy toward the DPRK from between 2001 and 2004 arguably made matters worse. Instead of moving in a direction that was consistent and likely to yield results, Washington insisted on an approach that struck many in Asia as a dead end. The State Department's noon press briefings notwithstanding, none of the other parties in the six-party talks—none of them—saw the United States as moving in the right direction. They mobilized diplomatic resources in support of the talks, but it would be hard to assert that any honestly believed that the multilateral process, as set out and practiced by the United States, would solve the problem. Despite constant protestations to the contrary from ranking officials in Washington, there was no real unity in approach. The more that trumpet blared, the less convincing it became. The agreement on the basic point that North Korea should not be allowed to go nuclear was never a sufficient base to sustain negotiations, particularly in the absence of a truly effective diplomatic strategy. Diplomacy increasingly became a scarecrow, and, in this case, the crows were not buying.

Tokyo

Few people would argue that the timing is right for movement in DPRK-Japan relations. Prime Minister Koizumi may be laboring mightily to hold the window open, but that is barely enough to keep hope alive, and hardly sufficient for substantive progress. The particulars of the internal Japanese political situation may change, but the main features have been locked in place for several years and the outlook in the near term is for more of the same. Relations with North Korea occupy a peculiar place as a domestic political, not a foreign policy, issue, subject to cross pressures, internal maneuvering by the ruling Liberal Democratic Party (LDP), and media hyperbole that makes serious thought virtually impossible.

The most obvious problem is the powerful emotional pull of the decades-old abduction cases. Utilized effectively for domestic political purposes, this issue has become increasingly difficult to solve. But a look at the history of DPRK-Japan relations over the past 30 years suggests that the abductions issue is as much a symbol as a cause, and that a large part of the overall problem stems from the vagaries of Japanese politics.

There is an impression that Japan-DPRK relations started to make progress only in 1990, when Shin Kanemaru visited Pyongyang and brought home two crew members from a Japanese ship, the Shosei Maru, who had been held for several years. But in fact, the North appeared ready to move ahead with improved relations as early as 1971, almost as soon as the Sato government left office, and before President Nixon's visit to China. Sato's successor, Tanaka Kakuei, was interested in normalizing relations with both China and the DPRK. By the time of Tanaka's downfall, in 1974, a certain floor had been set for progress in Japan-DPRK ties. This was not a step the North Koreans took lightly. In fact, it was a major development in DPRK foreign policy, given that "Japanese militarism" had been a major source of disagreement between the DPRK and the USSR in the late 1960s, with Pyongyang arguing against any improvement in relations with Japan.

When they first dipped their toe in the pool of Japanese politics, the North may have found things relatively simple. The 1970s were years of LDP dominance in Japanese politics, when factional bosses were key to decision making, and working with the factions was a key to getting things done. This was a game the North Koreans could play well—money being an essential element in making the game work, not just with the

LDP but with other political parties as well. Yet, the whole time the system was changing. After a succession of weak prime ministers in the 1980s, by the early 1990s the old-style politics had passed. The North Koreans did not know how to work the new system. And at the same time, new roadblocks on the way to improved relations appeared—missiles, the nuclear issue, and a new focus on the abductions.

The opening for diplomacy between North Korea and Japan has always been fairly narrow. For reasons of history and what might be termed national chemistry, it is relatively easy for either side to say or do something that will cause the other side to dig in its heels. The upshot is that when multilateral talks began in 2003, Japan was probably the least ready of any of the players, the timing in Tokyo was (and remains) the least ripe, and the drag from Japanese public opinion and politics on any multilateral diplomatic process has been the most severe. This is not for want of effort by key players in the government of Japan. But it is, in part, a function of the fate of the Japanese foreign ministry, the decline in the influence of experienced diplomats, and a shift to the right in Japanese politics in recent years.

The first Koizumi trip to Pyongyang, in September 2002, is a good example of the difficulties of timing in Japan. From all outward appearances, the summit should have been a breakthrough, and Kim Jong-Il's admission that the DPRK had kidnapped Japanese nationals should have marked the beginning of a new, positive phase in relations. Instead, under domestic political pressure, the deal fell apart in Japan almost as soon as Koizumi got off his airplane.

Although it is hard to quantify, it would also be a mistake to underestimate the basic antipathy Japanese still feel toward Korea. The sudden popularity of South Korean soap operas over the past year, while interesting in its own light, hardly indicates a major shift in opinion. Japanese media are still filled with breathless, two-dimensional portrayals of North Korea that skirt the edges of racism.

The challenge for Japan in sustaining the diplomatic track with Pyongyang is more difficult than most observers can imagine. Efforts to reproduce with the North the Japan-ROK negotiations that ended in the 1965 normalization agreement are doomed. The political system that helped produce that agreement no longer exists in Japan, and the political connections between the DPRK and Japan differ vastly from what existed in the 1960s between Seoul and Tokyo. The United States, closely allied with both Japan and the ROK, could lend its weight then to support a successful outcome. There is nothing similar to support or sustain Japan-DPRK negotiations, and without that as a floor, nothing that can keep Tokyo engaged in six-party talks or sustain the compromises that would have to be made to make the negotiations successful.

Seoul

The ROK's position on dealing with Pyongyang has been reversed almost totally in the past ten years. In 1995, Seoul's approach to North-South relations was, in grossly simplified form, "The answer is 'no,' now what is the question?" Today, the approach is more nearly described along the lines of, "The answer is 'yes,' whatever the question."

In one sense, there is no doubt that the window is open. Some observers worry that there may in fact be no window at all, simply a hole in the wall. This broad opening and generally positive approach may or may not be useful vis à vis Pyongyang, but in any case it has set up tensions between Seoul on the one side and Tokyo and Washington on the other, strengthening the image of divisions and thus weakening efforts at a broad, balanced multilateral diplomatic approach. In other words, there is a reasonable argument to be made that the timing is not really good now for Seoul to take part in multilateral diplomacy with the North, although for equal and opposite reasons, from what the timing was in 1995.

Sometime soon after Kim Il-Song's death in July 1994, then-ROK President Kim Yong Sam decided he was not going to deal with Kim Jong-Il. Instead, he would bring about his downfall. ROK policy moved into a reflectively negative mode. The United States wanted to move ahead with liaison offices with Pyongyang, as called for under the Agreed Framework? Seoul was opposed. The United States wanted to offer emergency good aid to North Korea? Seoul was opposed. A three-man team of North Korean infiltrators landed in the South—a routine event—and then the submarine carrying them ran aground off the coast? Seoul wanted to stop its cooperation with KEDO, beginning its work in the North to build two light-water reactors as part of the Agreed Framework. The struggle was nearly constant, nearly all along the line.

Despite the bump caused by China's careless (or carefully calculated, take your pick) references a few years ago to the ancient Korean kingdom of Korguryo as part of the Chinese empire, there has been a general drift in Seoul's diplomacy toward China in order to balance Japan and the United States, not necessarily in that order. Some of this drift appears to have been the result of strategic calculation, first in the government of Kim Tae Jung, and then of his successor. The details of Seoul's calculations, the precise extent of the drift, and the extent to which it may yet develop are not the issue here. Rather, the issue is the impact that these developments have had on the ROK approach to the six-party talks. To the extent that the South sees China as a balancing, and even moderate, force in the talks, Seoul feels safer in opposing a tough U.S. position. To the extent that South Korea, sitting across the DMZ from the North Korean army, is not prepared to close ranks with the American position, Pyongyang is encouraged in its recalcitrance. This may sound oversimplified, but it is not.

There is no appetite in South Korea for confrontation, the North is not seen as a threat, and there consequently persists a serious gap between priorities in Washington and in Seoul. This gap may have been widened in recent years, but it goes back 20 years and more. South Koreans have often become nervous, and sometimes angry, when the United States seemed to be going too far in pushing a confrontation for reasons of U.S. interests (e.g., nonproliferation). Washington's insistence that Seoul ease off from dialogue with the North in summer 1992 infuriated top ROK officials. South Koreans could be equally annoyed when the United States did not go far enough to protect what were seen as ROK interests. No one disagrees that it would be good if Seoul and Washington could coordinate much more closely in their policies toward North Korea; no one knows how to do it.

Fogging the diplomatic window further, the recent eruption of tensions between Seoul and Tokyo—tensions that have been just beneath the surface for years—means that the chances of a U.S.-ROK-Japanese unified diplomatic position, a real rather than a rhetorical unity that could have an impact in Pyongyang, have further receded. Seeing such fissures, the North has little short-term incentive for making concessions. Anyone in the North Korean leadership advocating concessions when the opposition is so clearly divided does not have a leg to stand on.

In the South, the issue of dealing with North Korea is not only emotional but also highly politicized. That does not encourage nuances in the policy, nor does it permit shifting course easily. The tactical shifts necessary for diplomacy receive exaggerated attention in the press and the National Assembly, and the ROK Foreign Ministry is not known for its ability to buck contrary opinion from either quarter. Press stories, no matter how distant from the truth, generate criticism that makes it difficult for South Korean diplomats to stay the course, especially in times like these, when the Foreign Ministry is under scrutiny from the Blue House as not being Korean enough.

The question here is not whether ROK policy is right or wrong in the context of inter-Korean relations. It is whether circumstances are right for Seoul to cooperate in a multinational diplomatic effort designed to prod the DPRK into dismantling its nuclear weapons program—which is Washington's stated goal.

Beijing

Beijing is probably as ready as it has ever been to participate positively in a diplomatic effort involving North Korea. In 1997, when the

Chinese joined the four-party talks (U.S.-ROK-DPRK-PRC), they were noticeably hesitant, feeling their way through and around the various issues on the table. Before the talks, the DPRK had made it clear it did not want the Chinese involved—consistent with its longstanding position that the PRC, having withdrawn the Chinese People's Volunteers in 1957, had no direct role to play in permanent peace arrangements on the peninsula. For the most part, the PRC delegation hung back in the talks, neither wanting to play nor wanting to be seen as playing a major role. There was no sense that the four-party talks were crucial to resolving an immediate crisis. And, because there was no pressure for a settlement, the talks meandered, foundered, and then expired, leaving the Chinese the space they needed to remain bland and relatively unexposed.

By contrast, in 2003, Beijing was concerned that the Korean situation was on the edge of getting out of hand. It moved quickly to stabilize things by arranging first three-party, then six-party talks. Washington's complaint that Beijing was not doing "enough" to pressure the North was beside the point. The time was right for constructive Chinese participation in the process. It simply was participation not geared to achieve the same ends Washington had in mind. It was never a good bet that the PRC would exercise the sort of leverage Washington hoped would substitute for a coherent U.S. policy toward North Korea.

Having noted that the Chinese have become more active and involved in the Korean nuclear issue than in the past, it would be fair to suggest that the PRC did not insert itself in the diplomacy because it wanted to see a negotiated solution. Instead, it wanted the talks as a shield, to prevent something worse—direct military action by the United States. Many would argue that the United States would never have chanced such a move, but in the atmosphere fed by public and private U.S. rhetoric at the time, such a development seemed possible in early 2003.

Over the past few years, with the diminution, in both perception and fact, of U.S. leadership in the region, it is not surprising that Beijing might see an opportunity to fill the vacuum. It is impossible to say what China's position on the diplomacy might be if there were still strong U.S. leadership, and a united U.S.-ROK-Japanese stance on the question of dealing with North Korea. In the absence of those two factors, it was almost inevitable that the Chinese should see the situation in its broadest geostrategic terms, not focused on the North Korean nuclear issue but rather on a more fundamental question—who will be the predominant power in Asia for the rest of the century? U.S. inability to deal with the North Korean problem over the past four years has ensured that the Chinese would be both more involved and, to some extent, less "useful."

Moscow

Moscow's role in the talks is limited, as Russia has sought to claw its way back, so far unsuccessfully, to being a player in Northeast Asia after a decade of cutting itself out of the action. If Russia is playing a significant role in the diplomacy on the North Korean issue, that fact is well hidden. No doubt Russia has passed messages, but that is not the same as influencing the situation. Ever since Foreign Minister Shervardnadze had his ears pinned back by DPRK officials for saying that Moscow was about to recognize the ROK, Russia has had little influence on the peninsula. Boris Yeltsin had no use for North Korea, and Pyongyang had only disdain for him. The situation improved markedly with Vladimir Putin's rise to power. Kim Jong-Il seems to have developed good personal relations with Putin, but sure signs have yet to emerge that those relations translate into the policy realm.

What Next?

It is easier to criticize than to fashion solutions that work. "More sticks," is an often-heard suggestion, usually made out of frustration or ignorance rather than careful calculation. But the concept of "sticks," admittedly like the concept of "windows," offers mental shorthand that can lead down false trails. Sticks, real sticks, are used either to threaten an animal (think of the dog beaten so often it cowers when you simply raise your hand) or to prod it in the right direction—think donkey or dumb ox. But North Korea is not a dog, or a donkey. There are no "sticks"—either applied or threatened—that will simply cause it to respond in the "right" way.

There have been few times when the North has responded to the threat or application of force. The Korean War is hardly a good example. The 1976 Panmunjom incident is not a good example either, because there is no evidence that the United States' sudden threat of force dissuaded the North from taking more aggressive action. To the contrary, almost as soon as the incident took place, the North signaled that it hoped to contain the problem and not have it grow into something bigger. It did not take Kim Il-Sung long to pass the necessary apology to defuse the situation. Similarly, in 1994, the common wisdom notwithstanding, there is little evidence that the North meant to go to the brink—much less over it—by unloading its nuclear reactor. At worst, Pyongyang realized this action would cause a spike in tensions, which it hoped to fix in short order. In this version of events, Jimmy Carter did not talk Kim Il-Sung into a solution so much as push the United States onto the right path, leading back to diplomacy.

If not sticks, then "carrots." But this is another term that gets us thinking the wrong way. The archives in Pyongyang may someday show that the North Korean leadership was encouraged to take positive steps because of inducements, but as a general rule, this group seems disinclined to move in any direction—especially one that looks antithetical to its long-term interest—just for a suitcase full of cash. The big, defining decisions are not made because of carrots.

The North's basic posture of neutrality in the Sino-Soviet conflict, its decision to encourage a continued U.S. presence on the peninsula— these fundamental policy lines were reached on the basis of strategic calculation. The Agreed Framework did not come about because the North was "bribed" by the promise of two light-water reactors. The Kumchang-ri agreement of 1999, which allowed the United States to inspect an underground site in the North, was not about getting access through a bribe of grain shipments. Critics like Nicholas Eberstadt repeat the accusation, but the United States could not have gained that agreement by bribing the North with grain even if it had made the effort. No amount of grain at that time would have induced Pyongyang to allow inspections of an underground site if there were not already a deeper policy motivation to engage in and improve relations with the United States. Carrots can be helpful, not in getting the North to go in a direction it firmly opposes, but in easing the way for a decision in the leadership. In Pyongyang, as in many capitals, it is important to be able to make the case that a decision to retreat was not, in fact, a concession.

For the Agreed Framework, for the Kumchang-ri agreement, and even for some measure to elicit DPRK cooperation on terrorism, the timing was right because both the United States and the DPRK had decided that moving toward improved, nonhostile relations was in their separate interests. Whatever the shortcomings of the Agreed Framework and the results that flowed from it, these could have been addressed and, to a large extent rectified, because the window for the necessary follow-up diplomacy was open.

By contrast, the timing has been wrong for the six-party talks that began in 2003. The preparations appeared to be even worse. The concept of the talks was not thought through, the execution was clumsy, and the results have, consequently, been negative. There was little comprehension in Washington about what it would take to keep such a complex process on track, and no stomach for doing it. In fact, it appears that many at senior levels in the administration either did not want or never believed the diplomacy would work in the first place. Indeed, it could not work as long as the United States completely ruled out serious bilateral talks with Pyongyang even within the six-party setting.

Consequently, over the past several years, rather than putting in place the building blocks for a multilateral approach, Washington allowed more and more necessary pieces to fall away. The human capital—the experienced diplomatic team built up over a number of years—was squandered and even the remaining, isolated pockets of expertise were ignored. There were only episodic displays of self-discipline on the part of senior officials, up to and including the president. Commitment to building an effective multilateral approach required displays of restraint and good sense when speaking on the North Korean issue. To be fair, there was some of that, but not nearly enough, and the atmosphere for negotiations, as a result, was never good.

It is likely that by now, Pyongyang has re-examined its own position on the feasibility, if not the value, of improving ties with the current administration in Washington. It is a hallmark of the DPRK that it rarely closes options for itself. It would not have survived this long if it operated on the assumption that it has permanent enemies. Certainly, the North remains prepared to talk with the United States. The question to be probed in such talks is whether, over the past couple of years, Pyongyang has put itself in a position that it can no longer discuss returning to the status quo ante with its nuclear program, to say nothing of dismantling the program completely.

The other parties have gone along with six-party talks largely to keep the United States in check. But the gaps between them and Washington have widened, not narrowed. We have not gained ground but lost it. The U.S. conception of where the talks should lead and, most important, how they should proceed, is shared only piecemeal by the others. The differences become more pronounced the more negative the situation becomes.

The circumstances still existed for dealing with the North Korean nuclear issue in 2001 and 2002—if Washington had freed itself of several pernicious, politically borne myths about the lessons from the previous eight years of engagement with Pyongyang. The window began closing in 2003, when the United States rejected bilateralism and insisted on a multilateral approach. The complexity of such an approach required considerable forethought and preparation. It received little of either. Real lessons of an earlier failed, multilateral effort with North Korea (the four-party talks of 1997–99) were ignored. And potentially useful lessons from KEDO's ongoing, relatively successful multilateral effort were put to the side.

Good timing is important, and rare. Something is almost always seriously out of kilter. More often than not, many elements are working against diplomatic progress while only a few support the effort. Careful preparation, geared to current realities, will not work wonders, but it can create conditions that render a diplomatic initiative less fragile, more prone to bounce than to shatter when—as inevitably happens—it hits a bump.

Preparations could not have overcome many of the basic problems already facing us in Northeast Asia in 2002. Nothing would have changed the domestic political situation in Japan, for example, or altered the ROK government's basic posture on pressing inter-Korean engagement with little regard for the status of the nuclear question. But better preparation might well have buffered the process, dampened the differences between the key trilateral parties (U.S.-Japan-ROK) and made it possible to take better advantage of those bits of progress that eventually did emerge from the first three rounds of six-party talks. If multilateral diplomacy on the North Korean nuclear issue is to find a real window of opportunity, it will need a better sense of the constraints on each of the parties, fuller preparations, and an abundance of the crucial element that was most in short supply the first time around—U.S. leadership.

NORTH KOREA TODAY:
POLITICS OVERLOADED AND SECULARIZED

Haksoon Paik

North Korean politics is overloaded by the difficult tasks of securing two vital interests: national security and economic development. For North Korea's economic reform and opening to succeed, a favorable international environment in which foreign trade with and foreign investment in North Korea can be expanded is required. Thus far, however, the North Korean nuclear problem has prevented the international community from trading with or investing in North Korea.

On the one hand, the North Korean leader Kim Jong-Il is under heavy pressure to achieve both goals. He needs not only to enhance domestic economic performance but also to seek resolution of the nuclear question in the international arena and secure security assurances from the United States. Being aware of the contradictory aspects of these objectives and the structural constraints on his ability to attain them, Kim Jong-Il appears to have strategically disconnected them, lest his economic efforts be thwarted by the prolonged nuclear confrontation with the United States.

On the other hand, North Korea appears to have been secularized significantly by the breakdown of orthodox socialist politics in recent years. Military-first politics and practical-gain socialism prevail in North Korea where the party took precedence over the military and the *juche* idea was the official ruling ideology.

This paper aims to answer the following questions in order to understand North Korean politics today. What are North Korea's current policy priorities? How did the country's economic policy and economic situation influence its policy priorities? What constraints does North Korea face in achieving its policy goals? How seriously has the nuclear issue prevented North Korea from attaining these goals? What strategies has North Korea adopted to secure its policy objectives under the existing constraints? How much has North Korea been secularized by the breakdown of orthodox socialist politics in North Korea? How stable is the North Korean political leadership and what are the prospects for power succession? What is the current state of affairs in inter-Korean relations? How have North Korea's policy priorities affected those relations? How do current inter-Korean relations influence North

Korean politics? Finally, what is wrong with the U.S. policy toward North Korea, and what can South Korea do to resolve the North Korean nuclear problem in a peaceful way?[1]

Policy Priorities

As is the case for any country, achieving national security and economic development are two of North Korea's vital tasks. Generally speaking, they go hand in hand, but the environment must be favorable in order to achieve both. In the case of North Korea, economic recovery and development have been heavily constrained by the developments in the security arena, particularly those related to the United States.

National Security and Nuclear Resolution

The North Korean leadership appears to have resolved simultaneously to seek nuclear resolution and attain security assurances from the United States and enhance economic performance at home. Unless the North Korean nuclear problem is resolved and security assurances from the United States (and other six-party participants) are obtained, North Korean economic recovery and development will be limited by its isolation from the international community. Under such circumstances, it is not surprising that North Koreans tend to think that "security is absolutely an important aspect of what they need to do to move beyond where they are now in terms of the reforms that they'd like to take place, in terms of relationships they'd like to develop with South Korea and Japan" and that "they view these really as impossible without getting beyond the current state of affairs with the U.S., and primary among that is a security assurance."[2]

North Korea's preoccupation with promoting national security has much to do with its hostile relations with the United States, the only country with which North Korea has been in conflict since its birth in late 1940s, including the war in the early 1950s. In the format of armistice, both countries are still at war.

Indeed, though decades have passed, North Korea's policy toward the United States, since the collapse of the Soviet Union and the East European socialist states, has been consistent: to officially end the Korean War at the earliest possible time, to sign a peace agreement, and to normalize relations with the United States. Any seemingly provocative actions that North Korea took against the United States were intended not to sever the relationship but to bring the United States back to the negotiating table. North Korea wanted to make a deal with the United States to resolve the festering issues between the two so that both countries could improve and normalize their relations.[3]

North Korea appears to have come to the six-party talks assuming that the goal of the U.S. policy is to denuclearize the DPRK. It also seems to have assumed that it could strike a comprehensive give-and-take deal with the United States by strategically giving up its nuclear weapons and weapons program through multistage actions. But the United States' lack of political will to solve the nuclear problem early together with stalled six-party talks and the stigmatizing of North Korea as an "outpost of tyranny" led by a "tyrant" disillusioned the North Korean leadership. From the perspective of the North Korean leadership, it had become a target for the U.S. campaign to spread freedom and democracy. The leadership likewise perceived that U.S. policy toward North Korea was regime change and system collapse instead of denuclearization and nonproliferation.

North Korea responded to the regime change policy defiantly and forcefully: it announced its possession and manufacture of nuclear weapons, its intention to expand its nuclear arsenal, and its decision to boycott the six-party talks indefinitely, until the United States met certain conditions.[4] North Korea's offensive put the United States on the defensive and threw the latter's predicament into stark relief. Neither the United States nor the other six-party participants could marshal effective countermeasures or counter resources to undo North Korea's nuclear manufacture and possession. This impasse effectively forces the United States to admit the failure of its North Korea policy and to correct it in order to resolve the nuclear crisis.

Economic Recovery and Development

North Korea is in the midst of an historic transition, from a traditional orthodox socialist economy to a practical-gain socialist economy with expanding market elements. North Korea introduced historic economic management reforms on July 1, 2002. The reform measures included: abolition of free rationing of food and daily necessities; discontinuation of subsidies to factories and firms for carrying out production or distribution activities; decentralization of economic planning and management except for some key strategic areas; expanded autonomy in business administration for firms and factories; introduction of capital goods exchange markets; introduction of prices based on real production factors and decentralization of price decisions; elevated role of currency in economic management; raised salaries to meet the rising cost of food and daily necessities; and the devaluation of the North Korean currency against the U.S. dollar.[5]

North Korea's July 1, 2002, reforms were a watershed event in the country's history, and their scope has been consistently enlarged ever since. The leadership proclaimed that the reforms had been conceived and carried out according to "our own style, ingenious economic management system and method suitable for developing realities and conditions of our country."[6]

The spirit that cut across all these reform measures can be summarized thus: "no free ride," "no averaging out," and "practical gain should be a top priority." The North Korean government named its economic policy "practical-gain" or "real-gain" socialism and emphasized the importance of making real profits in running factories and businesses.[7] Firms and factories are evaluated by the real profits criterion; those that fail to achieve such profits are punished. Korean households must hold to a similar standard; unless they earn their own living, they will drop out in the new economic environment, where the government does not ensure their livelihood and daily necessities.

North Koreans have recently become more dependent on money than on their government for their survival; North Koreans understand that "money talks." One of the negative components of this mindset is a widespread attitude that "money is everything," "money can do anything," and "I have to survive even by deceiving others." Support for collectivism and socialist egalitarianism is disappearing and individual selfishness prevails substantially across all social strata. Naturally, party cadres and government officials were repeatedly warned that greed for material gains is the first step toward ideological degeneration and that they could avoid falling victim to self-interest, materialism, and individualism by enhancing their level of revolutionary fervor.[8]

In late 2002, North Korea took dramatic measures to increase economic access to the outside world and improve relations with Japan. The designation of Sinuiju as a special administration district, Mount Kumgang area as a special tourist zone, Kaesong as a special industrial zone, and the DPRK-Japan Joint Declaration in Pyongyang (Pyongyang Declaration) all point to this new economic outlook.

Constraints

Several structural constraints, both domestic and external, prevent North Korea from achieving its policy goals. The two most conspicuous domestic constraints are first, the North Korean leadership's mentality of "being besieged" by hostile external powers, and second, the military's precedence over other state apparatus.

North Korea's "siege mentality" is the negative side of North Korea's long confrontation with the United States and Japan, and its isolation from international community. It also explains North Korea's defensiveness about its policy toward the "outside world." Siege mentality sometimes incites an offensive, confrontational attitude and approach to the outside world. It engenders distrust and hinders the North Korean leadership in its effort to widen its *Weltanschauung* and accommodate the outside world in dealing with sensitive issues. Siege mentality also causes time to be squandered when cooperative actions are called for. North Korea's loss of almost one year before it responded to the Clinton administration's goodwill in 2001 is one typical example. Siege mentality weakens decision making by heightening distrust of others.[9]

The precedence of the military characterizes North Korea's entire policymaking process and helps to predict the outcome of the country's power struggles and resource distribution. Kim Jong-Il has carried out military-first politics since the unprecedented economic hardship and famine in the mid-1990s. The military has had a big say in making policy—security-related and otherwise. North Korean generals are not simply professional military officers but also politicians who hold top high-ranking positions in the party and the National Defense Commission and are involved in decision making at the top level. In making U.S. policy and nuclear policy, the military has had more power and influence than any other groups in the country.

With respect to external structural constraints on North Korea achieving its policy goals, the two most salient are the North Korea-U.S. hostility and what might be termed legitimacy competition with South Korea.

When President George W. Bush came to power, he reversed the Clinton administration's policy toward North Korea, took up the issue of North Korea's highly enriched uranium (HEU) program in October 2002, and accused North Korea of clandestine pursuit of its nuclear program in violation of the Agreed Framework and the Nuclear Nonproliferation Treaty (NPT). These actions launched a new wave of anti-North Korean policy, which discouraged North Korea's efforts to secure a favorable international environment for the economic reform that it had introduced only a few months before.[10] They also drove a wedge between North and South Korea and between North Korea and Japan, at the precise moment that North Korea was accelerating inter-Korean relations on the one hand, after the historic June 2000 inter-Korean summit, and North Korea-Japan relations on the other, with Japanese Prime Minister Koizumi's September 2002 visit to Pyongyang.

The Bush administration, arguing that North Korea "admitted" the existence of the HEU program in the talks with James Kelly in Pyongyang, retaliated by stopping the delivery of heavy fuel oil (HFO) to North Korea. This maneuver practically killed the Agreed Framework, the foundation upon which U.S.-North Korean relations had been built. In response, North Korea removed the International Atomic Energy Agency (IAEA) inspectors and inspecting cameras from Yongbyon nuclear reactor and pulled out of the NPT in January 2003.

With North Korea's expulsion of the IAEA and its withdrawal from the NPT, the United States effectively lost a vital channel for firsthand information-gathering, along with its control mechanism and leverage over North Korea's nuclear-related activities. In other words, the United States now fell into a structural dilemma: it could not prevent North Korea from going nuclear if North Korea wanted to do so. This predicament continued until recently, when North Korea announced its manufacture and possession of nuclear weapons in February 2005.

How seriously has the nuclear issue prevented North Korea from attaining its vital national interests or policy goals? It appears that North Korea has been cornered and reluctantly pursued the nuclear option, risking the stakes it otherwise could have secured from the United States, had the United States been willing to negotiate. It is known that the North Korean leadership once truly believed in the value of possessing nuclear weapons, but subsequently realized that pursuit of nuclear option would be at the expense of improved relations with the outside world, including the United States. North Korea had demonstrated its strategic acumen when it signed the Agreed Framework in 1994, in which it played the nuclear card in exchange for securing its external survival through an improved relationship with the United States in the realms of security, diplomacy, energy, and the economy. However, when George W. Bush was elected, Kim Jong-Il faced an enormous obstacle in carrying out his strategy of nuclear resolution through dialogue and negotiations with the United States.

North Korea showed consistency in its strategic thinking when it came to the six-party talks in Beijing and put forward a concrete nuclear resolution proposal a multistage, comprehensive package deal based on the principle of simultaneous action at each stage. But the United States showed no serious response to North Korea's willingness to negotiate. Tragically, the U.S. government appears to have shifted its policy toward North Korea from denuclearization to regime change and system collapse. More importantly, North Korea perceived the shift in such a way that it must have elected to announce the manufacture and possession of nuclear weapons in order to protect itself from redefined U.S. objectives.

It is worth re-emphasizing that North Korea's seemingly provocative actions are geared to catch U.S. attention and bring the United States to the negotiating table. North Korea wants to make a deal with the United States. Unfortunately, North Korea's actions have often been misinterpreted in precisely the opposite way, particularly because North Korea has behaved provocatively in times of rising tension or when external strategic environments were perceived to be unfavorable. Ironically, the North Korean leadership views such tense periods as the best times for action, because then they are most likely to catch the full and serious attention of the United States and the international community. The September 1998 test firing of the multistage ballistic missile Taepodong I and the February 10, 2005 announcement of the manufacture and possession of nuclear weapons are cases in point.

Another external structural consideration that has constrained North Korea in formulating and implementing its policies has been authority over or competition for loyalty of the Korean people with South Korea. North Korea believes that it must fend off the possibility that South Korea could substitute for North Korea in the minds of the North Korean people. Unlike Vietnam, which has already achieved territorial unification, or China, which treats Taiwan as a lesser competitor, the North Korean leadership is instinctively preoccupied with "legitimacy competition" with South Korea, and this influences its policymaking. Such "legitimacy preoccupation" indeed, the very consciousness of competing with South Korea has always prevented North Korea from taking more dramatic, bolder cooperative measures toward the South, except on those occasions when cooperating with South Korea would not hurt the North's interests or when South Korea was weakened and thus unable to pose a threat. Kim Jong-Il's summit talks with South Korean President Kim Dae-Jung in June 2000 after South Korea's economic collapse and the IMF bailout at the end of 1997 are but two examples of this syndrome.

Strategies

What strategies could be employed in North Korea to overcome the constraints that prevent the North Korean leadership from achieving national security and economic development? Again, North Korea's tragedy can be attributed in large part to the inherent conflicts between these two policy goals, possessing and developing nuclear weapons on the one hand and urgently needing economic recovery and foreign assistance on the other. North Korea suffers from this contradiction, but it must explore ways to resolve it. As noted earlier, the North Korean leadership has sought to overcome it by disconnecting and then separately prioritizing economic development from nuclear weapons development, so that the former is not thwarted by the latter.

For Kim Jong-Il, achieving both of these vital interests, especially under current circumstances, has not been easy. Despite the increasing tension and security threat resulting from the Bush administration's hostile policy, however, North Korea introduced dramatic market-oriented reforms, fully aware that such measures would undermine the existing socioeconomic order and could lead to instability and even chaos. In other words, in July 2002, North Korea's introduction of market elements at a time of heightened security threat from the

United States was a critical choice: for domestic security through better domestic economic performance. Kim Jong-Il elected to strengthen the domestic system, which he thought he could achieve under the circumstances, rather than promote external national security, which then seemed unlikely to improve.

Some historical background for this critical choice is useful to understand its significance. It is noteworthy that North Korea's top priority since mid-1990s when it experienced an unprecedented famine on a massive scale has been economic recovery and development. It was natural that, beginning in 1998, North Korea advocated and pursued the policy of "building up a strong and prosperous state" more than any other in order to feed its people and secure economic recovery and development.

It is also noteworthy that North Korea's pursuit of economic recovery and development coincided with the engagement policy pursued by the Clinton administration in the United States and the Kim Dae-Jung government in South Korea. President Kim Dae-Jung came to power in 1998 and launched the Sunshine Policy toward North Korea, which helped the United States to see that engaging North Korea was beneficial for promoting its own national interests.

As a result, North Korea was then less concerned about security threats from outside, which freed the leadership to concentrate on economic recovery and development. It was clear that achieving domestic system security was more important for North Korea than concentrating its energy on external national security, given that the United States and South Korea had adopted less confrontational stances.[11] Put differently, the North Korean leadership preferred to achieve domestic economic recovery and development than to confront the United States with hostile policy. And, since the U.S. security threat was greatly diminished, it did not present an obstacle on the road to economic development.

Accordingly, after 1998, North Korea strengthened its policy toward the United States by taking positive steps: officially ending the Korean War, signing a peace agreement, and normalizing relations. Such a series of positive measures was possible particularly through the good offices of various South Korean leaders, beginning with President Kim Dae-Jung. Thereafter, the historic inter-Korean summit talks in June 2000; the visit to Washington, DC, by Jo Myong-rok, North Korean Vice Chairman of the National Defense Commission, in October 2000; and U.S. Secretary of State Madeleine Albright's exchange visit to Pyongyang in the same month—all of these reflected North Korea's strategy to establish a more favorable external survival structure. Strengthening domestic system security, which economic failure and famine had so critically undermined, was a crucial element of that strategy.

President George W. Bush's coming to power in January 2001 and his pursuit of an anti-North Korea policy threw cold water over the developing relationship between the United States and North Korea. More than anything else, the task of achieving national security against an external threat, including hostile U.S. policy, re-emerged as a top policy priority. North Korea now began to suffer greatly from an unfavorable international environment, which seriously incapacitated the North Korean leadership in meeting its economic recovery and development needs.

Under these circumstances of increasing security threat from the United States, North Korea introduced market elements in July 2002. There was more to this critical choice than meets the eye. It reflected the North Korean leadership's strategic choice to de-link the priority of accomplishing economic development from that of achieving national security, and the resultant change in policy priorities. Economic recovery and development have now become the focus of attention for the North Korean leadership.

At the same time, North Korea demonstrated its intention to get out of this dilemma by making diplomatic efforts to get security assurance from the United States through nuclear negotiations. As noted earlier, North Korea has taken the position that it absolutely needs security assurances from the United States to facilitate reform and also to improve relations with the United States and Japan to bring about economic recovery and development.

Given this revised position, North Korea faced a serious setback when it could not start real negotiations with the United States. The Bush administration felt neither the urgency nor the political will to resolve the North Korean nuclear issue and chose not to come to the negotiating table in a bilateral format even within the multiparty talks. The fact that the United States was caught in the Iraqi war was no doubt one reason for its inability to concentrate more on the six-party talks. More importantly, the Bush administration's bullying posture, which ignored North Korea's interests, intentions, and capabilities, failed not only the progress of the six-party talks but also North Korea's plan to attain U.S. security guarantees and to concentrate economic recovery and development through a give-and-take deal in the nuclear resolution.

North Korea's inability to implement its strategy impelled it to undertake provocative actions, again, to bring the United States to the negotiating table. It announced its manufacture and possession of nuclear weapons, its intention to expand its nuclear arsenal, and its decision not to return to the six-party talks until the United States met certain conditions. This destructive offensive by North Korea immediately put the ball in the U.S. court. Likewise, it put the United States on the defensive, at a time when it had no problem-solving strategy or effective countermeasures to employ against the North Korean offensive. The United States now had to continue its earlier policy, only to fail or be forced to revise it in order to accommodate the new developments.

Within the context of North Korea's provocation, it is important to understand that nuclear weapons, or even developing nuclear weapons, are not the ultimate goal per se. They are instruments with which to achieve specific higher-level goals, such as national security and economic development.

Eventually, if certain milestones are ignored during this weary tug of war, North Korea may not be persuaded to give up its nuclear weapons and may harden its position to possess nuclear weapons on a permanent basis at whatever cost. Recently, on September 19, 2005, in the joint statement of the fourth round of the six-party talks, it was agreed to denuclearize the DPRK and the Korean peninsula as a whole, but North Korea does not appear to be prepared to discuss the dismantlement of its existing nuclear weapons and weapons program as part of the six-party process. Such discussions and inspections could take place only after the United States and North Korea have greater mutual trust and have established normalized relations.[12] This means that only trust-building and successful negotiations—even though they will be time-consuming—can dismantle North Korea's nuclear weapons. To begin the process as soon as possible, good-faith negotiations between the United States and North Korea are crucial.

In addition to its economic reforms, the North Korean leadership sought economic recovery and development by expanding and strengthening its economic cooperation with South Korea. North Korea is known to have had high expectations for the policies of the Roh Moo-hyun government in the South. President Roh was elected with a campaign pledge that he would continue to promote the Sunshine Policy of the Kim Dae-Jung government and seek a more mature and equal relationship with the United States. But President Roh's policy toward North Korea soured because North Korea was believed to possess a secret HEU program, and South Korea collaborated instead with the United States in order to resolve the nuclear crisis.

Despite the growing tension between them, however, both Koreas have one thing in common: both want to keep economic cooperation alive and to expand the scope of that collaboration for political as well as economic reasons. Unfortunately, North Korea could not get enough economic cooperation from South Korea, mainly because the United States, at the height of the nuclear confrontation, pressured the Roh government to limit the scope of inter-Korean economic cooperation to the status quo level.

North Korea Secularized: Military-first Politics and Practical-gain Socialism

The prevailing description of North Korean politics today is that it is overloaded by the two vital tasks of achieving national security and economic development. Yet how might current North Korean politics be qualitatively characterized?

Current North Korean politics adheres to the concept of secularization, two indicators of which are military-first politics and practical-gain socialism. The precedence of the military over the party and other power apparatus is a sign of the breakdown of the orthodox socialist politics in North Korea, where the party traditionally took priority over the military. The military's priority accommodates realities in terms of the change in power and power relations.

Long before the post-2002 nuclear standoffs and the 2002 introduction of economic reform, North Korea advocated military-first politics in 1995 (fully in 1997) and the buildup of a strong and prosperous state in 1998 as the mainstays of political stability in a volatile and destabilizing atmosphere. North Korea's military-first politics was designed to encourage the military to play a leading role in safeguarding the existing regime, to advance economic construction, and to guide the people to follow the military's examples. Also note that the military-first politics represents Kim Jong-Il's political need to entertain the military, the country's most powerful and potentially dangerous power institution, at a time of unprecedented political and economic difficulties in North Korea.

Using military-first politics, Kim Jong-Il intensified ideological indoctrination programs, urging the people to equip themselves with revolutionary optimism in order to overcome the pending crisis. At the time, when North Korea celebrated the tenth anniversary of Kim Jong-Il's military-first politics, the military-first idea even appeared to have replaced the *juche* ideology as the official ruling idea and slogan.

This decline of the ruling *juche* ideology is the other sign of the secularization of North Korean politics. Currently, in addition to military-first politics, practical-gain socialism and the practical-gain mindset prevail in the government's economic policy and the daily lives of North Koreans. While *juche* emphasizes independence and self-reliance, practical-gain socialism consciously or unconsciously stresses the importance of interacting and cooperating with the outside world for economic benefits. North Korean society appears to have become much more secularized than before.

What ideology will hold people together as North Korea secularizes still further? The *juche* idea is undoubtedly embedded in the current military-first ideology, but *juche* itself is not emphasized as explicitly as before. North Korea argues that the military-first (song'un) idea represents the new higher stage of the *juche* idea. Kim Jong-Il is lauded as the founder of the military-first idea, which is invoked as the country's official ruling ideology. Practical-gain socialism has more to do with making economic reform and performance a success.

Political Stability and Power Succession

Facing the formidable task of overcoming the structural constraints and revealing limits to its strategies for survival, North Korean politics today is overloaded by the simultaneous tasks of securing national security and economic development. Yet what North Korea vitally needs to sustain itself, first and foremost, is political stability.

No doubt Kim Jong-Il is firmly in control and North Korea does enjoy political stability. The party, the government, and the military are loyal to Kim Jong-Il and his policy lines. Kim also appears competent in accommodating, balancing, and controlling the power elite and in mobilizing the people for loyalty and compliance.

However, Kim Jong-Il constantly faces the nagging question of how to strengthen the legitimacy of the North Korean system and how to prove his ability as a leader under the current circumstances. He is sandwiched between the domestic demand for better economic performance and the external demand to resolve the nuclear problem. To prove himself as a leader, he must perform in some critical areas: to effectively indoctrinate the people so they comply voluntarily with the leadership's new policies; to flexibly and smoothly accommodate the changes and developments inside and outside North Korea; to deal proactively with outstanding security and international issues; and to provide daily necessities for the people and achieve macroeconomic goals.

The year 2005 is a special year in that it marks the 60th anniversary of the founding of the Korean Workers' Party, the 60th anniversary of the liberation of the Korean nation from the Japanese rule, the tenth anniversary of the military-first politics, and the fifth anniversary of the June 15, 2000, North-South Joint Declaration.[13] The year 2005 is also a politically and historically important year for Kim Jong-Il to prove his ability as a leader by making a breakthrough in security and international issues and improving the sluggish economy. Otherwise, it will not be easy for him to strengthen the legitimacy of his rule and, thereafter, open a new era for himself. Even more important in 2005 is that North Koreans will have to celebrate these special anniversaries, particularly the 60thanniversary, which possesses a special meaning as a 60-year-long life cycle is completed and a new one is begun, according to Asian culture.

The North Korean leadership began 2005 by declaring that the agricultural front will be the foremost attack front in economy.[14] Currently, every effort in North Korea is focused on producing more food in order to solve the chronic food shortage. No one wishes to celebrate the special 60th anniversaries in hunger. It is reported that high-ranking officials and party cadres have even been sent for one-year periods to provincial, county units to supervise the implementation of party and government policies related to agricultural production.

It is noteworthy that North Korea came up with another important choice to agree on a comprehensive denuclearization of North Korea in the fourth round of the six-party talks in September 2005 and that North Korea recorded the best harvest in 2005 in the past ten years. These two events appear to have given a significant break to the North Korean leadership, at least for the time being.

Since 2004, North Korea has witnessed generational change in the important positions in government, military, and industry. Younger cadres and officials in their forties and fifties were posted to these positions, which until recently had been held by the old guard. This change of generations was most remarkable in the realm of industry. Most of the managers of companies and enterprises in North Korea are now in their thirties and forties. Kim Jong-Il has apparently decided to take up the reins of the party, government, military, and industry and gallop them along his policy line so that his regime can survive as it faces mounting pressures from outside.

If North Korea is to successfully conduct economic reforms and nuclear negotiations with the United States, it owes that possibility to Kim Jong-Il's stable political leadership and his lack of political challengers. It is noteworthy that, as a leader, Kim Jong-Il has been flexible and competent enough to accommodate new ideas and policy choices, for example, as demonstrated by the dramatic reform measures of 2002.

In the long run, there will doubtless come a time when Kim Jong-Il's ability will be tested in terms of maintaining political stability and simultaneously accommodating more liberalized political demands. What is almost certain, however, is that the future North Korean leadership will be more responsive to, and accountable for, the needs of the people, particularly their economic needs.

Recently, the question of who will succeed Kim Jong-Il has drawn the attention of North Korea watchers. There is a rumor that his second son is the heir, but there has been no reliable hard evidence on this issue within North Korea, and it remains to be seen. But one thing is clear: North Korea cannot afford to suffer political instability over the succession issue when the political elite so desperately needs unity and stability to solve the problems it faces at home and abroad. No rational leader will allow his subordinates to discuss or even float the idea of power succession, which could make people rally around the heir apparent and accelerate the lame duck status of the incumbent.

Inter-Korean Relations

What is the current state of affairs in inter-Korean relations? How have North Korea's efforts to achieve its two policy priorities affected inter-Korean relations? And how does the current state of affairs influence North Korean politics?

Inter-Korean relations have been damaged and distorted by the conflict between North Korea's policy of ignoring South Korea's role in resolving the nuclear issue, particularly at the earlier stages of the six-arty talks, and its desire for South Korean economic cooperation and humanitarian assistance. How did this distortion influence South Korea's policy toward North Korea?

First, South Korea was disillusioned when North Korea tried to ignore South Korea's effort and role in nuclear dialogue and negotiation. As a result, in addressing the nuclear problem, the South valued inter-Korean cooperation less than its alliance with the United States. Yet it is worth pointing out that South Korea could not fully distance itself from North Korea and tried to continue its cooperative policy in the areas of economic cooperation, social exchanges, and humanitarian assistance. It did so mainly because it could not betray its South Korean constituency, which supported inter-Korean reconciliation and cooperation for the long-term benefit of the Korean nation. This conflict of interests called into question the legitimacy and effectiveness of South Korea's policy toward North Korea on both sides of pro- and anti-reconciliation forces in South Korea, and it undermined the support base of President Roh and his government.

In addition, inter-Korean relations fared poorly for the past two-and-a-half years because of U.S. pressure. The Bush administration used North Korea's HEU program as an excuse to cut off its relationship with North Korea. Influenced by these developments, North Korea concentrated more on the North Korean nuclear standoff than on inter-Korean relations in an effort to make a breakthrough in the former. It has been North Korea's pattern of behavior that it concentrates more on the U.S. relationship when U.S. policy threatens its interests. Thus, the North Korean leadership tends to see the inter-Korean relations in the context of North Korea-U.S. relations when it comes to serious security issues related to the defense of the regime and system from the U.S. threat.

President Roh Moo-hyun came to power through the critical presidential election in December 2002, when the North Korean nuclear crisis posed an increasing threat to South Korea's security interest.

Likewise, President Roh's North Korea policy was formulated and implemented under circumstances of nuclear threat. The United States also put considerable pressure on South Korea to bring its policy in line with that of the United States. However, President Roh's policy toward North Korea and his vision of inter-Korean reconciliation and cooperation did not entirely agree with those of former President Kim Dae-Jung.

First, President Roh has tended to treat inter-Korean relations as more of short-term, give-and-take relationship based on reciprocity (though not publicly expressed as such), while President Kim Dae-Jung treated them as a long-term proposition, based on the special relationship between two halves of the same nation.

Second, President Roh practiced linkage politics between inter-Korean relations and the North Korean nuclear problem, while President Kim refused to accept such a linkage. In other words, President Roh decided not to promote inter-Korean economic and other cooperation as long as the North Korean nuclear problem remains unresolved, whereas President Kim pursued inter-Korean national rapprochement and Korea-U.S. alliance in parallel. President Kim persisted in refusing quid pro quo not only for the nation's long-term interests, but also for the inter-Korean dialogue and open channels of communication that might in themselves ultimately resolve the nuclear problem.

Third, the Roh government, unlike its predecessor, has not had an independent and exclusive North Korea policy. President Roh's policy for peace and prosperity was not a policy directed exclusively toward North Korea; it was formulated to promote peace and prosperity not only on the Korean peninsula but also in Northeast Asia as a whole.

The most immediate and important objective of President Roh's "policy for peace and prosperity" was to remove and resolve the North Korea nuclear threat through cooperation with nations interested in Korea. Accordingly, President Roh elected to strengthen South Korea-U.S. alliance cooperation and put less emphasis on improving inter-Korean relations. His actions split his support base in South Korea and also significantly distanced North Korea.

How, then, does the current state of inter-Korean relations influence North Korean politics? To be sure, the prolonged standstill in inter-Korean relations has not helped Pyongyang's pro-inter-Korean reconciliation forces. Furthermore, the slow progress in economic cooperation with South Korea in the Kaesong Industrial Park, coupled with South Korea's faithful collaboration with the United States at the six-party talks, has apparently inspired disappointment with the Roh government. This disillusionment underscores Pyongyang's current inclination that any deal with South Korea except for humanitarian aid and economic cooperation should be realistic and minimal until

South Korea proves, to a significant extent, to be an independent and positive actor in nuclear and other security-related areas.

Conclusion

It is worth summarizing some of the problems with U.S. policy toward North Korea, and also some actions that South Korea might take in order to resolve the nuclear issue peacefully.

The U.S. policy in particular has serious problems in its key assumptions, evaluations, and predictions. First, the Bush administration appears to assume that if the United States and its six-party partners put collective pressure on North Korea, it will give in and unilaterally abandon its nuclear program. Second, the Bush administration seems to comprehend that North Korea has not given in so far because the six-party participant states have not exerted sufficient pressure. Third, the U.S. government is not ready to admit the existing conflicts of interest and potential ruptures among the six-party talks participants about what steps should be taken, especially when the United States employs negative, punitive measures against North Korea. All of these indicate that the United States has never properly taken into account North Korea's interests, intentions, and capabilities, let alone those of other countries. North Korea's February 10, 2005, announcement wasa serious blow, and the Bush administration's apparent lack of enthusiasm for implementing the September 19, 2005 joint statement of the six-party talks further highlights the U.S. negligence.

It now appears that the Bush administration believes it is offering several significant "incentives" to North Korea in exchange for cooperation in the nuclear dialogue and negotiation. First, the administration repeatedly mentioned "no attack, no invasion" of North Korea. But no attack, no invasion announcements are not security assurances or guarantees in themselves. The difference between no attack, no invasion announcements and true security assurances is that the latter presuppose a change in U.S. policy toward North Korea—accepting the country "as it is" and meeting it in good faith as a negotiation partner. The former is merely lip service that requires no change in policy. North Korea even acknowledges that a written security guarantee remains only a sheet of paper if U.S. policy toward North Korea does not actually change from hostility to peaceful coexistence.

Second, the Bush administration distinguishes between "regime change" and "regime transformation." Such a distinction will make no sense to the North Korean leadership and indicates that the United States plainly does not accept the North Korean regime "as it is." The Clinton administration, too, used the expression "regime transformation."

But the Clinton administration conceived of North Korea's gradual transformation into a market-oriented, democratic regime by helping the North to introduce changes through engagement with the United States, whereas the Bush administration seeks to transform the North Korean regime without acknowledging North Korea's self-initiated reforms and gradual change to date.

Third, the Bush administration has repeatedly promised to consider a big benefit package to North Korea—including energy-related assistance—if North Korea returns to the six-party talks and first makes concessions; the same promise was repeated in the six-party joint statement. But North Korea does not appear ready to return to the negotiating table because of an unrealized fancy aid plan—distrust between North Korea and the United States runs too deep for such a simplistic proposal. Rather, what is required is a series of incentives that could provide North Korea with excuses to resume negotiations and make concessions. This means that the United States and other six-party talks participants have to accommodate North Korea's demands to a significant extent.

At least for the moment, these three incentives have neither been perceived nor accepted as such by the North Korean leadership to resume negotiations with the United States through the six-party talks. Regardless of North Korea's having gone nuclear, it is only through direct negotiations based on a comprehensive give-and-take that the country's nuclear programs can be dismantled and removed.

An idea of establishing a direct negotiation channel between the two Koreas has gained support among South Koreans since the second-term Bush administration has failed to show any flexibility in its North Korea policy, and no new, effective solutions have otherwise emerged. Under these circumstances, the logical choice left for South Korea is to open a direct inter-Korean channel for nuclear negotiation. While the U.S. government has no leverage or control over North Korea's nuclear-related activities, an inter-Korean channel could be an additional support channel for achieving the goal of nonproliferation in North Korea.[15]

Notes

[1] Some of the ideas and arguments in this chapter was presented at a seminar hosted by Center for Northeast Asian Policy Studies and the Korea Initiative at the School of Advanced International Studies (SAIS) at Johns Hopkins University on "South Korea's Democracy and Diplomacy," Brookings Institution, Washington, DC, Tuesday, March 23, 2004. For the complete event transcript, see http://www.brookings.edu/fp/cnaps/events/20040323.htm.

[2] "The North Korean Deadlock: A Report from the Region," Brookings/Asia Society Briefing, Brookings Institution, Washington, DC, January 15, 2004.

[3] *Rodong Shinmun,* January 9, 2003.

[4] *Rodong Shinmun,* February 10, 2005; *Korean Central News Agency,* February 10, 2005.

[5] "Kyongje Puhungul wihan ch'angjowa Pyonhyok: Pon'gyokjokuiro Ch'ujindoenun Kyongje Kwalli Kyeson" (Creation and Reform for Economic Rehabilitation: A Full-scale Economic Management Reform), *Choson Sinbo,* July 26, 2002. See also other economic management reform-related articles in *Choson Sinbo,* July 26 and August 2, 2002.

[6] "Let Us the Party, Military, and People Wield Higher the Great Power of the Military-First in a Single-Minded Effort," New Year's Joint Editorial," *Rodong Shinmun, Chosun Inmin'gun, Ch'ongnyon Chonwi,* January 1, 2005. See also *Choson Shinbo,* December 12, 2004. *Choson Shinbo* is a pro-North Korean newspaper published by a pro-North Korean residents' league in Japan. Cited in *Yonhap News,* December 12, 2004.

[7] A North Korean economic journal argues that *silli* (practical-gain) is something that demands of the workplace and the workers could obtain while giving priority to fulfilling national and social interests. *Kyongge Yon'gu,* March 2004.

[8] *Yonhap News,* January 10, 2005.

[9] See Robert Carlin, "Talk to Me, Later," chapter 2 in this volume.

[10] It was known later that North Korea had planned to introduce the economic reforms in January 2002, but President Bush's naming of North Korea as part of the "axis of evil" in his State of the Union speech made North Korea postpone the introduction of the reforms until July 1 that year.

[11] Note that "national security" and "system security" are conceptually differentiated here. National security has more to do with fighting the security threat from outside, whereas system security has more to do with fighting the security threat at home.

[12] Joint Statement of the Fourth Round of the Six-Party Talks, Beijing, China, September 19, 2005.

[13] The year 2004 was also a special year for Kim Jong-Il: it marked the 40th anniversary since beginning his work and career at the Korean Workers' Party, the 30th anniversary since being named "Party Center" and de facto heir to Kim Il-Sung, the tenth anniversary since the death of Kim Il-Sung, and the de facto tenth anniversary since being named the Chairman of the National Defense Commission, the highest government office in North Korea.

[14] See "Let Us the Party, Military, and People Wield Higher the Great Power of the Military-First in a Single-Minded Effort," January 1, 2005.

[15] Haksoon Paik, "What is the Goal of the U.S. Policy toward North Korea: Nonproliferation or Regime Change?" PFO 05-30A: April 7, 2005, Policy Forum Online, Nautilus Institute. See http://www.nautilus.org/fora/security/0530A_Paik.html.

NORTH KOREA: HOW TO REFORM
A BROKEN ECONOMY

William B. Brown

Ten years ago, in the summer of 1995, in Washington and in Seoul it was fashionable to predict the imminent collapse of North Korea's political system, and even the state itself, following in the footsteps of its Soviet cousins. Looking back, while clearly an errant forecast, it is easy to see why the pundits and the analysts thought the way they did. Kim Il-Sung had died the previous summer, abruptly ending a 40-year dictatorial reign. Kim's son and carefully groomed successor, Kim Jong-Il, was demonstrating no leadership ability just as the country was suffering a massive agricultural failure. A nuclear-weapons dispute with the United States had brought on a costly full-scale mobilization of the country's million-man army. And for those with access to more sensitive information, it was clear that the country's industry had essentially shut down; almost nothing of commercial value was being produced. Night imagery of the peninsula showed, quite literally, that the lights were out in North Korea.

A Continuing Analytical and Developmental Failure

By now, in mid-2005, sentiment in Washington and in Seoul has all but shifted 180 degrees and, again, not without reason. The Kim dynasty has, after all, demonstrated that it has more lives than a cat. Most remarks on North Korea now include the word *resilient* and focus on how impervious Pyongyang is to change. Despite their wide tactical differences, policymakers in both Washington and Seoul are now resigned to live with Kim Jong-Il, seemingly giving up on improving human rights and peaceful unification and only demanding that Pyongyang end its most dangerous project, the manufacture of nuclear weapons. All kinds of inducements are likely to become available if only North Korea takes a few steps that, on the surface, would seem to help the regime last another 50 years.

Again, however, this conventional wisdom may prove to be in error. Just as fear of North Korean instability led to more than $10 billion in Western, Chinese, and South Korean contributions to regime stability, overconfidence in regime resiliency may deter needed reform and lead the country and its people to further calamity. The truth, of course, is that no one really knows what will happen to North Korea, even over a period as short as the next ten years. This chapter looks at what is needed for economic reform to take place, reform that likely would save the country but which equally likely would force big changes in the socialist system and the Kim regime. Such reform is thus a middle scenario, bracketed by collapse on the one hand and continued isolation on the other. But whether it is a likely scenario is not at all clear. Reasonable people might put equal bets on each of these three outcomes.

One thing is clear. Kim Jong-Il stands at the center of a dilemma that will have important repercussions for his own legacy and the survival of the North Korean state. So far, he has shown a willingness to sacrifice the country—witness the million or so starvation deaths in the man-made famine of the mid-1990s—to his own ambition. Even so he has shown some inclination toward reform, removing in 2002 the centerpiece of his Stalinist controls, the public rationing system for food and other essential goods and services that guaranteed something akin to a slave system in which everyone is dependent on the largesse of the state. In doing so he allowed private markets to take a tentative hold on the economy. And now, the big powers of the region have offered a tempting proposition—all he has to do is drop his advertised nuclear weapons program and he will get lots of help in joining the market-driven East Asian economy.

Will Kim Jong-Il take what some might see as the bait, a poison pill that ultimately will destroy his socialist system? Or will he be able to grasp the moment and truly lead North Korea out of its morass? Again, no one can really know. My sense is that Kim Jong-Il is ultimately a weak leader, incapable of driving his nation successfully through politically dangerous but economically necessary market reforms. And, unfortunately, the mantle given him by his powerful father is large enough for him to monopolize power, preventing anyone else from taking the reins. In a nutshell, Kim appears to be reactive, not visionary, believing that the reforms needed by his countrymen would spell the end to his personal regime. Even so, Kim's inability to drive reform does not necessarily mean that reforms won't happen. North Korea's current weak central state is under a withering torrent of pressure from internal market forces—forces driven by desperate people in search of food and by factory workers who have lost their factories. Kim and his regime may thus be driven, kicking and screaming, into what they see as a vile market economy.

Clouding our picture of North Korea's economy is an absence of data and analysis. North Korea itself produces little in the way of information on economic conditions or policies. Interestingly, however, where information gaps appear, the South Korean government and others step in, acting as spokesmen for the Pyongyang government. For example, Pyongyang itself rarely appeals for foreign aid, instead allowing foreign donors to plead its case. And the most widely used economic statistics for North Korea are published by South Korea's central bank based on what at best are educated guesses of economic activity. The South Korean analysts do an admirable job of compiling bits and pieces of data, but the objectivity of their entire exercise is open to question. After decades of saying nothing positive about North Korea, official Seoul now attempts to put North Korea in the best possible light, trying to prove the efficacy of the Roh administration's politically charged engagement policy. South Korea's president, for example, recently proclaimed North Korea's reforms to be "irreversible" and Seoul's Unification Ministry seems to exaggerate Pyongyang's verbal commitment to reform.[1] Again, Seoul might be right, but its arguments are hardly convincing given the huge risk to South Korea itself should policies be implemented that are based on overconfident, some might say hopeful, analysis.

The South Korean government is not the only one at fault in issuing politically correct analysis. Western and international aid groups, having bought their access to North Korea with several billion dollars in food aid over the past decade, produce volumes of survey data but are unable to answer basic questions about the impact of the aid on North Korea's macroeconomy. Most damaging has been the reporting of the World Food Program (WFP), which for years has spread North Korean propaganda regarding the cause of the country's persistent malnutrition and disease. Now, in its latest report, after finally dispensing with the "bad weather" argument, the WFP worries that free markets are raising the food costs for the urban elite and the legions of privileged state workers, without considering the benefits that market activities and higher prices and wages are creating for the impoverished farmers and day laborers. So, by WFP's argument, food aid must continue to pour into the cities with no regard to its impact on the third of the population that are farmers or, for that matter, the hundreds of thousands of miners and manufacturing workers who should be employed in export-oriented endeavors.[2]

Meanwhile, European countries, which traded with and invested in the North extensively in the 1970s, but which have yet to receive payments on several billion dollars in government and private sector loans made to Pyongyang for now derelict industrial plants, managed to put on a conference on economic development in Pyongyang last fall without even mentioning the stinging but politically difficult debt default issue.[3] European government and academic functionaries act as if Pyongyang's lengthy pattern of not paying bills is of no importance to European businesses whom they expect to work with North Korea. But, of course, it is. Since the 1970s there has been almost no European–North Korean trade even though there are no political constraints on such activities.

American academics are hardly any better. In thousands of panel presentations of domestic and foreign economic issues, last January's American Economic Association annual meetings produced no papers on North Korea's critical economic situation. The profession has become so tied to statistical data that when a government does not produce data, economists have nothing to say.

There are some exceptions. Several think-tank researchers have helped to focus attention on the North Korean developmental problem in excellent books and articles on the topic[4] but their organizations generally lack the resources to undertake substantial firsthand research. And some South Korean government researchers, carefully distinguishing themselves from their government institutions, have published excellent reports on North Korea's banking system.[5] Interestingly, some of the best analysis may now be coming out of China and Japan where economists and newspapers are putting an acute eye to the potential for doing business with North Korea's problem-plagued but potentially lucrative economy.[6]

This chapter does not begin to fill this analytical void but it attempts, from an economist's perspective, to view what is happening in North Korea. *It argues that large changes are under way, but that the impetus for these changes is as yet unclear, at least outside North Korea. The crux of the question is whether the changes result from a top-down decision to reform or a bottom-up unleashing of market forces that a weakened regime can no longer restrain.* Any policymaker, businessperson or humanitarian worker needs to address this question before engaging with the North Koreans. If Pyongyang is resisting a bottom-up transformation, economic aid may be forestalling or even preventing reform. Given the small size of the country compared with the large size of potential foreign influences, such aid might be inadvertently keeping alive a comatose system, with disastrous results for the population. This is not to say unequivocally that no aid should be given. Even if reform is unwanted, aid properly placed and with substantial skill may still advance reform in a stealthy manner. But that implies that the aid givers must be more skillful than the regime stalwarts with whom they deal.

On the other hand, it is possible that Pyongyang is searching for a better way. One is reminded of the late 1970s when few if any outside specialists understood the dramatic nature of changes that were occurring in China's economy—even the collapse of the entire commune and cooperative farm system went generally unreported. If Pyongyang is intent on reform, as the South Korean government asserts, a dramatic solution to the economic and social problem can be forged relatively easily once the nuclear problem is resolved. The key in this case is to learn from what has occurred in China and South Korea, North Korea's neighbors and perhaps the two most successful economic reform stories of the late twentieth century. Their main lesson, as we discuss in the later parts of this paper, is that while outsiders can help on the margin, the key to reform and progress lies in giving ordinary workers the tools and incentives to produce for the future. And the best tool they can have is a well-working monetary system that encourages and rewards their savings and their investments. Dumping aid commodities on a country that produces commodities and avoiding discussions on finance and debt in a country that desperately needs capital are hardly helpful to a regime that might, at its heart, want to build a modern economy.

A Broken System

The story of North Korea's economic breakdown is by now well known but perhaps not so well understood. The aid community, with the best access to firsthand information about North Korea, has persistently colored its reporting to protect its privileged access to North Korea. In a situation best likened to a hostage situation, the aid providers argue in private that if a clear picture were portrayed in public Pyongyang would revoke their visas and no help would enter and people would starve. Of course people starved anyway and ten years later, with gloomy forecasts still right around every corner, these aid and humanitarian groups are beginning to play the issues in a more straightforward manner.

Food shortages are a symptom but not a main cause of North Korea's misery. Pyongyang's own statements explain the problem as one of bad weather; lack of access to U.S. technology, capital and markets (the so-called U.S. blockade); and the collapse of North Korea's allied states. One is tempted to think of a poor orphaned child, forced to go it alone. Pyongyang fails to mention that its limited access to world markets is the natural reaction of businesspeople not to deal with a country that is unreliable in its agreements and never pays its bills. As for an "embargo," what is to be made of a country that does not even attempt to enter the World Trade Organization or other international trade and finance organizations. The complaint against the US treatment of North Korea is particularly faulty. Like China three decades ago, with only a modicum of effort there is little doubt that North Korea could have access to what it apparently thinks is the all important U.S. market. But it also doesn't seem to understand that access does not mean credit. Credit must be earned in a way that Pyongyang does not seem to appreciate.

Aid and humanitarian groups tend to focus on other issues, such as natural conditions in the country that make it difficult to support agriculture, and North Korea's weak technology and infrastructure. Missing in their stories, however, is how easy it would be for North Korea to afford commercial imports of foodstuffs if only minimal priority were given to exports of minerals, metals, and other manufactured products. A single well-working nonferrous metals mine, of the type developed in North Korea by Japanese colonists prior to World War II, could earn enough foreign exchange to meet the country's food import needs. Prior to the 1990s North Korea regularly imported grain to make up the difference between domestic production and needs. It is difficult to understand why over the past decade Pyongyang has accorded the provision of food such low priority and why it has acquiesced to beggar country status. Again the most likely rationale for this tragic situation is the lack of reasonable leadership in Pyongyang.

Pyongyang correctly lays some of the blame of its industrial collapse—almost all major factories in the country have been shuttered for more than a decade—on the collapse of the Soviet economic bloc and its trading system. Even though North Korea was never formally a member of the Soviet regional system, its economic planning mechanisms were connected tangentially to the Soviet planned economy and considerable industrial trade occurred. Thus when Soviet and East European factories closed or shifted to market-based transactions in the early 1990s, North Korean factories were forced to compete for their business and generally lost.

More difficult for the Kim Jong-Il regime to acknowledge is the coup de grâce of North Korea's Soviet-styled economy—the death of Kim Il-sung in July 1994. The elder Kim is highly revered but, ten years later, his son can hardly blame the still faltering economy on the absence of the commanding father. It would make his own tenure look too dismal. But in part this is true. In the small, centrally controlled system that Kim Il-Sung had developed over his 40-year reign, Kim senior played the role of the essential micromanager, personally allocating resources and materials within the relatively simple industrial economy. He did this without the use of money or budgets—simply by the force of his personality and his close relationships with the managers of the country's 50 or so major industrial establishments. All without the use of money or markets, coal was moved from mines to chemical fertilizer factories, and the fertilizer to state farms, and the food to the public distribution centers, given out without charge as rations to the entire population. Annual and longer-term plans were developed to formalize this structure, but these plans never worked well. Instead, whenever there were disputes among the factories or the agencies, Kim could personally settle the issue and the needed transfers were made. Western analysts continually joked about Kim's "on-the-spot guidance" but this, in reality, probably kept the country running. And when the country faced real shortfalls, extensive aid from the Soviet bloc and China was always available to fill in the gaps.

When Kim died, this arcane management-by-fiat system died with him. His son had been well prepared to take over management of the economy, but evidently has lacked the personal ability to command resources. Coal mines thus began to flood for lack of electricity to run the pumps, even as electric power plants shut down for lack of coal.

Rail transportation instantly froze up for lack of steam coal and industry froze up for lack of rail transport. Without chemical fertilizer and power for irrigation pumps, the rice and corn harvests failed and the people, without recourse to money, trade, or markets, began a quick march to malnutrition. Tragically, with no one in charge, the absence of money and markets in the 1990s prevented the people from moving or even trading for essential goods and services. Andrew Natsios thus labels the situation as a silent famine in place.[7]

By 1996 or 1997 North Korea's economy, if not its political system, had indeed collapsed. An economy, by one definition, is a social system that allows the specialization of labor. By the late 1990s, specialization of labor had essentially ended for millions of farmers and industrial workers. Hungry coal miners abandoned their mines and scratched bark off trees to find something to eat while freezing farmers abandoned their fields and combed the hillsides for heating fuel. Without the "great leader" or a central plan to tell them what to do, and with markets and money strictly illegal, trade between coal miners and the farmers simply stopped.

Adaptation and Foreign Aid

That autarkic situation, or *juche* (self-reliance) economy as cynics might put it, is not the end of the story, as we have since found out. People, and even economic systems, adapt to hardship and North Korea's economy has rebuilt itself somewhat from the dire situation of the late 1990s. Foreign aid has been critical to this rebound but so has spreading grassroots-level private activity, filling in for the absence of the planned economy. Perhaps most important, money, often in the form of foreign currency, has quietly re-entered the economy and has begun to support the creation of a market economy.

Foreign aid is most visible in the delivery of food aid, which in the decade since the 1994 famine began has amounted to about $3 billion from the West, continuing even today. The World Food Program this year counts some 6.5 million recipients of its aid in a population of 22 million, funded mostly by the governments of the United States, Japan, and South Korea. Additionally, China provides in volume terms approximately an equivalent amount of food aid.[8] Of a minimal physical requirement of about 6.5 million tons of grain per year, North Korea produces about 4.8 million tons and foreign charity provides the rest. Amazingly, for a mineral rich and agriculturally poor country, North Korea now purchases commercially almost no food. This is a large change from its historical pattern in which food products were imported (1945–90) or in the centuries before the country was divided, when they were transferred commercially from the agriculturally rich south in exchange for coal and manufactured products from the more industrialized north.

This overall food situation has not changed significantly since the Western food aid program went into high gear in 1996 and 1997. Outright famine has been alleviated by this aid program, but malnutrition has not—WFP in spring 2005 reported that its surveys show about a third of the population is still chronically malnourished. And, according to the UN Population Fund, life expectancies have dropped about five years over the past decade[9]. The WFP warns of another famine if its food aid requests are not met for 2005.

Less visible but perhaps more important is energy aid. China delivers, apparently at no cost to North Korea, essentially all of North Korea's crude oil needs from the large Daqing oilfields in Manchuria to a refinery the Chinese built in the 1970s just inside the North Korean border near Sinuiju. Russian deliveries to a similar refinery in northeastern North Korea stopped many years ago after North Korea stopped paying for deliveries. U.S. delivery of a not insubstantial volume of heavy fuel oil (500,000 tons per year) ceased in 2003 after Pyongyang ended its cooperation on nuclear fuels. As with food, North Korea in the 1980s commercially imported crude oil from several Middle Eastern countries but no longer does this, apparently unwilling to give up precious foreign exchange or devote the effort needed to export products and earn funds needed to purchase petroleum.

Even with huge inflows of this commodity aid, Pyongyang can no longer fully support its public distribution system (PDS), the rationing mechanism that the regime has used since 1958 to effectively control the population. Following the famine, and with continued insufficient public disbursement of food, activity in the small and legal farmers' markets and in the large illegal urban markets surged. And as market activity expanded, the PDS pipeline sprung more leaks as collective farms began to divert production to the much more profitable markets. Over time this market activity expanded beyond foodstuffs and went far beyond the capacity of the government to control, with literally hundreds of thousands of people congregating in urban markets every day, even in Pyongyang, trading products and services within sight of the governing elite. Initially the currency in these markets was North Korean won and a scattering of Japanese yen, but won-denominated prices soared, fueled by money that was withdrawn from the large but meaningless won savings accounts that people had accumulated.[10] As a flood of newly minted money reached the markets, won quickly lost its value, and traders resorted to barter and to the use of Chinese, Japanese, and even U.S. currency.

The July 2002 Reform or Readjustment

By mid-2002 this market activity had apparently gotten out of control, with massive illegal markets operating even in Pyongyang city, off-limits but clearly visible to foreign visitors. Government department stores, with fixed but meaningless prices, moreover, were empty. On July 1, in its most dramatic economic move since markets were deemed illegal in 1958, Pyongyang snapped its official ration-controlled prices to the much higher black-market prices and encouraged everyone to use the markets. Salaries (generally paid only to state, Workers Party, and state-owned enterprises employees) were increased severalfold in a one-time jump to allow these public workers to afford the new prices. Presumably nonsalaried workers would cope and even benefit by privately selling whatever products and services they generate at the much higher market prices. And with rationed stores selling produce at market prices, the ration system formally ended for most people. Finally, the won was devalued by 98 percent, matching the existing black-market rates. The net effect of this move was to erase all of the monetary savings in the system, starting everyone over with essentially zero monetary wealth.

By now some modest external analysis has been performed on these policy changes. Almost all analysts predicted a huge increase in inflation and this is indeed the case. As predicted, the jump in prices proved not to be a one-time step movement but launched spiraling inflation that continues to the present. Even at the time it was apparent that Pyongyang made a huge mistake in not taking the price changes one step further and issuing a new currency—allowing some but not all of the old currency to be exchanged for the new currency at a reasonable rate of exchange. This would have allowed the public to retain some faith in the country's central bank, the issuer of currency. Instead, no one has any reason not to expect Pyongyang to again devalue its money and thus they trade it as fast as they can for foreign currencies or hard goods.

Figure 4.1 shows the inflationary response in terms of price of rice, North Korea's main food commodity. Other consumer prices similarly have soared.

Figure 4.1

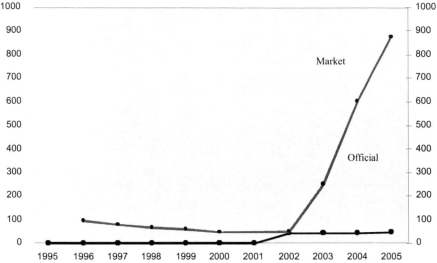

North Korea Rice Price: 1995-2005
Won per Kilogram

Some analysis, especially given by the South Korean government, mistakenly in my view, also sees the July 1 measures as "opening the economy" to the outside world.[11] This view does not recognize that Pyongyang has always been open to its own monopoly brand of foreign trade and investment. North Korea, like all socialist countries, has always engaged in trade with non-socialist economies whenever it was allowed and has always attempted to bring in foreign investment. Since socialist trade and investment are monopolized by the state, however, market economies have to create rules as to how they are to deal with them. Partially for this reason the GATT was created after World War II and entrance into the WTO is still a requirement for a country like North Korea to participate in trade on a normal basis with competitive market economies. This is not just a U.S. requirement but is true for all market economies. Since the 2002 policy measures, North Korean foreign trade has expanded but largely through informal activities that flow across the increasingly porous border with China, not as the result of official policy. And the level of trade with the outside world remains only about half the level of the 1980s.

It may be understandable that South Koreans, and to a lesser extent Americans, see North Korea as "opening up," but in both cases it is their own countries that have lifted restrictions and, in South Korea's case, given big incentives to trade with the North, rather than changes in

64

the North. And except for politically motivated investment from South Korea, there has been no new foreign investment in North Korea since 2002, and no prospects, given no efforts by Pyongyang to improve upon its dismal credit rating.

We are left then, even three years after the 2002 policy measures, unable to answer the important questions as to what Kim Jong-Il was thinking then and what he is thinking now.[12] Is this an effort to truly *"reform"* the economy or is an effort to regain *control* over deteriorating and out of control black markets?[13]

In the North Korean context, if even the first step of reform—letting supply and demand rule in the production and distribution of goods and services—is the course Kim Jong-Il has intentionally set his country upon, this will result in an enormous transformation of the entire social system. It will then be reasonable to expect a Chinese- or Russian-like transformation to lie fairly close at hand, likely beginning within a year or two.

The problem for analysts is that most of the same tactics that would suggest reform could have been employed by the state simply in a one-time effort to regain control over the marketplace. State-owned stores would offer high enough prices to producers to induce them to sell to the state—and high enough prices to consumers to cover the government's procurement costs. Instantly, the high-profit margins on the black market—gained for instance by buying rice at the ration price of 0.2 won per kilogram and selling it in the market for 50 won per kilogram—would disappear and the merchants themselves would disappear.

The Current Contradiction—Hyperinflation in a Fixed-Price Society

If controlling out-of-control markets was Pyongyang's intention in 2002 it surely did not work. For as soon as the won was devalued so suddenly and so sharply, the North Korean populace learned not to hold on to it. Hoarding of hard goods, swapping won for hard currency, and buying everything off the shelf, ensured a sudden and sustained boost in won-denominated market prices, creating something close to hyperinflation in a country that until a few years earlier had only known fixed prices.

Since 2002, market prices have continued to soar, more than doubling every year at an annual inflation rate something above 100 percent. Official prices for rationed goods and for wages and salaries apparently have remained at the levels set following July 1 and, therefore, are now as much out of balance compared with market prices as they were before the reforms. This leads to many inconsistencies and contradictions. The World Food Program, for example, in its spring 2005 request for food aid donations, exemplified this confusion when it stated that at the current exchange rate of about 2,400 won per dollar (up from 150 won per dollar in July 2002 and 2 won per dollar in the 40 years prior to July 2002), the average official wage in North Korea is only about 1–2 dollars month.[14] Thus, the WFP explains, an urban (government) salaried worker must work all month just to earn enough for a few cups of rice. But it failed to point out that the government worker earns a ration card that gives him the rice and that the nongovernment worker, in the market, can earn many times that amount. After all, whoever sells the rice earns that amount of money.[15]

Figure 4.2

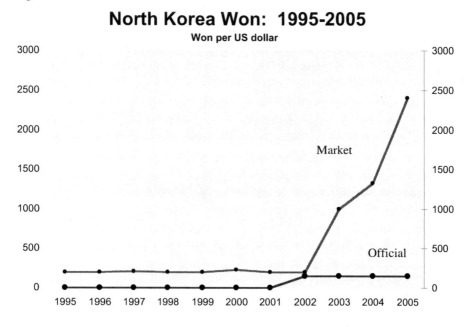

North Korea Won: 1995-2005
Won per US dollar

With nominal state-set salaries again so low as to be meaningless, it is the access to perks of state employment, especially the PDS food rations that are offered such workers, plus state-provided housing, education, and health care, that holds the state's workforce together. Rations are raised and lowered, presumably based upon food availability to the PDS, not necessarily to the country at large. Media reports last month stated that a 25 percent cut in rations this spring and summer indicates a shortfall of food is again occurring. This might be the case, but it might not if privately available food is increasing, either being grown on farms or imported via China. The WPF presumes the former but others, who see Pyongyang as on a reform tact, might suggest the other.

Whichever the case with food availability, clearly North Korea has by now created a particularly virulent form of a dual economy: one economy in which the state requisitions goods, sets prices, and provides rations, and the other economy in which production and distribution are determined in the markets. This can lead to a situation in which individuals who are able to arbitrage across the boundaries of the state and private economies stand to reap enormous profits. Both the market and the state are corrupted in this process, eventually to the point of state collapse, as occurred all across Eastern Europe.

These enterprising, ambitious, and often capricious individuals who overthrew the Soviet and East European regimes are now beginning to show up in North Korea. So far they seem to be a mixture of officials selling their authority and poor peasants and workers who have gambled right on the volatile markets. Interestingly, Russia media report that North Korean women may be in the driver's seat. Men are more likely to be employed at a state-set and minimal salary while women are more free to buy and sell in the markets, sometimes reaping substantial profits. How important this development is we don't yet know. Despite reports of several hundred newly wealthy North Korean families, and many high-value cars and other conspicuous consumption in Pyongyang, there is no evidence yet to suggest that they are a threat to the state.

Winners and Losers in a Dual Economy

Other than these few emerging tycoons, it is useful to consider who at this point in North Korea's transformation are the winners and who are the losers, at least compared with the command economy that existed in the 1980s and earlier.

Circumstantial and anecdotal information is all we have to go on but at least in theory the emerging market processes should reward those who can produce a good or a service and may penalize those who only consume. Probably a third or more of North Korea's workforce is employed by the state in essentially nonproductive occupations. These include the million-plus-man army, the Korea Workers Party bureaucracy, the ordinary government bureaucracy, and employees of derelict state-owned mining and industrial enterprises. These individuals receive state-set wages that are far below market wages but they have some access to the state's food ration system, residential property, health care, and the like.

With some important exceptions, these official classes are likely to be losers should real market reforms be under way and thus can be expected to be foot draggers. The exceptions may include some mining jobs—Pyongyang has authorized much higher mining wages to try to induce more mineral output—and those party officials who are in position to sell their privileged control of property and other rights. This later, often corrupt, element may turn out to be key to development of reform policy, as it has been in comparable situations in China and in Russia.

Winners in a real economic reform movement will no doubt be the current and past losers—the masses of industrial workers and farmers who live in astonishing poverty in North Korea. Their ability to provide real goods and services in a marketplace would be rewarded by those who need their output. Some elements of this are now present in North Korea, but individuals' ability to increase incomes is still dependent on their ability to improve their own productivity, difficult in the broken-down infrastructure that is apparent in North Korea.

Individuals who can unblock the many bottlenecks that have developed in the North Korean economy are likely to be the biggest winners. Many of these relate to transportation infrastructure and many to imported goods. The simple ability to move agricultural products from farm to city, either by fixing a truck or by use of once discouraged bicycles, can be highly rewarding in a market environment. Most likely, if given the freedom from state intervention, a new class of small business people will emerge.

Sustainability of the Current Situation

Three years after the July 2002 economic measures it is apparent that whereas major changes are occurring they are not likely to be in the direction that the regime would like to see. The most obvious problem indicator is inflation. Pyongyang does not publish inflation data, and the South Korean government for some reason stopped collecting such data once inflation appeared to become rampant. But anecdotal information from the media, from defectors, from travelers, and most of all from merchants involved in the China-North Korea border trade gives a pretty good glimpse of what is happening with North Korean prices.

The most prominent price indicator is the value of North Korean won. Pyongyang matched the 150 won per U.S. dollar rate in July 2002, but the new rate did not hold. The won has continued to devalue rapidly, falling by more than half in 2003 and 2004, and now 2,600 won is needed to buy one U.S. dollar. Prices of rice, corn, and other commodities also soar at a near triple digit rate. Clearly this inflation suggests a sustainability problem with the monetary system and thus the entire economy.

With rampant inflation another phenomenon has developed that must be a nightmare for the central bank and the country's social control apparatus. Since North Koreans do not trust their own money, they quickly exchange it for Chinese yuan and U.S. dollars whenever they have a chance. As much as 25 percent of transactions in North Korean markets now use foreign money.[16] As foreign money use expands, this undercuts the ability of the North Korean government to procure goods and services from its own people, or even to pay wages. And without access to foreign credit, the government itself can easily become starved for funds, much as can occur in a currency-board economy like Hong Kong or Argentina.

These monetary problems suggest the current situation is not sustainable. Again, however, we need to be cautious in interpreting the very different economic and political system that is North Korea. If the border remains relatively closed and foreign aid continues to flow to the regime, the regime may be able to buy back the markets and re-establish control over its internal economy. There is likely a fine line between how much aid is needed to maintain the current chaotic system and how much aid would allow the government to move back to its old planned system.

Next Steps for North Korea—Is the Chinese River Shallow or Deep?

China's Deng Xiaoping often spoke of the hesitating, learning-by-doing approach that the Chinese have followed in making economic reform work since 1978. Most projects were described as experiments, not following a hard and fast policy line. Contradictions and partial solutions were often tolerated. Some people and regions were allowed to get rich; others stayed incredibly poor and remain that way today. Much progress has been made, but even in 2005, big challenges remain, especially the job of creating viable capital markets, the last and perhaps most difficult step in creating a sustainable market economy.

It is tempting to view North Korea as just beginning a similar transition process, 25 years later, guided by Beijing, which remains its main benefactor. And the 2002 measures probably put North Korea in about the same situation as China was in 1978, after Chinese rural markets were legalized but before the communal farm system was abandoned. It is important, therefore, to understand what happened next in China. To the surprise of many, Deng Xiaoping included, the simple unfettered ability to sell goods into private markets quickly pulled apart the core of the Maoist revolution. Within only four years, by 1981, the entire commune and collective farms system collapsed and one billion Chinese peasants were freed to make independent decisions and to profit from hard work. The Chinese peasants responded with an enormous increase in productivity, from fields every bit as denuded as are North Korea's, providing the surplus that continues to drive the economy today. This astonishing development was not a matter of policy; it simply happened as socialist controls were lifted and the peasants rejected their cooperative organizations.

The same revolution might happen in North Korea and in fact might be happening right now. The size of the tiny private plots has been increased and there are some reports of selling or leasing property.

But there are not very many such reports, and observations of others indicate that the state and collective farms are holding together despite the emergence of free markets. One reason might be that the large inflows of food aid from overseas—aid that goes to the urban areas and to the government—limits the potential gains to the private production of food and other products. And in fact one wonders whether the Chinese collective farm system would have collapsed so suddenly had the equivalent of a hundred billion dollars of grain flooded the country in 1978 and 1979. With cities supported by foreign food, the Communist Party would likely have prevented radical changes in the countryside that allowed the peasants to begin to move.

There are other differences with China that need to be considered if North Korea can be expected to follow a Chinese reform path.

- First is the breakdown of North Korea's monetary system. The Beijing government has always been concerned with inflation and never let prices get out of control to the extent Pyongyang already has. Inflation at close to 10 percent annual rate may have contributed to the Tiananmen crisis in 1989. Had inflation reached 100 percent per year, it is not at all clear that the Chinese reforms would have held together.
- Second is access to foreign credit. China prior to reform practiced a conservative financial policy, borrowing little from abroad and paying back debts even under the worst situations. Thus, when embarking on reform, Beijing had easy access to foreign credit with which to import modern factories and technology. In contrast, in 2005, it would be hard to find any country with a worse credit rating than North Korea.
- Third is China's position in the 1970s as largely an agricultural society with a state sector much smaller, proportionally, than is North Korea's today. It's not clear that the one half or so share of North Korean workers who are productive can carry the load of the half that are not productive. And with wage bills growing out of control, Pyongyang must immediately face the issue of unproductive state-owned enterprises, an issue that Beijing has been able to postpone for three decades.

These differences suggest that Pyongyang may have a more difficult path to follow than has China. But it would be misleading to indicate that this path is impossible or that, in Deng's metaphor, the river is too deep or too swift to find the stones. Pyongyang has several important advantages.

- The country's existent industry and its mineral and hydropower resources can form the basis of export-driven development, providing proportionally a much larger lift to the North Korean economy than could natural resources to the Chinese.
- North Korea is a small country in a very dynamic and rich neighborhood. One could hardly pick better geography for integrating into the global economy.
- North Korea's smaller economy can insert itself into the world economy with much less friction than the giant Chinese economy.

Lastly, rapprochement with Japan would likely include the provision of $5–$10 billion in colonial-era reparation payments, giving North Korea a boost similar to that which Japan gave South Korea in the 1960s. If used wisely, these funds could anchor a new North Korean money and banking system, restore external credit, and kick-start foreign investment. If not used wisely, such aid could stymie reforms and maintain a comatose system for decades to come.

Our Next Steps

The South Korean government's assertion that North Korea has "irrevocably" launched itself on a "reform" path is coloring all of its decisions relating to economic interchange with the North.[17] If this were indeed the case our collective policy development could be quite easy. But the confidence exuded by Seoul seems to be the result of hopeful politics, not careful analysis. North Korea has taken an important step in legalizing markets but assessing such moves as irrevocable suggests an important misunderstanding of the large economic and political forces at play within the country.

Figure 4.3. Checklist for Economic Reform

(Y under way, X not observed)

1. * Continuation of inflation—(means market forces are at play)	Y
2. * Changes in relative prices, i.e. rice versus corn	Y
3. Big new public sector wage increases to match inflation	X
4. Reset of Public Distribution System (PDS) prices	X
5. Complete elimination of PDS (end of rations)	X
6. Increase in specialized (not rice/corn) farm production	Y
7. Increase in foreign currency circulation or (see 7)	Y
8. A new North Korea won (say *juche* won)	X
9. * Breakdown of collective farms—private farming	?
10. * Non-kin employment in new, larger, private enterprises	X
11. New central government turnover tax	?
12. * Intense budget debates, government layoffs	X
13. Public attention to Chosen (central) bank policy	X
14. Substantial increase in exports	X
15. Substantial increase in foreign equity (mining) investment	X
16. Official use of "reform" word	?
17. Increase in cross-Yalu border trade	Y
18. New interest in WTO membership	X
19. New interest in U.S. commercial liaison office	X
20. Foreign enterprises directly pay North Korean workers	X
21. ** Central Bank uses high interest rates to absorb currency	X

* Key Items. All five together are necessary and perhaps sufficient evidence of real reform.
** Would suggest must faster reform. Park Chung He (S. Korea 1962) like reforms in process.

In this situation, and in the absence of direct signals that it wishes to reform, the best course of action may be a neutral one: to treat North Korea as a normal country and one not deserving of any special treatment. This would mean large changes in the way we and others deal with Pyongyang.

1. Cessation of all government-to-government commodity and cash aid. Normal countries do not receive foreign aid. Economic aid is perhaps the most intrusive weapon the United States has in its arsenal and such a weapon has to be used with great intelligence. Used blindly, aid likely only serves to reduce the incentives to produce and to reform. North Korea, more than anything else, needs to learn to be more productive and commodity aid is harming that cause.

2. Removing so-called sanctions on North Korea except where North Korean companies or agencies violate U.S. or internationally accepted laws. And where these laws are broken, the United States and others would vigorously prosecute. This again is how normal countries treat each other.

3. Most-favored-nation trading basis with North Korea would not be set until and unless Pyongyang begins to negotiate membership in the WTO, just like any other country. One can imagine a China-like WTO membership process only much accelerated. But until the process begins, the United States would continue to apply very high tariffs on North Korean-made goods, to include products made in the South Korean investment zones.

4. Investment would be allowed and perhaps even encouraged but only in direct compensation or equity terms. Pyongyang deserves treatment as any other country and any other country that does not pay debts does not obtain credit. A debt work-out scheme with membership in the IMF or other financial institutions might be encouraged.

5. North Koreans would be free to enter the United States but would face the same scrutiny as other international visitors and violations of laws would be punished severely. Diplomatic activities would be allowed in a reciprocal relationship to U.S. diplomatic access to North Korea.

By treating North Korea as a normal country, the United States would not be out of step with the other industrial countries. These countries have all had more intensive commercial relationships with Pyongyang in the past and have been burned in the process, so trade and investment does not occur in a meaningful way. Nor do they offer much aid. Japan is somewhat an exception, but its commercial relationships with Pyongyang have plummeted in recent years as criminal North Korean activities have been exposed.

North Korea has two special relationships with which the concept of normal treatment is unlikely or impossible. One is China, which acts as North Korea's final guarantor, except in financial dealings. As the "lender of last resort," Beijing does have different obligations and is unlikely to end all aid to North Korea. But in the absence of other aid flowing into the North, Beijing would derive an increase in leverage and hopefully will use such leverage to obtain better results. A common misperception does need to be removed. Chinese and others assert that a collapsing North Korea would endanger China as swarms of North Koreans cross into China. This type of collapse already happened in North Korea in the 1990s and many North Koreans already live in China. Political collapse is far more sudden and if this were to happen, as in Eastern Europe or Afghanistan, ethnic Koreans would return to North Korea, not the other way around. China should consider that unreformed, North Korea is far more dangerous to China than it would be with reform.

The other special relationship is South Korea. With care, South Korea can promote itself as a useful partner of North Korea, not as an acquisition waiting in the wings. But it needs to show much more resolve in the face of military and political slights. The United States might encourage Seoul to continue some of its cross-DMZ activities in much the same role that Hong Kong played with regard to China, before China began to reform. Outright aid from the South should be ended but investment projects, where it is clear that both sides can profit from continuing operations, might be continued. A good example of such cooperation is the Kumgangsan Tourism project, at least as renegotiated following the bankruptcy of the South Korean partner. And the Kaesong project might proceed if it can be guaranteed that South Korean firms directly employ and pay the North Korean workers, not subjecting these workers to the slave system that exists in the rest of the country. Fertilizer payments and other gifts for hypothetical meetings, however, need to end.

The result of these actions would be to reduce for a time the already low level of U.S. interchange with North Korea, but they would set the foundation for much-improved economic relations to develop very quickly in response to specific North Korean moves.

A clear decision by Pyongyang to move toward economic reform, for instance by taking measures to free the farms and factories, and to develop a normal fiscal system with hard budget constraints that would fight inflation, could then be welcomed by the United States. A careful and sophisticated aid program could be initiated that would focus on helping Pyongyang create a viable monetary system, a key requirement if reforms are to succeed. Japanese reparations could boost North Korean reserves and help it begin to re-establish credit. Applications for WTO and IMF/World Bank/ADB memberships could proceed quickly and trade relations thereby normalized. Pyongyang would then be well situated to proceed in the manner of Beijing, or even faster in the manner of South Korea following its reforms in the early 1960s.

South Korea in the 1960s, in fact, offers Pyongyang and the United States the best model for development that anyone has come up with, and that model includes a big change in U.S. aid policy. In 1962 the United States stopped its commodity aid program for South Korea—ten years of food aid that nearly devastated the South Korean farm economy—and in its place began to help Seoul build monetary stability and a vibrant banking system. Once South Korean inflation had been defeated, and an appropriate banking system set up, the South Korean economy set off on its world record-setting expansion that has brought it from the poorest of the poor countries to middle-income status in two generations. North Korea is now the poorest of the poor. Once set on a similar path, there is no reason to expect anything less from North Korea.

The important nuclear issue is beyond the scope of this chapter, but the author suggests a similar approach could be applied as well. North Korea arguably has the right to develop nuclear weapons, but such developments have hugely negative consequences. Almost any country in the world can have nuclear weapons, but normal countries choose not to because the costs far outweigh the benefits. For starters, accepting a nuclear North Korea would mean, as in the Cold War, a situation in which there are big advantages for more powerful countries to employ preemptive tactics in uncertain situations. In North Korea's case, more powerful countries include each of its four neighboring states, as well as the United States. The chance of mistake then becomes much higher and the costs fall disproportionately on the weak country. It is difficult to expect ordinary trade and investment to develop under such circumstances no matter how benevolent the outside world wants to be.

Notes

Information in this paper is accurate as of May 30, 2005.

[1] See speech by President Roh Moo-hyun in Los Angeles, California, November 15, 2004. "I have noticed many signs of North Koreans' strong desire to reform and open their country. It's very clear that North Korea accepts market economics and that is an irreversible situation," found at http://www.nkzone.org/nkzone/entry/2004/11/controversial_s.php#more. Also see Unification Ministry report of March 2005, found on its web page: http://www.unikorea.go.kr/en/northkorea/northkorea.php?page_code=ue0403&mode=view&ucd=eng0303&ewn_num=158&cur_page=1. The ministry claims that North Korea now uses the word "reform" to categorize its economic policies.

Except for perhaps occasional uses of this important word, North Korean officials generally refuse to use it.

[2] See press conference for WFP in April 2005. http://www.nautilus.org/napsnet/sr/2005/0528A_Banbury.html The European and Japanese media asked sensible questions on the impact of ten years of food aid and the donors provided no answers. See http://www.nautilus.org/DPRKBriefingBook/agriculture/WFP_Projects.html.

[3] See EU web document on the delegation. http://www.delkor.cec.eu.int/en/highlight/NK%20Press.htm.

[4] Marcus Noland, *Avoiding the Apocalypse: The Future of the Two Koreas* (Washington, DC: Institute of International Economics, 2000); Nicholas Eberstadt, Ahn Choon-yong, and Lee Young-sun, *A New International Engagement Framework for North Korea* (Washington, DC: Korea Economic Institute, 2004).

[5] An excellent paper was published in 2004 by An Ye-Hong, chief of the North Korea Research Unit of the Bank of Korea's Financial Economics Research Unit, as translated by FBIS, March 26, 2004.

[6] See "Need for Reform and Opening," in *Heilongjiang xinwen*, November 5, 2004, as reported by Foreign Broadcast Information Service

[7] Andrew Natsios, *The Great North Korea Famine* (Washington, DC: U.S. Institute for Peace, 2001).

[8] Chinese food aid is difficult to tabulate. Some if not much of the international humanitarian aid arrives via China and is thus included in Chinese export data to North Korea. Some grain is provided through annual trade agreements in which North Korea is supposed to barter other products, for example, coal, but always falls short. North Korea thus ends up with large trading debts to China, which are regularly forgiven by Beijing. And, additionally, Chinese provinces send small amounts of explicit aid deliveries to North Korea.

[9] See http://www.nautilus.org/napsnet/sr/2005/0528A_Banbury.html.

[10] For decades, individuals had received money wages but were unable to spend the money since in the absence of markets, it was the ration coupon that was the major constraint. Money simply piled up in savings accounts, withdrawn only for special occasions.

[11] *Understanding North Korea's Economic Reforms* (Seoul: Korea Institute for National Unification, April 2005).

[12] Kim Jong-Il telegraphed the price measures in a speech to his legislature later published by South Korean newspapers. The speech is somewhat ambivalent, decrying the existing system, which Kim complains gives equally to all no matter how much they produce, and so he promises to end free and equal distribution. He speaks about improving profits (for the state) yet he does not quite support the free determination of prices based on supply and demand. It is as if the state can reset prices to reflect scarcity value and then only pay workers for their performance.

[13] The term "reform" when applied to an economy has a very specific and strong meaning in modern Chinese and North Korean usage. Essentially it means moving away from state-set fixed prices to market-determined prices, and from a central planning mechanism to reliance on the laws of supply and demand. In the former, the state determines what is produced and to whom income is distributed;

in the latter, it is the market that makes those determinations. Initially in China, reform may not have included a shift to labor markets—where wages also are determined by supply and demand—but by now to a large extent it has. Reform in this context does not necessarily mean full adoption of capitalism—where capital also is traded in markets—but in China it is now very close.

[14] Other sources give the won per U.S. dollar rate as 2,600 and 2,500 for March and April respectively.

[15] See http://news.bbc.co.uk/2/hi/asia-pacific/3575726.stm. Such statements point to both the incompetence of WFP economic analysis and to the contradictions now vividly apparent in the North Korean economic system. No one anywhere in the world can live for $1–2 *a month* and North Korean officials live reasonably well compared with their rural compatriots. The WFP seems not to understand that a so-called high food price means that someone has the money to bid up the price. Money of course circulates in this system—probably faster and faster in a system where everyone worries over the next devaluation—pushing up prices.

[16] Author's interview with a North Korean official, summer 2004.

[17] See speech by President Roh Moo-hyun in Los Angeles, California, November 15, 2004.

THE PRESENT AND FUTURE OF THE KAESONG INDUSTRIAL COMPLEX

Yeung Sueng Dong

The theoretical logic behind inter-Korean economic cooperation is the creation of synergy by combining the South's comparative advantage in capital and technology with the North's comparative advantage in labor and land. Since summit talks began, inter-Korean economic cooperation has progressed based on this logic. After several false starts, the Kaesong industrial complex began operations intended exclusively for the use of South Korean companies. For now, companies are operating in the park under a pilot program before full operations are to begin. Yet, now in the early operations of the park, one can see—if only partially—what the site could develop into once full operations are put into place.

Although the Kaesong project is not the first case of cooperation between the two Koreas, it is the latest stage of the economic relationship between South and North Korea. In Kaesong, South Korean companies are capitalizing on low rents, and the low wages and relatively high skills of North Korean laborers. The logistics of the operation are quite good as within a 100-kilometer radius of the park is a potential market of more than 20 million consumers. The combination of the low cost of labor, land, and logistics, paired with South Korean companies' capital and technological capabilities has the potential for creating very dynamic synergies. Questions regarding logistics and infrastructure have arisen. But the problems are beginning to be reviewed or resolved early on in the beginning phase of operations.

What will be more difficult to overcome is the political and military concerns, particularly of the United States government. Early setup and consultation was made between the South Korean and U.S. governments as they related to the Wassenaar Agreement on Export Controls for Conventional Arms and Dual-Use Goods and Technologies and the U.S. Export Administration Regulations (EAR) and Commerce Control List (CCL). The coordinated efforts cleared the way to allow 15 companies to begin operations in the industrial park. Less effective have been efforts at resolving the rise of North Korea's nuclear ambitions, and attempts to coax the North into a more open and cooperative engagement with the international community.

Development

Early development efforts began with Daewoo's Nampo industrial complex, which ceased operations in the late 1990s. Samsung Electronics followed with plans to build a 1.65 million square meter electronics multi-complex in June 1999, temporarily securing a site near Kaesong. North Korea had, by this time, become familiar with the concept of an industrial complex. The process of selecting a location for the complex took a few turns. Hyundai first suggested Haeju after considering approachability and circumstances of land transportation and electricity supply.

North Korea expressed a different view when its leader, Kim Jong-Il, offered Shinuiju during talks with former Hyundai president Chung Ju-yung in October 1999. The final selection was made when Chung Mong-hun, former president of Hyundai, and Kim Yoon-kyu, president of Hyundai Asan, visited North Korea on August 2000. They agreed with North Korea's leader on constructing a 66 to 132 million square meter industrial park in the Kaesong area. Later on an official agreement on the complex's construction was signed between South Korea's Hyundai Asan, North Korea's Korea Asia-Pacific Peace Committee, and the National Economic Cooperation Federation.

The North Korean government appointed Hyundai Asan as the developer of the industrial complex. Hyundai Asan acquired permission to use a 66 million square meter site and secured an exclusive business license on the site's general construction in December 2002. Hyundai Asan went on to conclude an agreement with Korea Land Corporation in December 2002. Thereafter, the license for the project's initial phase covering 3.3 million square meters—including rights on financing, design, supervision, and sales—was transferred to Korea Land Corporation.

The industrial park's development faced continuous delays. Hyundai Asan and the North's Korea Asia-Pacific Peace Committee signed an "Agreement on the construction of Kaesong Industrial Park" in August 2000. The groundbreaking ceremony was held three years later, on June 30, 2003. The actual groundwork for construction started about ten months afterwards, in June 2004.

Hyundai Asan and Korea Land Corporation later received approval from the Ministry of Unification to enter into a partnership for the construction project's initial phase of development. Hyundai Asan still has the licenses on the construction project's secondary and tertiary phases. These involve rights for development and tourism on a 62.7 million square meter area in Kaesong, including the 23.1 million square meter industrial complex.

Meanwhile, construction of the complex raised the need to secure a smooth flow of labor and capital between the two sides. Both governments reached an agreement to construct a highway and reconnect the Gyeonggi railroad. They also agreed on terms for employee border control, customs, and quarantine. Railroad and highway construction commenced in September 2000, and both will soon be ready for service. The North subsequently enacted a Kaesong Industrial Complex Law and ten supporting regulations after consulting with the South.[1] This institutionalized the development and operation of the industrial park.

There are several reasons why the development of the complex has been delayed. First, it took a long time for the South Korean government and Korea Land Corporation to plan an institutional framework that would guarantee lucrative terms of investment and independent corporate management. After great patience and effort, the typically rigid North Korean government made considerable concessions. Second, negotiations for guaranteeing safe passage and low rents made no progress, although such factors were essential to the project's development. Fortunately, the agreement on safe passage was concluded this year. Also, developers from the North and South signed the lease contract last March. The necessary conditions have now been met to fully carry out the project under the Ministry of Unification's plans for developing the project (Initial Phase Approval for the Co-Development of the Kaesong Industrial Complex, issued in April 2004). Currently, a pilot project is under way with 15 South Korean companies operating in the 92,400 square meter trial site. The project's purpose is to check out the legal, systemic, and investment environment prior to making the 3.3 million square meter complex fully operational.

Objectives

Doubts have been raised as to whether trade and investment outside the industrial park is advancing under the same idea. Inter-Korean economic cooperation prior to the summit talks was haphazard and still remains so in terms of making consistent plans for cooperation. The North's comparative advantage in labor and land is being utilized, but several factors have prevented them from being used to their maximum extent. For example, the South's unilateral announcement on April 7, 1988, went against the North's denial of inter-Korean economic cooperation, causing trade between the two countries to commence indirectly. It was difficult to maintain true competitiveness as problems naturally arose concerning payment and unnecessary expenses. In order to secure stable payment, such circumstances developed into trade based on consignment processing. But even consignment processing started to show its limits: the inability to provide technical guidance and the unreasonable payment and high distribution cost caused by sea transport.

The summit talks produced an agreement between the South and the North on balanced development through economic cooperation.

Systematic preparations were subsequently made according to this agreement. However, political restrictions made it difficult for the North Korean market to accommodate the South's capital and technology. Setting up an exclusive industrial complex like the one at Kaesong is expected to enhance the level of systems and social overhead capital (SOC) up to that of the South. This project will also be an opportunity for the North to attract capital and technology from the South. Unlike their previous trade with and investment in the North, South Korean companies are showing more interest in the Kaesong industrial complex project because they consider it a chance to truly capitalize on the synergies to be gained between the North and South in general. It might be possible to say that inter-Korean economic cooperation is moving in a normal direction through the industrial complex project.

Operations

What Is Happening in Kaesong Now?

In 2004, a total of 92,400 square meters out of the overall 3.3 million square meters of the complex were sold to 15 South Korean companies. Land lease contracts were concluded on June 14, 2004. The groundwork was finished at the end of the same month and the time is almost at hand to start raising factories. The preparatory committee for the establishment of the Kaesong industrial complex management organization is making arrangements with the North on the factories' design, equipment supply, and plans on manufacturing, sales, and employment.

The South Korean government only approved companies that pose no risk of having their equipment or material taken out to the North. Seven companies were first approved by the Ministry of Unification on September 8, 2004, four more were approved on September 17, another two received approval on October 19, 2004, and two more on January 26, 2005. Nine out of the remaining 12 companies are now building factories. There are about 400 workers from the South and around 1,900 from the North. Around 750 among them work for the 15 South Korean firms. The groundwork is being done by about 1,400 workers and supervised by around 150 on-site managers.

The South Korean government will grant KRW 109.5 billion to construct the complex's initial infrastructure. Waste water is first being processed through a self-treatment facility and then passes to an undercurrent facility. Meanwhile, the North has provided a 66,000 square meter landfill site outside the complex to incinerate waste. Five tube wells are to be developed, each to be shared by three companies.

Support of external infrastructure will only be provided on the trial site within the industrial complex. Since March 2005, commercial power amounting to 15,000 kW of electricity has been made available as well as 100 fixed telephone circuits for communications. Under an agreement on electricity supply, South Korea's Korea Electric Power Corporation was awarded sole rights to carry out the design, construction, and operation of electric power distribution to the complex. Communications are enabled by a fiber-optic cable that directly connects the industrial complex to the Kaesong telephone office and then to Munsan in South Korea. The calling charge will be US$0.40 per minute or lower according to the telecommunications agreement. As a reference, telephone charges are US$0.80 per minute between China and South Korea and US$0.50 between Japan and South Korea.

The South Korean government has decided to enforce an investment guarantee system to prevent the incoming companies' competitiveness from being weakened by increased initial investment and risk due to the political instability of the inter-Korean relationship. This system provides unsecured loans and provides up to 90 percent financial aid on losses up to KRW 2 billion. A public announcement is scheduled for early 2006 that leases are available for the complex's remaining 3.3 million square meters of space, at which point companies will be allowed to move in from the end of 2006.

The Comparative Advantage of North Korean Labor

Labor is one of the prime comparative advantages the North possesses. The quality and quantity of the North's labor force is generally rated very highly with respect to its cost. Among an estimated total population of 22.37 million as of 2002, the working-age population above fifteen years of age was approximately 16.93 million (see Table 5.3). The economically active population was 11.8 million and 69.7 percent of this group actually participated in economic activities. Such a high participation rate compares with an estimated factory operation ratio of around 30 percent and hints at the existence of excessive employment or unnecessary labor. This seems to dispel any questions about securing an adequate supply of labor. Yet, a greater agricultural population than that of the South means North Korea's agricultural sector should be absorbing its labor force (see Table 5.4). This matter is linked with the restructuring of the North's agricultural production and industries in general. Thus, there might be a temporary shortage of labor if a large-scale business project gets under way.[2]

Table 5.1. Development Status of the Kaesong Industrial Complex Project

Category	Major details	Date
Development	• Legal/institutional foundation laid with the conclusion of an agreement on a 66 million square meter development between the Hyundai Asan (South) and the Korea Asia-Pacific Peace Committee (North)	Aug. 22, 2000
	• Agreement concluded on the change in business between Hyundai Asan and Korean Land Corporation (initiated by KLC for the first phase)	Dec. 26, 2002
	•Ground-breaking ceremony of KLC's development office	Dec. 11, 2003
	• Opening ceremony of Hyundai Heavy Machinery Maintenance office	Dec. 22, 2003
	• Related contracts such as rent and compensation fee for installations concluded	April 13, 2004
	• Completion ceremony of KLC's development office	Oct. 21, 2004
	• Agreement on electricity supply concluded	Dec. 3, 2004
	• Agreement on communication device supply concluded	Dec. 30, 2004
North Korea	• Kaesong Industrial Complex Act announced	Nov. 27, 2002
	• Sub-regulations relating to development and company formation promulgated	June 29, 2003
	• Sub-regulations related to labor and taxes promulgated	Oct. 1, 2003
	• Regulations regarding management organization, entry, visit, residence, and customs promulgated	Dec. 17, 2003
	• Sub-regulations relating to foreign currency management and advertising promulgated	Feb. 27, 2004
	• Prescriptions for real estate promulgated	Aug. 25, 2004
	• Prescriptions for insurance promulgated	Oct. 11, 2004
Agreement between South and North Korea	• Agreement for customs, communication, and quarantine adopted	Dec. 8, 2002
	• Agreement on economic cooperation of four areas, such as investment guarantees, implemented	Aug. 20, 2003
	• Agreement on passage between Kaesong industrial complex and Mount Kumgang concluded	Jan. 29, 2004

84

Specifics and major trends	• Hyundai Asan and Korean Land Corporation approved as joint business parties by the Ministry of Unification	Dec. 27, 2002
	• Ground-breaking ceremony for the initial phase of land development for the Kaesong industrial complex	June 30, 2003
	• Cooperation in the initial phase of 3.3 million square meter development approved by the Ministry of Unification	April 23, 2004
	• Contract regarding companies moving into the pilot site (15 companies) concluded	June 14, 2004
	• Completion ceremony for building sites of the pilot site	June 30, 2004
	• Preparation team for foundation of Kaesong industrial complex project assistance team organized	Aug. 16, 2004
	• Selection of cooperating businesses (7) in the initial phase of the pilot site approved	Sept. 8, 2004
	• Selection of cooperating businesses (4) in the second phase of the pilot site approved	Sept. 17, 2004
	• Assistance team for Kaesong industrial complex project established	Oct. 5, 2004
	• Selection of cooperating businesses (2) in the third phase of the pilot site approved	Oct. 19, 2004
	• Opening ceremony of management committee and a ground-breaking ceremony of companies located in the pilot site	Oct. 20, 2004
	• Opening ceremony of Woori Bank located in Kaesong Industrial Complex	Dec. 7, 2004
	• Completion ceremony of Livingart (ceremony celebrating the first manufactured product)	Dec. 15, 2004
	• Completion ceremony of SJ Tech, Co. Ltd.	Dec. 28, 2004
	•Selection of cooperating businesses (2) in the fourth phase of the pilot site approved	Jan. 26, 2005

Source: Ministry of Unification, *Status of the Kaesong Industrial Complex Project*, February 2005.

Table 5.2. Status of Companies to be Located in the Pilot Complex

	Company	Line of business (sub-classification)	Major products	Investment (billions of won)	Area purchased (square meters)
Initial approvals	Samduk Trading	Footwear manufacture	Footwear	4.96	8,045
	Munchang Co.	Sewing; apparel	Airplane working apparel	3.8	5,365
	Bucheon Industries	Electric power supply; control devices	Wire harnesses (electric wiring components)	4.5	8,045
	Magic Micro	Electronic components; video devices	Lamp assembly (for LCD monitors)	3.0	4,026
	Yongin Electronics	Electronic components	Transformers, element coils	4.0	8,045
	Daewha Fuel Pump	Automobile components	Automobile fuel pumps	5.08	4,026
	Taesung Industries	Plastic products	Cosmetics containers	6.0	8,045
Second approvals	SJ Tech	Plastic products	Semiconductor component containers	4.0	5,365
	Hosan Ace	Ordinary machinery	Fan coils (air cleaner components)	2.6	3,300
	Shinwon	Sewing; apparel	Apparel	3.79	8,045
	Living Art	Other metals	Kitchen utensils	4.5	3,300
Third approvals	Romanson	Watches and components	Watches and jewelry	15.58	8,646
	TS Precision	Semiconductors and electronic components	Semiconductor mold components	2.8	5,365
Fourth approvals	JCCOM	Communication and broadcasting equipment	Optical communication components/materials	4.3	5,867
	JY Solutec	Other machinery	Automobile and electronic components and molds	5.0	8,045

Table 5.3. North Korea's Economic Activity Participation Ratio, 1999–2002
(Units: thousands; percent)

Year	Total population	Population over 15 years of age (A)	Economically active population (B)	Participation ratio (B/A)	South Korea's participation ratio
1999	22,082	16,379	11,367	69.4	63.4
2000	22,175	16,574	11,548	69.7	63.7
2001	22,253	16,741	11,685	69.8	64.0
2002	22,369	16,926	11,797	69.7	64.3

Source: Korean National Statistical Office, Ministry of Unification.

Table 5.4. Comparison of South and North Korea's Agricultural Population
(Units: thousands; percent)

Year	South Korea		North Korea	
	Agricultural population	Ratio	Agricultural population	Ratio
2000	4,031	8.6	8,160	36.8
2001	3,933	8.3	8,189	36.8
2002	3,591	7.5	8,232	36.8
2003	3,530	7.4	8,288	36.8

Source: Korea National Statistical Office.

As for the qualitative aspect, North Korean workers are comparatively excellent. Compulsory education lasts for 11 years and the school attendance rate is almost 98 percent. South Korean companies that bring in clothing from the North under consignment processing positively rate the technical capability of most North Korean workers. This implies that, considering the level of education, workers in North Korea are better at acquiring technology than their counterparts. Another important attraction is smoother verbal communication. Most firms that enter an overseas market encounter difficulties in accurate technical guidance and management because of cultural heterogeneity and differences in language. Labor disputes frequently occur due to lack of communication skills and understanding local culture. Such problems have caused many firms to completely withdraw from their overseas businesses. In North Korea, technical guidance is occasionally difficult due to political reasons. Still, firms and workers both desire technical guidance as it actually requires less time because direct verbal communication is possible. South Korean firms regard this point as one of the greatest advantages in entering North Korea's market.

The North's labor force is also competitive because of its wage level. Since the North undertook economic reform measures on July 1, 2002, an exchange rate was set at 145 North Korea won per dollar. A monthly minimum wage was fixed at 2,000 North Korean won as well. However, such details have not yet been officially reflected in the North's foreign investment law. So it is hard to precisely assess how much actual change there has been since 2002.

The minimum wage that the North designated for Kaesong industrial complex was US$57.50, including social insurance. On October 22, 2004, Yong-sul Kim, vice minister of North Korea's Ministry of Trade, gave a briefing at a consultative meeting with the World Federation of Overseas Korean Traders Association at the People's Palace of Culture in Pyongyang. In the briefing, he explained that the minimum wage of North Korean workers at foreign-invested firms had been lowered to €30 (approximately US$38) from between US$80 and US$120. Moreover, Kim emphasized that North Korea's minimum wage was lower than that of its counterparts, including China, India, and Thailand. The background to this measure was the realization, after the heavy devaluation from 2.1 to 145 North Korean won per dollar that followed the North's economic reform measures, that wages would have to be adjusted. South Korean businesspeople had also been pointing out that wages in North Korea were too high. Whether the same wage standard will be applied to the Kaesong industrial complex is still unknown, but it is likely to be equally applied. Meanwhile, all kinds of taxes and utility costs have also been incurred.

At absolute prices, North Korea's exchange rate and minimum wage at foreign firms are fixed at a higher level than ordinary local wages. Still, wages have been brought down significantly compared with China or Vietnam. Of course, it is impossible to compare wage levels alone since fixing wages involves the labor force and business environment as well as overall price levels, SOC, and other business-related systems. Nevertheless, North Korea's wage level is still lower than that of China or Vietnam judging from what is seen at the Kaesong industrial park. Basing calculations on a real exchange rate may lower wages outside the complex to less than the US$38 announced at the World-OKTA meeting. The wage of unskilled labor was between US$10 and US$30 when Vietnam and China first opened their markets.

Development of North Korean Land and Logistics

The fact that the North Korea borders China and Russia gives it a geographic advantage; North Korea could be Japan's entrance to the Northeast Asian market. The realization of the North's potential in this regard has recently grown as lively discussions have been held on forming an economic bloc in Northeast Asia. Although a fair amount of restriction exists in reality, there is no doubt about competitiveness that could be created by combining the abundant resources and labor force of China, Russia, and North Korea with the capital and technology of South Korea and Japan. Therefore, reforming and opening the North Korean market and improving inter-Korean relations is essential to forming a northeastern economic bloc. North Korea's geographic location is also quite significant in this regard.

Although transportation logistics by sea, rail, and highway have been problematic and have prevented the reduction of transportation costs for materials and products between the North and South, on December 15, 2004, it took seven hours for kitchenware manufacturer Livingart—the first company to commence production at the complex—to sell 1,000 pots manufactured at the Kaesong complex at a department store in Seoul (the company employs about 270 North Korean workers to manufacture an average of 1,200 pots a day). This symbolic event showed that products manufactured by the North's cheap labor can be released in real time at markets without passing through a warehouse. It emphasized the probable competitive edge North Korean–manufactured products could gain in South Korea's market due to the close geographic proximity.

At the Kaesong industrial complex, the North's comparative advantages meet with the South's capital and technology, with the result being increased competitiveness. Meanwhile, South Korean companies are becoming less attracted to consignment processing at Pyongyang because of unstable systems and an uncontrollable local environment. This represents a major change in inter-Korean economic cooperation as its focus shifts from consignment processing to direct investment in Kaesong.

Initial Estimates of Profits

Since operations are still in an early phase, it is not possible yet to talk concretely about the industrial complex's profitability. Yet, some basic assumptions can be made primarily based on the players participating in the complex's development and operation.

To begin, North Korea is being paid in U.S. dollars for rent, labor, and utilities. It further expects to receive US$16 million according to the lease contract concluded on April 14, 2004. The lease contract breaks down to US$3.3 million for rent of the 3.3 million square meter site to codevelopers Hyundai Asan and Korea Land Corporation (US$1/square meter), US$4 million for construction of office space used as a customs and employee-border control area, and US$8.7 million accounts for demolition of buildings that were on the site prior to construction.

Apart from slight positional distinctions, North Korean workers are generally paid US$57.50 a month including US$7.5 for social insurance.

Wages are paid through an external recruiting agency in North Korea because of its inadequate financial system. Approximately US$110,000 is paid to about 1,900 North Korean workers each month. Furthermore, as mentioned above, a communication fee is also paid at a rate of US$0.40 per minute for 100 fixed telephone circuits. Since South Korean companies are in charge of developing and operating the industrial park, there is not much benefit left for North Korea. It is a known fact that North Korea is dissatisfied with the deal in this respect.

Codevelopers Korea Land Corporation and Hyundai Asan have different perspectives regarding profits. Korea Land Corporation, as a public enterprise, puts the public's interest before profitability. It does not expect any profit since it sold the lots it developed at nearly half their cost of approximately US$100 per square meter. The government plans to cover the losses. Hyundai Asan, on the other hand, will generate positive returns from exclusive rights to build factories and various infrastructure for companies in the pilot project site. However, that profit will not offset the losses occurred from the Kumgang mountain tourism project. Nevertheless, Hyundai Asan is paving the way toward a favorable position in various future North Korea construction projects.

As for the 15 companies in the complex's pilot project, it seems that all the mechanisms for profitability are in place. These firms have inexpensively secured a site close to a metropolitan area that is has a market potential of 20 million consumers. Better yet, the risk compensation for investment is nearly 90 percent. Conditions for capital loans are relatively favorable as well. Even though all these are somewhat based on the special character of the pilot project, participating companies will potentially generate the highest profits from the complex's development. This is the very reason why South Korean small- and medium-sized enterprises (SMEs) are keenly interested in locating in the industrial park.

Issues and Opportunities

What Can Be Expected in the Future?

Two aspects need to be considered in order to gain insight into the future of the Kaesong industrial complex. One is the industrial complex's economic competitiveness; the other is the political and military circumstances. These two are indicators for forecasting the future success or failure of the Kaesong industrial complex. There are also administrative issues that are closely linked with meeting national security concerns and U.S. Export Administration Regulations.

At the moment, the development plan of the Kaesong industrial complex envisions that the 3.3 million square meter site will be fully allocated to companies by 2007. A total of 66 million square meters, including an industrial area of 26.4 million square meters and a 39.6 million square meter residential area, are slated for the project's second and third phases, but the exact size and detailed arrangements are still being discussed with the North. Although at this point it is hard to predict whether the Kaesong industrial complex project will be a success, a vibrant atmosphere is certainly present at the complex construction site.

Business and Economic Risks and Rewards

Considering economic factors only, the Kaesong industrial complex looks promising, which means it has a high growth potential. Obtaining a quality workforce at low wages is essential to realizing the growth potential. As discussed above, the minimum wage in North Korea is US$57.50 a month including social insurance; trained workers and managers are paid more. Competitors such as China or Southeast Asian countries do not stipulate minimum wages, but they generally range around US$100 a month. Thus North Korean workers are competitive in terms of wages.

The quality of labor at the industrial park seems good so far. According to a source from Livingart, the productivity of North Korean workers is less than half that of South Korean workers. Despite almost a month of preliminary training, some verbal communication problems, such as different use of vocabulary, turned out to interfere with enhancing productivity. But not much time should be needed to resolve such problems. In fact, productivity should already be improving quickly with respect to cases in China or other Southeast Asian countries. Improvement in North Korea can be rather shortened because direct verbal communication—the slight vocabulary differences aside—is still possible between employees and the employer. A potential downside to relatively smooth communication may be labor disputes, which could pose a greater political challenge.

Although there seems to be an adequate labor pool already in place, there has been concern over potentially larger projects requiring a greater supply of labor. If the 3.3 million square meter site is expanded up to 26.4 million square meters as originally planned, is the North capable of quickly providing the corresponding amount of labor? China has been consistently able to maintain a large labor supply for its agricultural sector thanks to its huge population of around 1.3 billion. North Korea's population of around 20 million does not seem to be large enough to sustain an adequate pool of labor. A solution, however, lies in the North's armed forces. There are approximately 1.1 million troops in North Korea, an absurdly large figure in view of the size of its economy. The Kaesong industrial complex is equipped with a system to effectively absorb the North's military personnel into the workforce, which may resolve concerns about labor supply.

The industrial park's market accessibility is another advantage that adds to its high growth potential. It only took about seven hours from Kaesong for Livingart's products to be displayed for sale at shops in the South. No other foreign production base is capable of delivering products in such a short time. The industrial park's location is what made this possible. North Korea has a total population of 20 million, and the South Korea's metropolitan area has strong purchasing power. This means that a basis is there to consume the products manufactured in the industrial complex. With the South Korean government's support, industrial plots are expected to be sold at less than 495,000 won per square meter. This is lower than the price of any industrial complex located in the Seoul metropolitan area.

Furthermore, geographical accessibility makes it possible to take advantage of the South's systematization of manufacturing. Passing through the cease-fire line is still inconvenient, but should ease in the course of time. Competitive products made by the North's labor and the South's capital and technology could even aim for the Japanese market. The worldwide trend seems to be in the direction of locating production bases near existing markets, making the Kaesong site an ideal production base for Northeast Asian countries such as the two Koreas, Japan, and China. Infrastructure at the complex is not yet capable of performing at the necessary level—a weak point in the short run—but it can be built over time.

South Korea is on the verge of becoming an economically advanced country; however, numerous SMEs are struggling because of a sharp increase in overall production costs. Companies that fail to increase their competitiveness have no choice but to move their production bases overseas to countries like China. If they do not do so, they will be weeded out. South Korean companies have a great option in relocating to the North. Still, there are many obstacles to overcome and South Korean companies do not have much time to spare, which may mean that the future of the Kaesong industrial complex hinges on how quickly North Korea can evolve into a genuine member of the international community.

Political and Military Concerns

Perhaps the greatest challenge government efforts face is resolving issues that specifically relate to the industrial park centering on strategic goods and designating a place of origin for Kaesong-produced goods. The South Korean government has many aspects it should consider in trying to prevent the handing over of strategic goods to the North. The industrial complex's special character is represented by the fact that South Korean companies are the end users of the complex and that the South will be in charge of managing the complex. Another aspect is that South Korea is subject to the Wassenaar Agreement. Then, there is the ultimate duty as a nation's government to protect its local firms.

The Strategic Trade Information Center, a governmental organization, was established in the South out of concern with these various issues. The organization will be responsible for controlling the export of strategic goods in advance or afterward. The United States basically understands the significance and gravity of the Kaesong industrial park and has confirmed that so far there have been no complications regarding the export of strategic goods. However, South Korea and the United States plan to closely and constantly negotiate on the export of items included in the U.S. Export Administration Regulations (EAR) and Commerce Control List (CCL).

In order to mark the place of origin as the Republic of Korea on products produced in Kaesong and carried into South Korea, according to the international rules of origin, over 60 percent of the product's material must come from South Korea. But export to other countries is likely to be problematic because exported items must abide by the importing country's own rules of origin. In the mid to long run, when negotiating free trade agreements (FTA) the South Korean government will accordingly try to get such products to be treated equally to those produced in South Korea.

Meanwhile, the government is also focused on developing adequate conditions for exporting products manufactured in Kaesong to countries like the United States and Japan. As part of such efforts, Singapore, under its free trade agreement with South Korea (November 29, 2004), treats products manufactured at Kaesong like those manufactured in South Korea.

Dong Figure 1. Free Trade Agreements and Goods Assembled in Kacsong

The recently concluded FTA between South Korea and Singapore treats products manufactured at Kaesong as South Korean products. The fact that such products have secured a market is encouraging. As in the case with Singapore, the government plans to seek identical conditions at FTA negotiations with other countries. Unfortunately, this is not a fundamental solution to securing markets. Although Singapore will treat Kaesong's products like those made in South Korea, other parts of the world will still treat them as North Korean products. Therefore, this matter can be fundamentally solved by normalizing relations between the United States and North Korea. -

Another problem occurred right after the selection of the 15 companies in the pilot project was completed. As a matter of fact, this problem, involving the U.S. Export Administration Regulations (EAR) against North Korea, was foreseen. The regulations stipulate that export is prohibited to an enemy country if more than 10 percent of a U.S. product or technology is included. The U.S. Department of Commerce does not apply these regulations on a country-to-country basis, but rather to individual companies. Various products carried into the North on a large scale complicate the interpretation on these regulations.

It took almost half a year for the 15 companies to assess whether all kinds of manufacturing equipment and raw materials violate the EAR. Considering this, it might take years to go through the same process with about two hundred companies to be involved in the complex's initial phase. Besides, North Korea is not the only country restricted by the U.S. regulations, so it is unreasonable for the South Korean government to ask for the U.S. to make an exception and increase the number of personnel in charge to spur the process. Unless relations between the United States and North Korea improve, the industrial complex could end up a business failure because of this delay regarding the U.S. EAR.

Legal technicalities aside, the place of origin for products made in Kaesong is clearly North Korea. Furthermore it is well known that the United States considers North Korea a terrorist state and imposes various economic sanctions. Ironically, the United States is the main target market for the low-to-medium priced products assembled in Kaesong. Even though the capital and materials are completely the result of South Korean corporate investment, it does not change the fact that Kaesong is in North Korea. This may mean giving up the United States as a major target market. The products may be targeted at Japan and the EU, but the fact remains that the U.S. market alone can generate enough demand to allow Kaesong to develop and enjoy economies of scale.

Political or military circumstances are generally assumed to be stable and are considered peripheral to economic factors. In some cases, political or military risks are willingly accepted if highly lucrative returns are guaranteed. However, the Kaesong industrial complex is located in the North near militarily sensitive territory just across the cease-fire line. Further complicating the issue is North Korea's nuclear ambition. It is undeniable that the fate of the industrial complex rests upon the outcome of some serious political and military issues.

Political and military insecurity is an impediment. Several previously mentioned problems regarding economic factors can all be resolved in time. Yet, within this time political or military factors may not be resolved, making the future of the complex bleak. Several incidents have already occurred that may have dimmed the future of the Kaesong industrial complex.

In a similar sense, electricity and communication supply may run into difficulties as the complex expands up to 66 million square meters. Also, in accordance with the cease-fire agreement, transportation is currently via a temporary road at the cease-fire line. However, passage across the cease-fire line could be jeopardized if the truce accord is substituted with a peace accord or if the nuclear weapons issue with the North deteriorates further. U.S. officials, based on these assumptions, have played down the role of the Kaesong industrial complex. The fundamental solution, then, is for North Korea to clear up its nuclear issue and work to have its name removed from the U.S. State Department's list of designated terrorist states. The future of the Kaesong industrial complex is closely tied to the resolution of political and military issues between North Korea and the international community.

Conclusion

Despite the myriad difficulties, development of the Kaesong industrial complex is steadily moving forward. Supporters of the project point out that the industrial complex will raise the level of inter-Korean economic cooperation from trade to investment. It is expected to contribute to relieving military tensions as well. Furthermore, there has been no evidence to support criticism that the complex itself will provoke political instability.

In practice, inter-Korean economic cooperation has two meanings. One is an expectation of pure economic interchange, where competitiveness is created by combining South Korea's capital and technology and North Korea's land and labor. The consignment processing project actively developed in Pyongyang is a representative case in making use of North Korean labor. But the Kaesong industrial complex has the advantage of using labor that costs US$57.50 a month and has, within a 70 kilometer radius, a metropolitan market of 20 million people. This is enough to draw the attention of struggling companies in the South. Besides, the South's capital is like an oasis to the North, which is in desperate need of foreign capital.

Considering economic factors alone, the industrial complex provides conditions that can enhance the competitiveness of a company's products. Simply put, the complex could be a promising production base for Northeast Asia. However, there is a time limit to improving noneconomic factors such as the political and military situation.

Another expectation is that North Korea will gradually change through economic interchange. A project that once seemed impossible due to the political and military confrontation between the two Koreas has become a reality. This implies that North Korea is opening up, even if slowly. Inter-Korean economic cooperation has grown from simple trading to commission processing, and now to direct investment. North Korea has changed enough to accept South Korean capital. Despite the fact that conversation between North and South Korea has been suspended, a host of agreements were made on economic interchange through the first half of 2004. North Korea has started to comply with the internationally accepted trade order through inter-Korean economic cooperation.

Based on these expectations, inter-Korean economic cooperation will help Korean companies increase their competitiveness and perhaps lead to the Korean peninsula developing into a center for the Northeast Asian regional economy. South Korea is pushing to become the hub for the region through the Korean peninsula's geographical advantage, and is forming a triangular economic zone with Seoul as the financial center, Incheon as distribution center, and Kaesong as the manufacturing base. South Korea means to be the bridge between China's fast-growing economy and Japan's advanced economy. The goal also includes intercontinental economic interchange spanning from Russia to Europe and from the Pacific to the United States. Kaesong has a significant role in realizing such a vision. To reach this objective, North Korea's participation is a must. South Korea's needs mostly lie in economic aspects, so its policies are also focused on the same goal.

Underpinning this drive is the U.S. stress on political and military factors rather than economic ones. From the U.S. standpoint, it is difficult to see how an economic bond can be created with North Korea as unreliable as it is. The view is that South Korea's actions provide another string for the tyrannical Kim Jong-Il regime to pull on with no hopes of profitability guaranteed to anyone doing business with the North.

Dong Figure 2. The Nuclear Row

On February 10, 2005, North Korea publicly announced it had nuclear weapons and that it will refuse to participate in the six-party talks indefinitely. This was enough to draw attention from the other five parties as well as the international community. This subsequently created concern over the fate of the complex. On the day North Korea made these statements, construction at the complex continued as usual. The press portrayed February 10 as an ordinary work day for laborers in the North. The Ministry of Unification made a presentation to the 15 companies involved in the pilot project to reassure them that the project will continue despite North Korea's announcement. The development of the industrial park seems to be continuing without much trouble for the time being. Nevertheless, the press and even the companies involved in the pilot project are uneasy about the change in the political-military situation. Simply put, there is anxiety that the complex might be shut down, as the political and military situation is not something the South Korean government can manage alone.

There is a risk of North Korea's shutting down the inter-Korean border anytime. And if this actually happens, the numerous facilities installed in the North's Kaesong industrial complex will fall into North Korea's hands. Some may think that the complex's development can wait until North Korea becomes a more fully integrated member of the international community. Nevertheless, the South Korean government's approach is also feasible in the sense of considering all options to resolve the problems with North Korea, as President George W. Bush has even pointed out himself.

Notes

[1] The regulations cover the complex's development; the establishment and management of firms, tax payments, and labor; the establishment and management of the complex's management organization, customs, entrance, exit and sojourn, foreign exchange management, and advertising and real estate.

[2] There are reports that rural-to-urban migration has increased in North Korea since it undertook economic reform measures from July 1, 2002. However, it is difficult to find proof of this movement.

Photographs of Recent Progress in the Kaesong Complex

Complete View of the Pilot Site

Factory Construction Site

Electricity Supply Works

Fire Station

North Korean Workers in the Complex

North Korean Workers in Practical Training

Accommodations in the Complex I (Cafeteria)

Accommodations in the Complex II (Green Doctors, the Hospital in the Complex)

HUMAN RIGHTS AND THE CRISIS
IN NORTH KOREA

David Hawk

Within the last several years human rights violations have joined nuclear proliferation, famine, and displaced persons among the interrelated crises in or with North Korea. For the May 2005 conference, "North Korea 2005 and Beyond," hosted by the Walter H. Shorenstein Asia-Pacific Research Center at Stanford University's Freeman Spogli Institute for International Studies, I was asked to address the human rights element of the Korea crisis. I have been asked to specifically address the following questions: What human rights abuses are there in North Korea? What is the evidence? Is the ROK addressing this? What has been the impact of the U.S. Human Rights Act? How can the United States and the international community make meaningful progress? What are the implications for U.S. policy? The following comments seek to address these questions and related issues.

The Violations

The DPRK contends, whether its diplomats know better or not, that concern about human rights in North Korea is a political or politicized instrument to bring down or suffocate the North Korean state. To the contrary, at its core, human rights are matters of universal values and international standards that apply to all nation states irrespective of the form of government. These international standards—negotiated by diplomatic representatives of the variety and growing number of nation-states in the post-World War II world order—define and set forth in the form of positive international law what states ought not do *to* their citizenry and what states should do *for* their citizenry to the extent that resources allow.[1]

There are several ways to match up what is known about North Korea's violations with the universal norms and international standards of human rights in the modern world. The first is to take the standards set forth in the Universal Declaration of Human Rights and simply compare those standards to what one knows, and/or what is generally known, about North Korea. Second, there have been three efforts under UN auspices to gauge North Korea's human rights performance: the "expert" analyses by the human rights treaty monitoring review procedures; the judgment by fellow UN member states rendered in the form of resolutions at the UN Commission on Human Rights; and the more recent evaluation by the Special Rapporteur on the DPRK. Additionally, North Korean human rights policy and practice can be compared with modern state practice in East Asia. And lastly, DPRK policy and practice can be examined in light of the recent developments in international criminal law.

The Universal Declaration of Human Rights and the DPRK

Try a test. Take a copy of the 1948 Universal Declaration of Human Rights, the major defining statement of human rights in the modern world. Go down the list of rights recognized and set forth in the Universal Declaration and, from what you know about North Korea, check them off one by one. Are those rights respected or violated in North Korea? It will be very surprising if this reckoning does not result in a long list of rights that are not respected or observed in North Korea. The United Nations has, however, already done this exercise formally, evaluating the DPRK's adherence to international norms and standards of human rights.

The UN's Evaluation of DPRK Violations (I): The Expert Analyses of the Treaty Monitoring Procedures

The rights set forth as general principles in the Universal Declaration were "elaborated" (negotiated by member states, a process that took 20 years) into positive international law in the form of full-fledged treaty systems in two international conventions: the International Covenant on Civil and Political Rights and the International Covenant on Economic, Social and Cultural Rights. When nation-states sign and ratify or accede to these treaties they are agreeing to respect and/or implement the provisions explicitly enumerated within these treaties.

One of the requirements of states parties to these international human rights conventions is to submit reports to the UN on the measures that have been taken to implement the provisions of the treaty. These reports are then examined by UN committees of individuals who were nominated by their governments and elected by the states parties but who serve in an individual, expert capacity.[2] These treaty implementation monitoring committees made up of some of the world's leading human rights experts (mostly in the form of constitutional and international lawyers from every region of the world and the global variety of legal and political systems) carefully examine the implementation reports submitted by the various states parties.

After meeting with diplomatic representatives of the countries whose treaty implementation report is under consideration, these committees—the Human Rights Committee and the Committee on Economic Social and Cultural Rights—then issue "Concluding

Observations" that enumerate "concerns" (where they think the state party is not in compliance with its treaty commitments or "obligations," as the lawyers put it) and "recommendations" (how to improve the situation and achieve better compliance).

For whatever reasons, the DPRK acceded to four of the seven "core" international human rights treaties.[3] Thus it is entirely legitimate and proper for other states and nonstate actors to hold North Korea up to the commitments and standards it has formally agreed to. The DPRK's reports to the treaty implementation monitoring committees are available on the UN website, as are the Committee's Concluding Observations.[4]

These UN expert bodies have found the DPRK to be in substantial noncompliance with—the lawyers' way of saying North Korea is in violation of—a considerable number of civil and political, economic, social, and cultural rights.[5] In turn, the list of recommendations is a veritable UN roadmap for human rights improvement in the DPRK and/ or for measuring human rights progress in North Korea.[6] Summaries of these recommendations are attached.

The UN's Evaluation of DPRK Violations (II): The Resolutions of the United Nations Commission on Human Rights

Unlike the UN treaty monitoring bodies on which experts sit in their individual capacities, the UN Commission on Human Rights is a subsidiary organ of the General Assembly on which 53 UN member states meet for six weeks a year to consider a large variety of human rights matters and where member state ambassadors or delegations vote according to the instructions of their respective foreign ministries.

The resolutions adopted at the Commission represent the considered findings and judgments of other governments within the modern interstate system. Beginning in 2003, under the sponsorship of the European Union (EU), resolutions passed by the Commission—by large margins—recognized and condemned the widespread and large-scale violations in North Korea.[7]

The UN's Evaluations of DPRK Violations (III): The Report of the Special Rapporteur on Human Rights in the DPRK

Owing largely to North Korea's refusal to cooperate with the UN in the human rights area as requested in the 2003 resolution, in 2004 the Commission called for the appointment of a Special Rapporteur on the human rights situation in the DPRK. Subsequently, Vitit Muntarbhorn, a highly regarded law professor at Chulalongkorn University, Bangkok, was appointed. His report is available on the UN website.[8] He outlines six "Specific Challenges":

1. the right to food and the right to life;
2. the right to the security of the person, humane treatment, nondiscrimination and access to justice;
3. the right to freedom of movement and the protection of persons linked with displacement [primarily in China and upon return to North Korea];
4. the right to the highest attainable standards of health and the right to education;
5. the right to self-determination/political participation, access to information, and freedom of expression/belief/opinion, association and religion; and
6. the rights of specific groups/persons: women and children.

Professor Muntarbhorn's fair, balanced, and independent perspective will likely become a central approach to the DPRK human rights crisis.

Modern State Practice in East Asia

Another way to look at North Korean human rights policy and practice is in the light of modern state practices in the DPRK's closest state neighbors in East Asia. The gap is huge and obvious; not only between North Korea and the modern industrialized democracies of Japan, South Korea, and Taiwan, or the newer, developing democracies in Mongolia, Thailand, Malaysia, the Philippines, Indonesia, and so on, but also between North Korea and other formerly Confucianist nation-states such as China and Vietnam, where the old Communist "ruling party" maintains a monopoly on political power, but where the state has withdrawn from overwhelming and overweening control over the day-to-day lives of the citizenry.[9]

The DPRK sometimes takes offense at being compared with is neighbors, particularly China, on the grounds that it is pursuing a Korean way. But of course, South Korea pursues a radically different and altogether more successful path to development, modernization, prosperity, and cultural distinction. The DPRK also used to contend that it offered an example for the entire third world to follow. But with the possible exception of Myanmar, all of the states of Northeast and Southeast Asia are following different paths from that of North Korea, and they are all doing better.

The Statutes of International Criminal Law

A final way to gauge the North Korean human rights situation is to compare the phenomena of DPRK repression to the recently established international criminal law standards. Up until the recent drafting of the (Rome) Statues for the International Criminal Court, crimes against humanity were largely a legal doctrine, existing largely in the international law books and minds of law professors for various acts not included within the legal definition of genocide and war crimes. Now, Article 7 provides a clear definition in positive international law of acts— proscribed and prosecutable—that are crimes against humanity.[10]

Unfortunately, the phenomena of repression now proscribed and theoretically prosecutable as crimes against humanity describe all too precisely the system of repression integrally associated with the North Korea system of preventive, lifetime "strict regime" detention at hard labor without any judicial process whatsoever in the *kwan-li-so* political penal labor colonies in which up to 200,000 North Koreans are imprisoned (and not only suspected political dissidents but sometimes generations of family members as well).[11]

Conclusion

North Korea contends to the UN that there is no human rights problem in the DPRK. When approached by NGOs in the UN coffee shops, DPRK diplomats contend that there are no human rights violations in North Korea, which of course would make it unique among UN member states, as nearly all have violations of one sort or another. However, when compared with international human rights standards, DPRK policy and practice can be summed up, in human rights terminology, as (1) a consistent pattern of gross violations of international recognized human rights, and (2) crimes against humanity. In plain English, violations: massive, systemic, and criminal.

Evidence and the Burden of Proof

Until ten years ago, North Korea was a veritable black hole of noninformation on the human rights front. For example, if one goes back and looks at the annual global reports of Amnesty International over the last 30 years, or the annual reports of Human Rights Watch over the last 20 years, all one will find (with two exceptions) is a few sentences saying that little or no information was obtainable on the DPRK.[12]

Human rights joined security and humanitarian challenges vis-à-vis the DPRK because of the increasing amounts of first-person and eyewitness testimony on human rights violations from North Koreans who in the mid- to late 1990s fled to China in search of food and thereafter became accessible—initially to South Korean faith-based organizations, NGO humanitarian aid workers, journalists, and scholars, who began to collect their stories and analyze the information they presented on the situation inside North Korea.

Shortly after 2000, growing numbers of North Koreans who had fled to China made their way to South Korea, where they became accessible to non-Korean academics, journalists, and human rights researchers. Previously, the small number of DRPK "defectors" to South Korea had mostly been diplomats, high-level Workers Party officials, and high-ranking military personnel allowed to travel abroad in the first place. After 2000, there has been a growing number of nonelite (many of mid-to-low *Songbun*, the DPRK's hereditary class structure), many of whom were substantially nonpolitical Koreans who initially fled to China in search of basic human survival for themselves and their families during the height of the famine crisis.

These North Korean "escapees" had terrible stories that began to circulate in South Korea, Western Europe, and North America. These former North Koreans, now accessible in South Korea, were the source of information contained in the 2002 Human Rights Watch report, *Invisible Exodus: North Koreans in the People's Republic of China*, the 2004 Amnesty International report, *Starved of Rights: Human Rights and the Food Crisis in the DPRK*, and my report for the U.S. Committee on Human Rights in North Korea on political detention and imprisonment (2003 in English, 2004 in Korean).

Caveats Regarding the Evidence

Some South Koreans are discomforted by the now substantial body of harsh and unflattering information available on human rights violations in the DPRK, perhaps because it is publicized by conservative media outlets in the ROK, or because it confirms or reinforces castigations by elected politicians in the United States, or because it is politically inconvenient as it annoys North Korean government officials. And there are some allegations by a small handful of North Korea refugees for which the evidence is too thin and weak to garner credibility. But, overall, the bulk of the testimony from the North Korean refugees now in South Korea will, overwhelmingly, stand the test of time, if, or when, North Korea further opens up. [13]

Recently an otherwise reputable South Korean NGO has challenged to the UN Commission on Human Rights the reliability of data collection and fact verification on reported information deriving from former North Koreans presently residing outside of the DPRK.[14] However, the UN Special Rapporteur found the testimony of North Korean escapees he interviewed in Mongolia to be "profoundly mov[ing]."[15]

Another example of a recent study that found the testimony of North Korean escapees presently residing in China to be entirely credible is the June 2005 Refugees International report, *Acts of Betrayal,* based on interviews between June 2003 and May–June 2004 with 47 North Koreans. RI's findings, based on the personal stories presented in this report, as analyzed by a former Oxfam (Boston) and UNDP official (Phnom Penh), is that "not since Cambodia under the Khmer Rouge has a government succeeded in creating such an all-encompassing reality of oppression and restrictions on the basic rights of the majority of its citizens."[16]

The Burden of Proof

There is a broad consistency in the testimonies of North Koreans interviewed in three different political environments: China, Mongolia, and South Korea. Until such time as North Koreans can be interviewed privately and confidentially within the DPRK, the burden of proof with respect to the data consistently reported by North Koreans who have fled North Korea remains with the DPRK. For example, if the information about extremely harsh and brutal prison conditions inside North Korea, including forced labor and ethnically motivated forced abortions and infanticide in particular, or the larger picture provided by the refugees, is not true, it would be very easy for the DPRK to disprove the allegations of the former prisoners by allowing the ICRC, UN human rights officials, the Pyongyang-based diplomatic community, or reputable NGOs like AI or HRW access to the labor camps, prisons, and detention facilities.[17] Until these facilities are open to international inspection, the testimony of the former North Korean prisoners stands.

Is the Republic Of Korea Addressing North Korean Human Rights Problems?

South Korea's approach to North Korea, as I understand it, is one of "deterrence-plus"—the "plus" part being policies of reconciliation and engagement with the DPRK. It would not appear that engagement with the North has led South Korea to dispense with military preparedness or cast off its security alliance with its preferred, if in some quarters resented, "off-shore balancer." Further, even the "plus" or engagement part of ROK policy has a strategic purpose—namely, reducing the threat that the quarter or third of the South Korean citizenry that resides within the range of DPRK's forward-deployed, hardened site, long-range artillery will actually come under hostile fire.

South Korean engagement with the North in its "sunshine" and "peace and prosperity" phase has always had a "basket three" component (as the humanitarian cluster of concerns in the Helsinki Accords, the Final Act of the Conference on Security and Cooperation in Europe was dubbed) centering, obviously, on alleviation of the famine in North Korea and family reunification (an urgent priority given the advanced age of the separated family members). Both of these issues—famine relief and family reunions—can be addressed in the language and analysis of human rights. And, through both engaging administrations, South Korea does, it should be noted, continue to receive and support the North Korean refugees who present themselves to South Korean ports of entry and/or consular officials, even if prominent reconciliation advocates eschew deliberate or large-scale North Korean refugee outflows when proposed as a political destabilizer.

Thus far, South Korean policy toward North Korea does not go beyond this to include the violations of human rights stipulated in the UN reports, resolutions, and analyses mentioned above. When asked, South Korean diplomats invariably reply that the resolution of the nuclear crisis must come first (a notion with which arms controllers and anti-proliferation advocates in the United States surely agree). Other ROK diplomats state that formal raising of human rights issues with DPRK awaits a Korean War peace treaty, that is, the replacement of the 1954 armistice with a full-fledged peace agreement in which the parties to that 50-year's previous conflict recognize each other's existence cum legitimacy and that a state of war no longer exists between them. These ROK diplomats point out that this was exactly the model of the CSCE (Helsinki Accords) and that only after the World War II borders were recognized and accepted did the parties on opposite sides of the Iron Curtain undertake regular, formal dialogue on human rights issues.

These arguments or approaches are not without merit. The downside is that they essentially delegate South Korean human rights policy toward North Korea to Kim Jong-Il and George Bush. An even more serious problem is that the DPRK nuclear crisis may not be resolvable, or at least resolvable in any time framework other than a very distant future. There is a viewpoint in South Korea that if only George Bush would be nicer to Kim Jong-Il, the North would not need a nuclear deterrent and DPRK's nuclear crisis could be easily solved and its nuclear warheads and fissile materials dismantled for an entirely reasonable price.

Maybe so. But maybe not. It could just as easily be the case that, when the DPRK says it supports the ultimate goal of a nonnuclear, weaponized Korean peninsula, this is a goal only to be realized following peninsular reunification on the basis of a political formula put forward by Kim Il-Sung.

North Korea's willingness to give up such nuclear weapons and fissile material it now possesses—as opposed to freezing or slowing down the development of additional warheads—is something that should be tested by a thorough negotiations process. But by the hallowed, if cynical, canons of "political realism," it should not be surprising if Kim Jong-Il or his likely immediate successors will be disinclined to irrevocably part with their main, if not only, bargaining chip. The DPRK nuclear arsenal is Kim Jong-Il's sole attribute of national/personal stature and prestige—membership in the elite club of (nine) nuclear powers, in the face of a continuing "legitimacy competition" with a confident and dynamic South Korea that has the world's tenth largest economy. Without nuclear weapons, North Korea is a mendicant state with an oversized army and failed economy, and a place that many foreign visitors describe as bizarre.

If the approach of wanting to solve the problems of "peace" and/or proliferation before tackling human rights seems initially reasonable, it is reasonable only if it is achievable in the near future. If a denuclearized and de jure (as opposed to de facto) pacified peninsula can only be achieved a decade or generation hence, there is much less ground for ignoring the immense contemporary human rights problems.

In the meantime, the ROK has had trouble finding its voice and its stance regarding the systemic and widespread human rights abuses in North Korea, most notably at the 2003 UN Commission on Human Rights where even though the ROK is a member state of the Commission it was "absent" (even though ROK diplomats were physically present in the room during the speeches and the voting). Subsequently, the ROK has "abstained" from utilizing the diplomatic vehicle of an explanation of vote (EOV). An oral intervention on agenda item 9 (under which the DPRK is considered) does not name the DPRK, but leaves little doubt about which UN member state is being described, for those in the room to hear it.

Sometimes there is something of "see-no-evil, hear-no-evil, speak-no-evil" character to South Korea's approach to North Korea, even beyond what might be encompassed by the oft-proclaimed asymmetrical nature of the engagement relationship. It remains unclear to me why it would not serve the cause of mutual respect and friendship for South Koreans to tell their kin to the north that the DPRK is going to have to take into account the growing concern in the international community with their human rights policies and practices if they seek to achieve greater integration into the global political economy—starting, though hardly ending, with North Korean cooperation with UN human rights officials.

Human rights matters suitable, indeed normal, for intra-Korean discussion would likely include unaccounted for South Korean abductees and unaccounted for and/or un-repatriated South Korean POWs. (Indeed, as these are clearly South Korean citizens, it would be abnormal for the ROK not to raise their situation and fate with the DPRK.) Another example of a human rights issue that strikes me as suitable for inter-Korean governmental-level discussion, particularly as South Korea increases investment and travel flows to the Kaesong industrial project, is the dreadful punishment meted out by DPRK police to forcibly repatriated North Koreans who had met South Koreans while residing in China in search of food or remunerative employment.

At the governmental and nongovernmental level, South Koreans are presently trying to figure how best to tackle the North Korean human rights situation. Hopefully, high-level North-South dialogue will resume—on a broad range of topics. And hopefully South Korean government officials will find ways to raise human rights issues with their North Korean counterparts. If security and political issues should be resolved by dialogue, surely there is also a good case for dialogue on human rights.

At present, North Korea will discuss human rights issues only with representatives of states with which it has diplomatic relations or, perhaps, that are in the process of working toward same. International humanitarian relief NGOs working in North Korea assert that they will be immediately expelled if they mention human rights. South Koreans active in inter-Korean dialogue assert that the North Koreans will either walk out or become hysterical if they bring up human rights. Still, ways to approach human rights issues need to be explored and taken up. Surely one of the most important long-term measures to promote human rights in North Korea is for human rights issues to be placed on the inter-Korean "engagement agenda." Most progressive South Korean governmental officials and civil society activists would not disagree with this in the abstract. But more immediately and concretely this has been rather more problematic.

Some advocates of engagement, reconciliation, and peace and reunification were initially put off that the extreme North Korean human rights violations were used by previous ROK military regimes to justify their own repression in the South. Some South Korean civil society activists are even more put off that the North Korean human rights issue has been taken up by the U.S. Congress and executive branch. Sometimes it is stipulated that this has "politicized" the issue. In its most extreme iteration, it is feared that the human rights issue is being raised to prepare U.S. public opinion for a military attack on North Korea in the name of democratic governance.

In a larger, more general sense, however, protesting repression is inevitably political. Repression by governments is political—actions by state authorities to cope with deep-seated social problems such as those involving racial, ethnic, or religious minorities, or actions taken to maintain political power. But if repression is political, protesting repression is also inevitably political. Almost always, the government being criticized sees such criticism as serving the cause of internal or external opponents and adversaries.

In my experience, raising human rights violations in Central America in the 1980s was intensely political, whether it was, for example, in regard to political murder by the U.S.-backed regime in El Salvador or depredations in Nicaragua against indigenous peoples on the Atlantic coast by the U.S.-adversarial Sandinistas. Attempts to link human rights considerations to détente with the Soviet Union in the 1970s, or to condition U.S. military and economic aid or trade policies to human rights in a variety of countries was—from the 1970s to the 1990s—always, and intensely, political. I do not understand how North Korea would be any different.

Further, in my experience, the political right uses human rights violations by leftist regimes as a rhetorical stick. And the political left, or what is left of it, uses human rights violations against rightist regimes. There are some conservatives who find it all too easy to minimize, obfuscate, and explain away violations by right-wing regimes, and some leftists who find it all too easy to minimize, obfuscate, and explain way violations by regimes nominally committed to some variant of socialism. Here, too, it is hard to see why it would be any different for North Korea.

What Is the Impact of the U.S. North Korean Human Rights Act?

Although the enactment of this law is an invaluable symbolic act of hopefully considerable political importance, it is too early to predict or describe its influence or impact.

The presidential envoy called for by the Human Rights Act has yet to be appointed, and the approach taken by him or her will be the largest determinant of the outcome or impact of the act. The tasks for the presidential envoy stipulated in the act are very good ones, including dialogue with the North Koreans (obviously they would have to be willing) as well as technical training and exchange programs (with and for North Koreans); working cooperatively with UN, EU, and other countries in Northeast Asia; consulting with relevant NGOs; making recommendations regarding activities funding opportunities envisioned in the act; and so on.[18] But whether, and/or how, the presidential envoy, once appointed, will do any of these things remains to be seen.

The act seeks to link increased humanitarian aid to the DPRK to improved end-use monitoring. But the Bush administration is not likely to increase humanitarian aid in the absence of a settlement to the North Korean nuclear issue.

The act expresses the will—in fact, the unanimous will—of the Congress that the United States should itself take some North Korean refugees. But the Department of State has already informed the congressional committees that the refugee sections of the act are unimplementable.

The North Korea Human Rights Act was, essentially, an "authorization" bill that was reported onto the floor of the House of Representatives and Senate from the Foreign Affairs and Foreign Relations Committees. Other congressional committees have to "appropriate" the actual funds necessary to implement the activities "authorized" in the act. But rather than providing funding for the activities explicitly mentioned in the act, the Appropriations Committee funded instead a U.S.-based human rights NGO to hold rallies and large-scale conferences in Washington and Seoul.

No funding for the activities actually envisioned in the Human Rights Act will be available until 2006 or 2007. Thus, assessing the impact of the activities mentioned in the act—including funding for the excellent work now done by Seoul-based human rights NGOs, increased Korean language broadcasting for Voice of America and Radio Free Asia, enabling NGOs to send small transistor radios with movable dials across the PRC-DPRK border, and so on—will have to wait even longer, if they are ever funded at all.[19]

The present inability to access the impact of the North Korean Human Rights Act notwithstanding, it nonetheless seems that the opposition to the act by "progressive" NGOs and legislators in Seoul was considerably wide of the mark. To take only three examples, why congressional concern for the end-use monitoring of bilateral American humanitarian aid to North Korea will be deemed by North Korea as threatening, and even damaging to bilateral North Korean–South Korean relations, is not self-evident, yet the ROK National Assembly members' letter to Senator Lugar (September 2, 2004) makes these assertions without explanation as to why this is so.

The South Korean NGO "Civil Society" Statement (July 22, 2004) has some wobbly logic. It asserts that "guaranteeing North Koreans the right to basic living must be pursued through unconditional humanitarian aid." But if food aid is provided with no conditionality whatsoever, then the recipients are perfectly entitled to divert it to domestic or foreign markets and pocket the profit from selling the free food unconditionally provided. How can this be consistent with "guaranteeing" North Koreans' rights to basic living?

Further, the South Korean NGO statement posits that "linking" aid to human rights considerations "contradicts" the protection of the rights of North Koreans. This view is at considerable variance with the mainstream human rights NGO approach in the United States, which has always been to seek the linkage of U.S. foreign aid and security assistance to human rights considerations. Certainly, South Korean human rights and democracy advocates did not oppose efforts by U.S. human rights NGOs to link U.S. policy and U.S. aid to human rights violations in the ROK in the 1970s and 1980s. Indeed, at the time South Korean human rights advocates strongly supported such linkage. Of course, many former North Koreans today who have escaped the DPRK and successfully obtained asylum in South Korea, where they have freedom of speech and a political voice, also support linking aid with human rights.

How Can the United States and the International Community Make Meaningful Progress?

On the one hand, there has been progress in putting North Korean violations on the international agenda, as seen most importantly in the recognition and condemnations of those violations by large majorities at the UN Commission on Human Rights, and also the U.S. congressional Human Rights Acts. Both UN and U.S. congressional condemnations are rare. Both will make it harder for severe DPRK violations to be forgotten, put aside, or swept under the rug.

Documenting and publicizing violations and seeking to put them on the international agenda is the fundamental human rights project (along with, to a lesser degree, technical cooperation projects of dialogue and/ or human rights education or training). To that extent, the last several years have seen quite considerable progress in the way the North Korea issues are handled. But once a human rights matter is on the international agenda, it is more or less out of the hands of human rights advocates and advocacy and rather more subject to the security, economic, and national/personal prestige factors that largely drive the international politics of states, and in whose shadows and interstices human rights advocacy thereafter takes place.

Still, a long-term perspective is needed. It took nearly 15 years from the Helsinki Accords to the fall of the Berlin Wall. It took even more years of advocacy and action until apartheid in South Africa became untenable. We should not expect North Korea to be different.

In this longer-term perspective, if North Korea wants to maintain the *juche* version of the "hermit kingdom" and maintain diplomatic, economic, and/or security relations with the surviving members of the socialist bloc or socialist-leaning states of the nonaligned movement, then there is very little that those outside of those blocs can do.

If, on the other hand, North Korea wants to join the international community and political economy of the 21st century—that is, have access to international bilateral and multilateral foreign aid and foreign investment and trade access to global markets—then there is a lot that other members of the international economy and community can do in the longer term in raising alongside the processes of economic, political,

115

and financial engagement the international human rights standards of the 21st century.

And, of course, it is precisely to the countries with which the DPRK does not enjoy normal political and economic relations—South Korea, Japan, and the United States—that North Korea now turns to (in its highly idiosyncratic fashion dubbed by some as "belligerent mendacity" and by others as a contorted "cry for help") to bail out and rehabilitate its collapsed economy following the withdrawal of Soviet foreign aid and the substantial commercialization of Chinese aid in the late 1980s and early 1990s. This would seem a potentially efficacious context for "positive linkage"—or, in other words, carrots.

Some examples of "positive linkage" follow.[20] Almost all scenarios for global economic engagement with the DPRK include a role for the United Nations Development Programme (UNDP). If North Korea wants a serious program of support from the United Nations Development Fund, then it can and should be required to engage in dialogue with the UN High Commissioner for Human Rights and the relevant human rights rapporteurs and other experts mentioned in the EU-sponsored resolution at the Commission. If the DPRK wants serious aid from the international financial institutions (IFFIES), then the international community can request access by the ICRC to North Korea's detention facilities. If the DPRK wants access to U.S. markets, then U.S. diplomats and trade representatives can raise issues of forced labor and DPRK cooperation with the International Labour Oragnization (ILO). If the United States, Japan, and the EU are going to be asked to finance very large-scale infrastructure projects—ports, power grids, and the like—then why not ask for the dismantlement of the political penal labor colonies, the operations of which are clear and massive crimes against humanity?

Policy Implications of Human Rights

The policy implications of human rights concerns cut a number of ways. In the short run, political realists, arms controllers, and South Korean reconciliation activists need not fret. If there is a deal on the table at the six-party talks, it is inconceivable that the United States would turn it down for reasons having to do with human rights. If the DPRK ever agreed to completely, verifiably, irreversibly dismantle (CVID) its nuclear weapons program, it is inconceivable that the United States would say "no, not unless you CVID the prison camps as well." CVID, of course, was more a slogan than a policy fit for negotiations. But if the DPRK ever does agree to Nunn-Lugar away its nuclear warheads and fissile materials and agree not to export missiles to U.S. adversary regimes in the Middle East, it is simply too much in the U.S. national interest not to accept. By the same token, if the DPRK declines to enter talks because, allegedly, Congress passed a largely symbolic human rights act or because the secretary of state uses the entirely accurate word "tyranny," is it conceivable that the DPRK has decided to accept the verification measures that would surely have to accompany any agreement? Or to talk about the allegedly nonexistent program for uranium enrichment?

On the other hand, it probably will have been noted that the available set of potential positive linkages noted above, which I would like to see utilized to pry or induce reform and human rights openness from the regime, are the same leverages that others will want to use and the DPRK will surely link to any conceivable resolution of the nuclear and missile proliferation crises. Utilizing the same set of carrots to promote both nonproliferation and human rights might require some uncharacteristically adroit diplomacy by North Korea's interlocutors.

Still, a lot depends on how the issues are framed if real negotiations actually get under way. Human rights considerations were factored into the resolution of Cold War conflicts in the heart of Europe in the 1970s; into the resolution of Cold War conflicts in Central America in the 1980s; and in Southeast Asia in the resolution to the Cold War conflict in and over Cambodia in the early 1990s. There is no reason to assume, at the outset, that human rights considerations cannot be factored into the a resolution of Cold War conflict on the Korean peninsula, particularly if a resolution goes in the direction of a "comprehensive" rather than a "trading-security-for-security" direction. In fact, the one element most in common among advocates of engagement as well as pressure toward North Korea is a preference for a "Helsinki approach."

In many respects, the best circumstance for promoting human rights in the DPRK is one in which North Korea is increasingly engaged with, not isolated from, the international community and in which serious and real economic development is undertaken in North Korea, provided that this means the DPRK will follow the Chinese/Vietnamese model of de-totalitarianization. But this also depends on a resolution of the nuclear standoff. In the absence thereof, it is hard to see either Japan or the United States contributing to rehabilitating and strengthening the North Korean economy.

To the extent that I understand the fundamental negotiating positions of North Korea and the United States, these are very far apart and unlikely to be bridged in the foreseeable future, even if the skirmishing over the shape of the negotiating table and bargaining leverage is resolved. If this is the case, the most that can be accomplished by human rights advocacy is to continue to document the DPRK violations and keep the issue on the international agenda in the hopes that the strategic and geopolitical issues can be better tackled five or ten years hence.

In the longer term, there is a different type of policy implication. While some engagement advocates fear that human rights concerns are raised in order to suffocate the North Korean regime and cause its collapse, more likely it is the other way around. It is not ongoing isolation but engagement that threatens the collapse of the Kim Il-Sungist regime.

Scholars have noted that the Kim Jong-Il regime is based on three legs: extremely thorough police state internal intelligence operations; the certainty of punishment for dissenting thought; and a monopoly on sources of information available to the populace. The last is breaking down already owing to the increasing availability of modern information technology. More North Koreans will obtain access to foreign (mostly South Korean) radio and TV. South Korean dramas, movies, and soap operas (in video tape and DVD formats) are already sweeping North Korea. More and more North Koreans will meet more and more South Koreans on various exchange programs and business opportunities. North Koreans will come to know that Kim Il-Sungism has fed them lies about South Korea and South Koreans. North Koreans will see what a modern, advanced, and prosperous Korea looks like. Freedom of information and increased communication with Koreans from below the 38th parallel will prove the spartan North's Achilles heel and likely result in a regime legitimacy crisis. This will be hastened by engagement not regime isolation.

The same is true, though to a much lesser degree, by the diminishment of tension and increased interaction with other nationalities, including the hated American imperialists. Unable to provide a good life to Koreans much beyond the privileged residents of Pyongyang, the *juche* kingdom has already lost much of its heavenly mandate. The raison d'être of the Kim dynasty has always been the seamless struggle against Japanese colonialism and U.S. imperialism. The social and political distortions of a theocratic garrison state will be increasingly pointless to many more North Koreans once American and Japanese embassies are sitting in Pyongyang. The dynamic most conducive to the demise of Kim Il-Sungism is the old-fashioned "revolution of rising expectations" after the geopolitical isolation has ended and the food crisis has bottomed out.

Notes

[1] Positive international law as opposed to what lawyers call "customary" international law.

[2] The Committee members do not speak or vote under the instruction of their various foreign ministries.

[3] The DPRK initially acceded to the International Covenant in the early 1980s when the Chun Do-hwan regime in South Korea was under intense domestic and international criticism for the massacre of prodemocracy students in Kwangju. The heavily propagandistic tone of the DPRK's initial reports under the covenant creates the appearance that the DPRK was offering a public posture

of commitment to human rights in contrast to the well-publicized contemporary repression in South Korea.

The treaties to which the DPRK acceded include the International Covenant on Civil and Political Rights; the International Covenant on Social, Economic and Cultural Rights; the Convention on the Elimination of All Forms of Discrimination against Women (CEDAW); and the Convention on the Rights of the Child (CRC). The other "core" international human rights conventions are the conventions against racial discrimination, torture, and genocide.

[4] *The Second Periodic Report of the DPRK on Its Implementation of the International Covenant on Civil and Political Rights*, UN Document no. CCPR/C/prk/2000/2, May 4, 2000; *The Second Periodic Report of the DPRK on Its Implementation of the International Covenant on Economic, Social and Cultural Rights*, April 2002; *Concluding Observations of the Human Rights Committee: Democratic Peoples Republic of Korea*, UN Document No. CCPR/CO/72/DPRK, August 27, 2001; *Concluding Observations of the Committee on Economic, Social and Cultural Rights: Democratic Peoples Republic of Korea*, UN Document No. E/C.12/1/Add.95, December 12, 2003.

[5] These include for civil and political rights: the non-independence and non-impartiality of the judiciary; the lack of an independent national human rights institution; the limited number of indigenous human rights organizations and the non-access of international human rights NGOs; lack of measures to deal with the food and nutrition situation; the fact that four of five offenses subject to the death penalty are essentially political offenses; the retroactive nature of punishment in the absence of law; torture and ill treatment by law enforcement personnel; the conditions of detention facilities; inadequate prohibitions on forced labor; pretrial detention practices; restrictions on domestic and international travel; the repression of freedom of religion; restrictions on the freedom of expression; restrictions on freedom of assembly and association; restrictions on citizen participation in public affairs; and the low level of women at senior levels of the public sector.

For economic, social, and cultural rights: the nonimpartiality of the judicial system; the lack of an effective individual complaint system in the field of economic and social rights; non-implementation of the right to work and the right of the individual to choose his/her career and workplace; labor camp punishments for persons who have traveled abroad without passports or travel authorization; nonrecognition of the right to strike and form trade unions not controlled by the ruling party; the lack of legal provisions to punish domestic violence; the social exclusion of orphans; the high rates of malnutrition of children and maternal mortality; and declining attendance rates in schools owing to consequence of natural disasters.

[6] It is sometimes said that the UN approach concentrates too much on civil and political rights and not enough on economic and social rights. This is an interesting observation. However, it should be noted that focusing on economic and social rights is a much more radical approach, sometimes going to the heart of a state's political economy and national priorities. It is also the case that such rights are sometimes much harder to implement. For example, compare the difficulties of ending public executions for essentially political offenses or the creation of a national human rights institution, a recommendation of the

UN Committee on Human Rights, with the establishment in North Korea of independent trade unions and collective bargaining and joining the ILO system, a recommendation of the UN Committee on Economic, Social and Cultural Rights.

[7] The voting on the resolutions was in 2003: 28 in favor, 10 opposed, 14 abstentions, 1 absence (ROK); in 2004: 29 in favor, 8 opposed, 16 abstentions; in 2005: 30 in favor, 9 opposed, 14 abstentions. (These are very substantial margins for "country-specific" resolutions at the commission, indicating the widespread recognition among UN member states of the extent and severity of DPRK violations, and also North Korea's isolation politically.)

The DPRK violations included, specifically: torture; public executions; extra-judicial and arbitrary detention; the absence of due process and the rule of law; imposition of the death penalty for political offenses; the large number of prison camps and the use of forced labor; sanctions against North Koreans who have traveled abroad; pervasive and severe restrictions on freedoms of thought, conscience, religion, opinion and expression, peaceful assembly and association; prohibitions on free movement internally and abroad; forced abortions and infanticide against forcibly repatriated women.

[8] UN Document. No. E/CN.4/2005/34, January 10, 2005.

[9] What I am referring to here is not so much allowing direct foreign investment or allowing foreign corporations to directly engage in mining or production or commercial distribution enterprises as it is allowing citizens the freedom of domestic and international travel, to chose their place of residence and profession or occupation, to converse with each other, or with foreigners, on a person-to-person basis or via the internet or telephone (including privately held cell phones), to listen to a variety of radio and TV broadcasts (i.e., radios without North Korea's fixed dials), and so on. Further, including the development of the rule of law, not only with respect to the enforceability of commercial contracts but also with respect to defendants' rights in the case of arrest, etc. If looked at from the governmental side, a diminution of constant police and party surveillance of the entire population, a diminution in the number of incarcerations for essentially political acts, and an end to state monopoly on information. In political science terms, the differences are systemic: while Vietnam and China remain nondemocratic, authoritarian regimes, North Korea remains totalitarian or corporatist.

[10] Article 7 reads as follows:

> When committed . . . against any civilian population: deportation or forcible transfer of population (forced displacement of persons from the area where they are lawfully present, without grounds permitted under international law); imprisonment or severe deprivation of physical liberty in violation of fundamental rules of international law; torture; murder; enforced disappearances (the arrest, abduction of persons, by or with the authorization, support or acquiescence of, a State or political organization, followed by refusal to acknowledge that deprivation of freedom or to give information on the fate or whereabouts of those persons with the intention of removing them from the protection of the law for a prolonged period of time); enslavement; and persecution (the intentional and severe

deprivation of fundamental fights contrary to international law by reason of the identity of the group or collectivity) on political grounds.

[11] For analytic descriptions and satellite photographs of North Korea's political penal labor colonies, see David Hawk, *The Hidden Gulag: Exposing North Korea's Prison Camps* (Washington, DC: U.S. Committee for Human Rights in North Korea, 2003), pp. 21–41, 89–117. Former political prisoners and guards at the *kwan-li-so* encampments attest to scores of thousands of prisoners therein. The overall and obviously very round number of 200,000 as the total labor colony population comes from former officials of the National Security Agency (*Kuk-ga-bo-wi-bu*, the police agency that runs the camps) who have "defected" to South Korea.

[12] The first exception was the mid-1970s cases of Ali Lamada and Jacques Sedillot, Venezuelan and French Communists respectively, recruited by the DPRK Foreign Ministry to live in Pyongyang and translate the works of Kim Il-Sung into Spanish and French, but who were imprisoned and tortured after they concluded (privately they thought) that the Kim Il-Sung personality cult was un-Marxist. After an international campaign, Lamada and Sedillot were released in the late 1970s and thereafter provided detailed accounts on the several prisons where they had been detained. The second exception was a 1988 report by Human Rights Watch/Asia and the Minnesota Lawyers Committee on North Korea, which provided legal analysis of the DPRK constitution and legal code but was almost entirely devoid of first-person accounts of violations.

The nonavailability of information on the situation in North Korea became acutely realized in the late 1970s and the decade of the 1980s when the international human rights movement tried to provide support to the South Koreans struggling for law and democracy in the ROK by documenting, publicizing, and protesting the imprisonment of South Korean students, religionists, and political oppositionists by the military authorities. During this time, few believed that North Korea was any workers' paradise, but the country was so isolated from the international community, there was next to no information available on which to base human rights campaigns.

[13] Prior to my current research on North Korean human rights conditions, I interviewed literally hundreds of Cambodian survivors of the Khmer Rouge genocide, scores of Rwanda survivors, and scores of victims of human rights violations in dozens of other countries around the world. I do not mean to equate the phenomena of repression in North Korea to those of Cambodia or Rwanda, but the nature of the survivor accounts is strikingly familiar. The former North Koreans I interviewed in Seoul would have to have the literary imaginations of a Kafka or Dostoyevsky to make up or invent the sufferings they survived and now describe. The accounts of some 35 former North Korean political prisoners can be seen in Hawk, *The Hidden Gulag*. Of the former North Koreans interviewed for that report, only two were unreliable or provided unusable testimony. One person really wanted to make a declaration against Kim Jong-Il, but that person's personal claims to imprisonment dissolved when pressed for details. One other person, who I do not doubt suffered greatly, answered my questions with literally incoherent non sequiturs.

[14] See Appendix 1 to chapter 7, by Kim Ki-Sik.

[15] *New Developments since the Submission of the Main Report by the Special Rapporteur, Vitit Muntarbhorn, to the Commission on Human Rights (E/CN.4/ 2005/34)*, UN Document No. E/CN.4/2005/CPR.5, March 22, 2005, p. 25.

[16] Joel Charny, *Acts of Betrayal: The Challenge of Protecting North Koreans in China* (Washington, DC: Refugees International, Washington, DC, April 2005), p. 2. The executive summary, based on the refugee stories comprising the bulk of the report, summarizes their stories as follows:

> In North Korea access to public goods—food, education, health care, shelter, employment—cannot be separated from the all-pervasive system of political persecution. The North Korean population is divided into three classes: core, wavering and hostile. The class status of each family is for life and transfers from generation to generation. Members of the hostile class are the last to receive entitlements, which is disastrous when a comprehensive welfare regime such as that established in North Korea collapses, as it did from 1994 onwards. Thus, an entire class of individuals is persecuted through the functioning of North Korea's political system. In the context, there is no meaningful way to separate economic deprivation from political persecution.
>
> In addition to the fundamental discrimination with the North Korean political system, the government further limits access to food and the economic means of survival through a variety of policies that control the lives of North Korean citizens. The government controls movement within the country by requiring travel passes to move outside one's community of origin. Since foraging for food or looking for employment wherever it can be found are essential survival strategies at times of food shortages, limits on travel further prevent North Korean citizens from meeting their basic needs. The government restricts the activities of international relief agencies, declaring certain areas of the country off limits and preventing independent monitoring of the relief supplies provided.
>
> Thus, most North Koreans crossing the border into China are fleeing state-sponsored denial of their human rights. Members of the "hostile class" and residents of areas deliberately cut off from international food assistance have an especially strong case to be considered refugees in the sense of fleeing targeted persecution. But the denial of basic rights extends more broadly, and the hunger that drives people to flee is the direct result of the political system that has been created by the leaders of the North Korean government. Not since Cambodia under the Khmer Rouge has a government succeeded in creating such an all-encompassing reality of oppression and restrictions on the basic rights of the majority of its citizens.

[17] The reports of the ICRC are provided only to the government concerned and are not made public. Reports by UN human rights officials or NGOs would be public documents.

[18] At present, unlike, for example, the Peoples Republic of China, the DPRK refuses to cooperate with UN human rights officials, but the presidential envoy can pursue with Maurice Strong, the UNDP and the UN SG special representative to North Korea, the "mainstreaming" or "Action Two[ing]" of human rights

in regards to the overall UN approach to North Korea. The EU is particularly important, as at present the DPRK is willing to discuss human rights issues with the EU members with whom the DPRK has normal diplomatic relations. The ROK has an ambassador at large for human rights who has extensive experience with North Korea, and with whom the presidential envoy should also collaborate.

[19] Radios produced in North Korea have fixed dials, allowing the listener to receive only the DPRK government channels. Radios with movable dials would enable North Koreans to listen to foreign broadcasts, particularly Korean language materials and South Korean programs broadcast in the adjacent areas of China with large ethnic Korean populations.

[20] "Negative linkage" such as sanctions and embargoes are sometimes complicated instruments for promoting human rights. And they are very hard to apply to North Korea owing to the DPRK's already substantial isolation. Except for China and South Korea, there is very little for the rest of the world to withdraw or withhold (exclusive of humanitarian famine relief). But both China and South Korea see potential state collapse in North Korea as profoundly contrary to their national interest.

Perspectives on North Korean "Displaced Persons"

Kim Ki-Sik

The human rights situation in North Korea has, in the last few years, together with the issue of the North Korean nuclear weapons program, become a matter of pressing concern to international society. Earlier, the main human rights concern regarding North Korea was one of humanitarian aid by the international community in response to the humanitarian calamity brought about by food shortages and massive famine resulting from severe flooding. However, over the last few years, the focus on North Korea seems have zeroed in on issues relating to the North Korean political system; this focus has become very much politicized. Today, issues of human rights in North Korea have become one of the most potent grounds for criticism of the North Korean system and for calling for a change in the North Korean system. The rise in criticism within international society of the human rights situation in North Korea, on the other hand, has aggravated the issues surrounding North Korea's nuclear weapons development and the conspicuous decline in humanitarian assistance by the international community to North Korea. These shifts have been brought about mainly by the issue of North Korean displaced persons and the testimony by some of the "escapees" about the human rights situation in North Korea.

The plight of North Korean displaced persons, highlighted by various attempts to enter foreign diplomatic facilities in China, has become an icon of the human rights issues concerning North Korea and the focal point of international society's concern. The shocking testimony by some displaced North Koreans has given rise to a critical perception of North Korea in international society and has been adopted as the major evidence of the anti–human rights nature of the North Korean system. The U.S. administration and Congress have in recent months made use of recent developments—and, at the same time, added weight to them—and have latched onto human rights issues, by the introduction of the North Korean Human Rights Act as a means to pressure North Korea and by using the issue of human rights as a grounds for the various policies aimed at bringing about the collapse of the North Korean system or a regime change. The key issue in these developments, however, is whether they actually contribute to a substantial improvement in the human rights situation in North Korea. This chapter aims to describe the situation of

North Korean displaced persons to the extent it can be corroborated, and to identify the characteristics of North Korean displaced persons based on an analysis of the motivation for their border crossing, and suggests some basic principles for addressing the human rights issue of North Korean displaced persons. This chapter aims to highlight the dangers of a politicized approach to the issue of displaced North Koreans and other human rights issues and lays out the basic orientation the People's Solidarity for Participatory Democracy (PSPD) has developed in addressing human rights issues in North Korea. It should be noted that this chapter avoids using the term "refugees," which is often used in international society, but instead uses the term "displaced persons." This reflects, as will be explained below, the complex characteristics of North Korean displaced persons and, at the same time, an awareness of the political implications latent in the term "refugees."

The Situation of North Korean Displaced Persons and the Issue of Human Rights

It is realistically not possible to ascertain the exact number of "North Korean displaced persons." The difficulty is similar to that of trying to ascertain the exact figures of "undocumented migrants" in Korea, the United States, or any other country. A report of the government of South Korea, in October 1999, estimated the number of "North Korean displaced persons" staying in various "third countries" to be between 10,000 and 30,000. A South Korean refugee relief organization, Good Friends: Center for Peace, Human Rights and Refugees (hereafter Good Friends), issued a report in 1999, based on its survey of 2,479 villages, indicating that some 300,00 North Korean displaced persons were "hiding out" in three northeastern provinces of China. In June 2003, Ruud Lubbers, the United Nations High Commissioner for Refugees (UNHCR), offered an estimate of 100,000 North Korean displaced persons in China.[1] A review of various reports points to an estimate of over 100,000. An unpublished report of the National Human Rights Commission of Korea also locates the figure somewhere between a few tens of thousands to a few hundreds of thousands.[2] The massive exodus of people from North Korea was triggered by the grave food crisis following a series of floods and related natural disasters in the mid-1990s. The origin of the phenomenon provides a valuable and important window for understanding the motivation of the exodus and the characterization of the "displaced persons," and for beginning to consider efforts for the improvement of the human rights conditions of the displaced persons and finding solutions to the very issue of exodus itself.

The recent easing of the food crisis in North Korea, the enactment of the North Korean Human Rights Act in the United States, and stepping up of law enforcement activities by the Chinese authorities in the wake of political and diplomatic tensions arising from the repeated entry into foreign diplomatic offices in China have been cited as having brought about a decline in the size of the exodus from North Korea.

While displaced North Koreans are found in most Asian countries, such as Mongolia and the countries of Southeast Asia, as well as Russia and other areas of what was formerly the Soviet Union, where there are substantial Korean communities, most are located in China. The survey by the National Human Rights Commission, mentioned above, found that most displaced North Koreans prefer to stay in China and hope to return to North Korea after accumulating some financial resources. Similar findings were made by surveys conducted by nongovernmental organizations.

According to the South Korean Ministry of Unification, the total number of displaced North Koreans who have been brought to South Korea was, at the end of 2004, 6,304. Relocation in South Korea has increased markedly over the past few years. In 2000, the number stood at 312, increasing to 583 in 2001, 1,139 in 2002, 1,281 in 2003, and 1,894 in 2004. The statistics show that 67 percent of the displaced North Koreans brought into South Korea are women. This may reflect the fact that most of the more recent displaced North Koreans are women, and that their livelihood is relatively insecure.[3]

The atrocious conditions and human rights abuses suffered by displaced North Koreans in the North Korea-China border areas have come a subject of serious concern. Due to the insecurity of their status, many are known to have been subjected to trafficking and serious exploitation. A 1999 survey by the Good Friends found that 40.9 percent of displaced North Koreans who found employment did not receive any wage aside from the provision of food and housing. Displaced women are known to have been forced into unwanted marriages following trafficking and some have been forced into prostitution. Unprotected displaced children suffer from hunger, malnutrition, and skin diseases due to long period of wandering in search of a livelihood. Many have been found to be suffering from serious psychological trauma.

The atrocious human rights conditions that befall displaced North Koreans stem from the very fact that they do not have legal status in China and are forced to live in hiding. The Chinese government conducts repeated roundups of displaced North Koreans and maintains a policy of force "repatriation" to North Korea. The aforementioned National Human Rights Commission survey found the Chinese authorities have intensified their roundup of displaced persons since the enactment of the North Korean Human Rights Act in the United States. The Chinese government is known to have established seven internment camps for apprehended displaced persons. Moreover, it carries out a regular forced repatriation, numbering 200 to 300 a week. The Chinese military is known to have been ordered to block the entry into China of the North Korean exodus and to expedite work of internment and forced repatriation.

The Motivation for Crossing the Border

The motivation for crossing the border seems to vary widely for individual displaced North Koreans. Some have crossed the border temporarily to secure food, medicine, or money, while others, driven by the difficulties they faced in North Korea, undertook the journey in search of a livelihood. Some crossed the border in search of a better life while others sought to escape punishment following some kind of criminal activity. Some were found to have abandoned North Korea for political reasons stemming from their critical attitude toward the North Korean regime, while others were pulled by family members who made the cross-border journey earlier. Finally, there are those who were induced to cross the border by groups that facilitate or orchestrate planned exits. In many cases, multiple motivations seemed to be at play.

In general, however, the central or root factor seems to be the food crisis and economic difficulties that have gripped most of the North Korean population (see Table 1). This generalization is borne out by the fact that the mass exodus began in the late 1990s following the serious aggravation of the economic and food crisis in North Korea. At the same time, both a set of push factors and of pull factors seems to be at play in the exodus phenomenon. While the various "economic" motivations for the cross-border exodus were conditioned by threats to livelihood and survival arising from the economic and food crisis (which characterized the earlier phase of exodus), the rapid economic growth in China seems to have been a pull factor, inducing a more voluntary "migration" in search of a better life, especially in the later phases of the exodus. An analysis by the Korea Institute for National Unification, a government-funded research center, found that while the number of North Koreans crossing the border declined with the gradual easing of the food crisis in North Korea, the motivation for border crossing began to shift in 2000 and onwards from a "search for survival" to one of a "search for a better life."

Table 1. North Korean Border Crossing by Types of Motivation

	Livelihood difficulty	Concern for punishment	Critical attitude toward the regime	Family reunion	Settlement in China	Family conflict	Others	Total
2000	127	66	52	51	13	2	1	312
2001	293	73	33	171	7	2	4	583
2002	606	93	96	259	37	39	9	1,139
2003	774	80	123	194	46	53	11	1,281
6/2004	463	44	63	148	2	39	1	760
Total	2,263 (55.53%)	356 (8.74%)	367 (9.01%)	823 (20.2%)	105 (2.58%)	135 (3.31%)	26 (0.64%)	4,075 (100%)

As of June 2004 (unit=persons)
Source: Division of Social and Cultural Exchange, Ministry of Unification

The various findings give little credence to the belief that the major factor or cause for the mass exodus is politically motivated, including a critical attitude toward or dissatisfaction with the North Korean system or regime. Furthermore, although economic factors were found to be the major motivation, it would be unreasonable to conclude that the issue of North Korean displaced persons can be linked to the issue of the North Korean system or regime, extending the argument that the North Korean system or regime is the root cause of the economic crisis that has fuelled the exodus. This is, however, not to deny that the unique autarkic and feudal socialist system found in North Korea is one of the fundamental factors that gave rise to the recent economic crisis. If the socialist system itself was a key motivating factor, then a similar exodus should have been found before the outbreak of the recent serious food crisis. It is worthwhile to note that China, a similar socialist state, is addressing the issue of economic problems through reform and liberalization.

Characteristics of North Korean Displaced Persons

Characterizing North Korean displaced persons is a very difficult matter. As pointed out above, the major motivation for border crossing for these people was economic. While the early border-crossers were driven by the sheer need of survival, more recently cases that can be categorized as economic migration in search for better life are increasing. The human rights issues that arise from the cross-border migration are while differing in degree fundamentally similar to those found among undocumented migrant workers in South Korea coming from various Asian countries or in the United States coming from various Latin American countries and Asia. That is issues of the threat of arrest, exposure to blatant exploitation, and human trafficking, and the like. Forced repatriation upon being apprehended by the authorities is a common problem for all undocumented migrant workers, be they in South Korea or the United States.

There are, however, some pertinent factors that make it difficult to view North Korean displaced persons in the same light as undocumented migrant workers in South Korea or the United States: the motivation for their border crossing is intrinsically linked to the very special conditions created by the food crisis. The extent and pervasiveness of human rights abuses suffered by North Korean displaced persons hiding out in China and other temporary settlements have been found to be extreme. At the same time, North Korean displaced persons are, despite the recent softening, liable to punishment when they return or are returned to North Korea. These particular circumstances have been behind the calls for recognizing them as refugees and according them the human rights protection stemming from such a recognition.

Although there is considerable debate as to whether North Korean displaced persons can be deemed refugees, a view has been presented that they can be recognized as refugees, even if the motivation for their border crossing is mainly economic, because they genuinely and justifiably fear persecution on their return to North Korea. Such a view has been spelled out by Vitit Muntarbhor, the Special Rapporteur on the Situation of Human Rights in the Democratic People's Republic of Korea, appointed by the United Nations Commission on Human Rights. In short, according to this view North Korean displaced persons may be deemed refugees so long as there is a possibility of their persecution.

There is, however, very little possibility for North Korean displaced persons to be recognized as refugees since the mandate for refugee status recognition, according to the UN Refugee Convention, lies with the government of the hosting nation. Although China ratified the UN 1951 Refugee Convention in 1982 and acceded to the 1967 Protocol relating to the Status of Refugees, it has yet to give any formal recognition to the existence of North Korean nationals in China who have fled from North Korea out of fear of political persecution.

Although it may be difficult to expect the North Korean displaced persons who have crossed the border into China because of the grave food crisis in North Korea to obtain mandate refugee status, they are genuinely displaced persons who are in need of the protection and the concern of the international community. They must be granted a status whereby they will not be subject to forced repatriation and will have access to temporary protection. The International Organization for Migration makes clear that the rights of undocumented migrants to life, to be free from slavery and forced labor, torture, and inhuman treatment, and to enjoy privacy, freedom of movement, freedom of thought and religion, and freedom of expression cannot be violated or denied. In addressing the issue of North

Korean displaced persons, it is necessary to take into consideration the inexorable conditions that drove them to flee from North Korea and the wide-ranging human rights abuses from which they have been found to suffer. These must be thoroughly eradicated.[4]

Changes in the North Korean Policy on the Punishment of Returning Displaced Persons

The North Korean government is known to have, in the early stages of the exodus phenomenon, deemed returned displaced persons as having betrayed the nation and the people, and to have subjected them to heavy punishment. It regarded the returnees as perpetrators of political crimes and incarcerated them in political prisoner camps. Their family members were forced to relocate to special controlled areas. However, as the size of the exodus mushroomed, the North Korean authorities began to develop differentiated responses according to the length of stay outside North Korea and the motivation for departure.

Since September 27, 1997, in easing punitive action against returned displaced persons, the North Korean government interned returnees in a "9/27 Shelter" (otherwise known as a "kkot-jebi" camp) for a period before they were released. (Only a special category of returnees was managed separately in Defense Ministry and Public Security Agency detention centers.)

The 1992 North Korean Constitution, in Article 86, stipulated that the betrayal of the nation and the people was the gravest crime and liable to heavy punishment. This provision was, however, repealed in 1998 Constitution, paving the way for softening the punitive measures in response to a massive increase in the exodus. The 1987 Criminal Code, in Article 47, defines illegal exit from the country as a traitorous act against the nation and stipulates a punishment of more than seven years of correctional labor. The 1999 Criminal Code, however, defines two types of illegal departure from the country: the simple crossing of the border, that is, persons who illegally cross the border, are liable to less than three years of correctional labor (Article 117), whereas persons illegally crossing the border into another country with an intent to subvert the Republic are liable to correctional labor of more than five years but less than ten. Persons whose crime is serious are liable to more than ten years of correctional labor or death and confiscation of their property.

The 2004 Criminal Code, in Article 233, redefined persons crossing the border found in the earlier versions as persons crossing the border into and out of the country. At the same time, the punishment reserved for this violation was reduced from less than three years of correctional labor to less than two years of labor rehabilitation. As two years of labor rehabilitation is equivalent to one year of correctional labor, the punishment is understood to have been reduced from three years of imprisonment to one year of imprisonment.[5]

In August 2004, the North Korean authorities announced that those who crossed the border for purely economic reasons would not be subject to criminal punishment. The National Human Rights Commission's survey of North Korean displaced persons found that persons who crossed the border in search of food were released after one week of summary internment, and no serious punishment was meted out to their family members. The U.S. Department of State report on North Korea also notes that North Korea, on the basis of an amendment of its criminal code, distinguishes between political border crossing and temporary border crossing due to economic reasons in meting out punishment. It found that punishment has been eased, with a stipulated maximum penalty of two years of labor rehabilitation for those who have crossed the border illegally for economic reasons, and that the treatment of returnees has improved. The findings reported by the U.S. State Department, however, differ considerably from the congressional information used in the deliberations over the North Korean Human Rights Act in 2004.

The overall picture is one of softening in the way the government of North Korea treats or punishes persons who have crossed the border, not withstanding the continuing human rights issue concerning the very punishment. At the same time, there appears to be an easing of the control over border crossing in the North Korea-China border area. This change is corroborated by an increasing number of North Koreans who have crossed the border into China going back into North Korea to recross the border to China accompanied by members of their family. There are also cases of returnees, subjected to forced repatriation by the Chinese authorities, re-entering China. Furthermore, there are cases, although they are not as common, where North Korean displaced persons who were relocated in South Korea re-enter North Korea and then return to South Korea via the North Korea-China border.

The Practical Dangers of a Political Approach to the Issue of North Korean Displaced Persons

The activities of various organizations facilitating the North Korean border crossings, such as the organized entry into foreign diplomatic offices and the exposure of the human rights situation among North Korean displaced persons and the general situation in North Korea, have contributed greatly in raising awareness in the United States and the international community of the issue of displaced North Koreans and the human rights situation in North Korea. However, some of the more extreme efforts of these organizations in carrying out planned border crossings have led to negative effects that could bring about an aggravation of the human rights situation of displaced North Koreans. There are many civilian organizations and activists, working on the basis of humanitarian principles, who provide valuable assistance to displaced North Koreans who find themselves suffering from grave human rights violations. However, there is a rising criticism in South Korea of some Christian mission organizations that seem to be intent on exploiting the issue of North Korean displaced persons for some political purposes and of some NGOs for their "planned border crossing" ventures.[6]

Some people involved in planned border crossings have been accused of exploiting displaced North Koreans for their own political or commercial objectives. The charge is that they have gathered together some displaced North Koreans, organized them to enter foreign diplomatic offices regardless of the possible danger involved, and then drawn media attention to their operations. Recently, there has been various verification that some organized brokers have been involved in some of the "planned border crossings," and have received money for delivering displaced North Koreans to South Korea. The South Korean prosecutor's office has recently taken criminal action against some of those identified as "brokers."[7]

Planned border crossings for passage to South Korea have given rise to problems of orchestrated mobilization of displaced North Koreans, sensationalism, and human rights abuse and criminal activities directed at displaced North Koreans. The media attention generated by planned border crossings for passage to South Korea has forced the enforcement activities of the Chinese authorities, creating extremely difficult conditions for most of the displaced North Koreans who hope to remain in China. These orchestrated efforts drive displaced persons into greater danger, by constraining the space for displaced persons and giving rise to the likelihood of more severe punishment when they are forcibly repatriated to North Korea.[8]

Although the seriousness of human rights issues in North Korea and the growing international concern about them have been a key factor in the growing activities of NGOs focusing on displaced North Koreans and the rapid politicization of the issue, the support of conservative organizations within and without South Korea, which have their own political or commercial objectives, cannot be ignored as another key factor. Some Japanese television networks that are known to be deeply involved in "planned border crossings" have employed Korean nationals to film the "border-crossing" ordeal. They have been accused of using the issue to generate angry, anti-North Korean sentiment in Japan.[9] It cannot be denied that the distortions and exaggerations of the human rights situation in North Korea, incorporating the issue of displaced

North Koreans, that began to circulate in volume stem in some way from this kind of intervention.

Some conservative religious organizations in the United States and the National Endowment for Democracy (NED) are known to provide support to various groups that raise North Korean human rights issues. The U.S. government is also known to have a plan to support North Korean human rights organizations in order to press North Korea on human rights issues through the vehicle of the North Korean Human Rights Act (2004) and the Annual Report on Activities in Support of Human Rights and Democracy (March 28, 2005).

The U.S. Congress enacted the North Korean Human Rights Act in 2004, paving the way for allocating $20 million per year from fiscal years 2005 to 2008 for humanitarian support for displaced North Koreans. The U.S. State Department's report to the House of Representatives International Relations Committee (pursuant to Article 301 of the North Korean Human Rights Act), titled State of Displaced North Koreans and the U.S. Policy on Displaced North Koreans, describes how the follow-up activities of the North Korean Human Rights Act have aggravated the human rights situation of displaced North Koreans and that the policy of protection for displaced North Koreans was not likely, in the present situation, to bring about the desired results.

The State Department report found that the governments of countries where displaced North Koreans are located vehemently oppose the entry of official U.S. government funds to support displaced North Koreans. At the same time, they also oppose the conduct of asylum application reviews in their own territories. As a result, the report indicates that the implementation of policies for the protection of displaced North Koreans will not be simple. The U.S. policy requires asylum applicants to present an urgent cause for settlement in the United States rather than South Korea or any other third country. It has been made clear that the United States will be selective in granting asylum to those whose border crossing is highly politically motivated or possess high-quality information. The report notes that there was difficulty in obtaining information about North Korean nationals seeking asylum due to the fact that North Korea has remained a closed society for so long. It also notes that difficulties have arisen in the asylum application review procedure due to the restrictions caused by the fact that North Korea is listed as a state giving assistance to terrorism. [10]

While the U.S. government is making many public pronouncements about humanitarian assistance for displaced North Koreans, stressing its own role, in reality, however, it does not envision granting asylum to any substantial number of displaced North Koreans. Instead, it is intent on transferring all the responsibility and burden for settlement of displaced North Koreans to the South Korean government. The United States has always insisted that displaced North Koreans seeking settlement should be directed to South Korea. Given, furthermore, that it insists on being selective in granting settlement to North Koreans, the U.S. policy for protection or asylum for displaced North Koreans is likely to lead to nothing much.

The real problem, however, lies in that the enactment of the North Korean Human Rights Act is creating even more difficulties for displaced North Koreans. China, since the introduction of the act, has stepped up its enforcement campaign, carrying out forced repatriation, and has begun to deal severely with persons who have been found to be involved in instigating "border crossings." Furthermore, the Chinese authorities are handing out heavy fines to ethnic Koreans in China who have been found to have provided hiding or assistance, thus weakening the capacity of the Korean community in China to provide protection for displaced North Koreans.

Lately questions are being raised concerning the trustworthiness of the testimony of displaced North Koreans. Although it is necessary to respect the experiences of displaced North Koreans and their testimony when it is corroborated by accounts of other people, the concern arises from evidence of exaggeration or false testimony by some displaced North Koreans in order to raise their worthiness. The most worrying is testimony of torture, biological experiments, forced abortion, infanticide, and the like, being conducted in "concentration camps," which have raised instantaneous outrage in the international community. Claims such as these remain to be verified. Even other displaced North Koreans are raising doubts about the veracity of such testimony.[11]

A Basic Perspective on the Issue of Displaced North Koreans and Some Insights

In order to move toward developing effective measures to resolve the issue of displaced North Koreans, it is imperative to undertake a comprehensive survey of the exact number of displaced North Koreans and their current situation, as well as the motivations for their border crossing and their thoughts about their future. Although it will not be easy to survey the situation of displaced North Koreans given that they are all in some form of hiding, a thorough survey of the situation is necessary to be able to produce a genuine and effective program of measures focusing on this issue.

It is clear, however, on the basis of the aforementioned survey of displaced North Koreans and the analysis of their motivation, and the extent of the seriousness of human rights abuses suffered by them, that their rights as migrants must be guaranteed and the practice of forced repatriation and punishment against those who have fled North Korea for humanitarian reasons must cease. The Chinese government must, in order to bring about an improvement in the human rights situation of displaced North Koreans, grant temporary residence and end the current policy of forced repatriation. Given that most of the displaced North Koreans express a hope to return to Korea after earning some income, the Chinese authorities should extend generous treatment in a humanitarian spirit. The North Korean authorities, who have already watered down the punishment of returnees either those who return voluntarily or through forced repatriation, should not impose any kind of punishment on those who were forced to cross the border because of the very threat to their survival. The authorities will need to lower the level of punishment even more for all displaced North Koreans.

There is no question that the exodus was triggered by the food crisis and is now continuing due to various economic motivations. The exodus is not likely to come to an end without a marked improvement in the food situation and economic conditions. Therefore, humanitarian assistance to North Korea by the international community aimed to deal with the food crisis, which is the indisputable cause of the exodus, should not be stopped or reduced for any political reasons, but rather maintained and even increased.

Given that reform and liberalization are thought to be vital for overcoming North Korea's current economic problems, which have propelled the exodus and spawned much of the grave human rights situation, an international-community effort that creates a positive environment is vital. Unless the current deadlock between North Korea and the United States is resolved in a comprehensive manner, which would then pave the way for North Korea's efforts in reform and liberalization, there cannot be a fundamental solution to the issue of displaced North Koreans.[12]

What needs to be stressed is that the issue of displaced North Koreans should never be exploited for political or commercial purposes. This is not in any way beneficial to the cause of improving the human rights situation of displaced North Koreans. Activities that induce border crossing or asylum seeking need to be curtailed; in cases where such support and assistance may be necessary, they should be taken up with great care. The various brokering activities related to border crossing need to be eradicated. The efforts to persuade displaced North Koreans to head for a third country with an ulterior motive of attacking the North Korean system or regime or with the intent to bring about its collapse, or the actions of those donor agencies that support organizations engaged in this kind of activity, are damaging the humanitarian principles of human rights protection and aggravating the general human rights situation. This can jeopardize the possibility of developing an environment conducive to a fundamental resolution of the problem of displaced North Koreans. Given this, these activities must cease. Related to this, the South Korean government must take care that its settlement policy toward displaced North Koreans does not become an inducement for planned border crossing. The U.S. government must also realize that the North Korean Human Rights Act and other human rights policy activities directed at North Korea are having an opposite effect in terms of the human rights situation of displaced North Koreans. It must undertake a thorough re-examination and reorientation of its policies.

Basic Perspectives on Human Rights Issues in North Korea

Civil society organizations in South Korea are well aware of the gravity of human rights issues in North Korea. Those issues cannot be minimized by arguing that North Korea is a special case, but must be subject to universal human rights principles. On the other hand, a critical approach is needed about the current politicization of human rights issues in North Korea and the simplistic attitude that fails to take into consideration the various interrelated and interconnected factors surrounding human rights issues. The civil society movement in South Korea is, at the same time, concerned about the negative consequences that may arise from an inappropriate manner of intervention in North Korean human rights issues.

There has been much debate and doubt about the policy objectives of the U.S. approach to the issue of the North Korean nuclear weapons development program. Is the United States working to bring about an end to North Korea's nuclear weapons program or an end to the system/regime that exists in North Korea? Similarly, these same questions are being raised about the U.S. human rights policy toward North Korea, as manifest in such actions as the North Korean Human Rights Act. Is it aimed at improving the human rights situation in North Korea, or is it guided by a goal of bringing an end to North Korea as it is currently organized? The general opinion of the civil society movement in Korea leans toward the latter.

Using human rights issues as a political vehicle for attacking a state deserves to be criticized as undermining the very principles of human rights. A human rights policy directed at North Korea couched in such a political motivation will only bring about greater internal control and closure; it will foster an even greater climate of confrontation and tension, aggravating the threat to peace in the whole of the Korean peninsula, and willingly, cynically, or inadvertently will lead to an deterioration of the human rights situation.

The PSPD is committed to finding an effective nexus of development rights, peace, and human rights. In short, the PSPD believes that a comprehensive settlement of the current conflict between North Korea and the United States over the issue of nuclear weapons development leading to the establishment of a system of peace in the Korean peninsula and creating an environment conducive to North Korea's reform and liberalization—is the clearest, surest, and most fundamental way forward for the improvement of the human rights situation in North Korea, including the issue of displaced North Koreans.

The two appended documents, including the recent written statement submitted to the UN Commission on Human Rights for the session on North Korea, describe the basic perspective of the PSPD on the issue of human rights in North Korea.

Appendix 1[13]

Commission on Human Rights, Sixty-first session, Item 9 of the provisional agenda

The Question of the Violation of Human Rights and Fundamental Freedom in Any Part of the World

Written statement submitted by the People's Solidarity for Participatory Democracy (PSPD), a nongovernmental organization in special consultative status

Approaches for Improvement of the Human Rights Situation in North Korea (DPRK)

Concerns over the human rights situation in DPRK are mounting, while views on how to improve it find little common ground and efforts to collect factual data run into grave difficulties.

We note that the fifty-ninth and sixtieth sessions of the UN Commission on Human Rights have adopted resolutions condemning North Korea's human rights abuses and the sixtieth session appointed a Special Rapporteur on the North Korean situation. The first report submitted by the Rapporteur in January 2005 is duly appreciated.

We note with appreciation the constructive elements suggested by the Rapporteur considering the underlying context in order to understand the issue of North Korea human rights, specifically the challenge for civil, political, social, economic rights and his recommendations. At the same time, we regret that the report has not sufficiently assessed positive actions by the DPRK government, such as the revision of the criminal law and efforts towards inter-Korean reconciliation and cooperation, initial signs of important changes. The main question is, we believe, how to link various recommendations for the improvement of the human rights situation in the DPRK with steps to transform the perilous environment surrounding the country, created by regional and global power politics, clearly beyond the scope of what one government could aspire to do, that impedes both local and international efforts to promote human rights in the DPRK.

In this regard, we would like to emphasize that the DPRK's active efforts must accompany the international community s pragmatic and consultative approach. We cannot deny that the DPRK government and its policies are at the root of various violations of the human rights of its people. Admitting that the most important responsibility for the worsening human rights situation is ascribed to the government would lead to affirmative steps for the improvement of human rights. The DPRK government should also open access to human rights information on its people. We hope that the DPRK government takes such initiatives and invites the international community to give necessary support to admit the DPRK as a member of the community.

At the same time, we hope and stress that the international community recognizes and works together on the external factors that affect the isolation of the DPRK and its confrontation with its neighboring countries. We need to recognize the real and potential effects of the economic sanctions, arms build-up, and large-scale military exercises constantly occurring in the region, which involve a questionable role played by the government of the United States. The impact of the security approach to human rights is worsening since the government of the United States took the path of labeling the DPRK a rogue state and a member of the axis of evil.

In great contrast, there has been a steady and substantial growth of mutual understanding and trust-building processes between the two Koreas. This should shed light on our thinking and actions in the future. The constructive role played by nongovernmental organizations in this process also deserves proper attention.

History and reality in Northeast Asia show that improvement of human rights in a country tends to work better with a careful review of conditions for and against peace than without. This leads us to take a more comprehensive and balanced review and actions. In this light, we put forward some principles of engagement in the human rights problems in the region, as follows.

First, the right to life and eradication of the conditions of poverty and famine should receive the utmost attention in considering the human rights issue in the DPRK. The improvement of human rights would be immaterial if there is sustained hunger among a large part of the population. The first priority in addressing the human rights issue in North Korea is the people's right to survival.

Second, international engagement in North Korea must not threaten peace in the region. Approaches attending conflict and confrontation with little practical alternatives cannot do much. The peaceful coexistence of all nations in the region is the basic premise for securing the human rights of the peoples in the region. This point is well taken in the development of the inter-Korea relationship and the cooperation between governments and nongovernmental organizations in the process. Least desirable in this situation are politically motivated approaches in the name of human rights, such as the North Korean Human Rights Act by the United States.

Third, the international community needs a set of principles for intervening in North Korean human rights issues: the intervention must be performed in a just, consultative, and peaceful way by actors equipped with ethical and human rights legitimacy. The engagement in human rights issues must promote a universal cause and thus selective actions informed by power politics must be strictly avoided.

Fourth, holistic standards of human rights should be applied to the human rights issue in North Korea, including standards not only of political and civil rights, but also those of economic, social, and cultural rights, and the right to development as agreed in the United Nations. A selective choice of standards will lead to weakening or even denial of the legitimacy of international intervention.

Considering these aspects, we recommend the following points be included in the discussion of the human rights situation in the DPRK in the United Nations Commission on Human Rights.

First, as the Special Rapporteur pointed out, the United Nations Commission on Human Rights should express a clear understanding of the highly complex internal and external contexts affecting human rights in the DPRK and recommend that it improve its human rights situation accordingly and through a holistic approach.

Second, the United Nations Commission on Human Rights needs to emphasize the necessity of continuing humanitarian aid to the DPRK, including food and energy, in order to assist its government in protecting the right to life of its people. In effect, the food aid provided by the international community since the 1990s has contributed considerably to the alleviation of North Korea's food crisis. Nevertheless, North Korea is still in urgent need of food and a social network for people is not properly working.

Third, as all human rights are interdependent and inalienable, the United Nations Commission on Human Rights should include the right to self-determination and the right to development in its review and recommendations to the DPRK. To this effect, it should review issues in international aid, sociopolitical policies, and the legal system, not excluding issues of military conflict, arms build-up, and economic sanctions in the region and the role played by all the governments involved. We urge that the UNCHR call for the relieving of military tensions and reducing militarization in the region to create favorable conditions for the improvement of human rights in both Koreas, and emphasize the need for trust building, consultation, and cooperation among all concerned governments in the region.

Fourth, the United Nations Commission on Human Rights should pay attention to the fact that North Korea complemented the principle of legality through, among others, revision of its criminal law in 2004. It is also reducing punishment of repatriated defectors. The UNCHR also needs to recognize that the North Korea government is imposing minor penalties on those who had escaped for economic reasons. Along with other positive signs, these form an important base for further steps.

Fifth, due to the difficulty of and political sensitivity in collecting accurate information, the United Nations Commission on Human Rights needs to emphasize the importance of data collection and fact verification before attempting to devise ways of improving human rights in the DPRK. For example, it needs to undertake a comprehensive examination of reported information on forced labor and infanticide, about which the last UN resolution expressed grave concern.

Finally, we urge the United Nations Commission on Human Rights to take specific measures to provide basic rights and freedom to persons escaping or temporarily leaving the DPRK and residing in the PRC. Escapees from the DPRK are now in the blind spot of human rights. It is the duty of the United Nations and the international community to protect the rights of these people. The DPRK and PRC governments need to do the utmost to protect the basic rights of migrants from the DPRK, and stop forced repatriation and punishment for those who escaped North Korea for humanitarian reasons. The UNCHR should also note the complexity of the situation caused by some undesirable effects such as that produced by the passage of the North Korean Human Rights Act in the United States and the work of "designed defection" of North Koreans promoted by some NGOs.

Appendix 2

The PSPD's Approach to the Issue of Human Rights in the DPRK

The PSPD considers the following points central to resolving human rights issues in the DPRK:

First, the DPRK government should do much more to improve the human rights situation for its nationals. The DPRK government has the primary responsibility to address the human rights problems confronting its nationals. Even though the current human rights situation in the DPRK is to a certain extent related to the political and economic sanctions taken by the United States and its allies, one cannot deny the impact that the failure of the system and policies of the DPRK government has had on human rights of its people. We urge that the DPRK government exert its utmost effort, both nationally and internationally, to protect and improve the human rights of the affected people. The DPRK's commitment to this end will lead the international community to accept the DPRK as one of its members and render it necessary support.

Second, the development of human rights regimes in international organizations like the UN has contributed to understanding human rights in a wider and deeper context. Efforts on an international level to protect human rights are certainly an outcome of the progress of mankind. In this respect, we strongly urge that all civil, political, social, and economic rights and the right to development be applied to the DPRK in accordance with the understanding achieved in the UN human rights bodies. A selective application is not only partial in its nature but deeply flawed and dangerous. We note that social and economic rights and the right to development are seriously threatened in the DPRK due to its economic crisis. We also note that civil and political rights are limited in the DPRK due to its unique political system.

Third, we assert that of all human rights the right to life takes the central and fundamental importance in our efforts to address the human rights situation in the DPRK. As pointed out in the Brandt Report to the UN in 1980, with starvation, there can be no peace. Equally, with starvation there are no human rights. Considering the serious economic difficulties experienced in the DPRK, its people's right to life should receive priority over other issues of human rights. We believe that the human rights intervention of the international community in the DPRK should start with humanitarian aid. The principle of indivisibility of human rights should form the basis of formulating a comprehensive understanding and approach to the issue: the interrelationship of the conditions and enjoyment of civil and political rights and social and economic rights must be examined in addressing the human rights issue in the DPRK.

Fourth, the human rights intervention of the international community in the DPRK must not threaten the peace process in the Korean peninsula. Without peace, there is little room for human rights. Peace on the peninsula is the prerequisite for the realization of human rights of both Korean peoples. The ROK and DPRK governments have been mutually forming a reconciliation and cooperation policy for peaceful coexistence with their peoples' strong support. However, the North Korean Human Rights Act adopted by the United States has induced many peoples to flee from the territory of DPRK. The act does not substantially contribute to improving the human rights situation in North Korea. It actually runs counter to the two Koreas' efforts at peace-building and a peace-based approach to other issues. This approach of the United States has rather contributed to creating new distrust and new confrontation between two Koreas. Such an approach produces effects tantamount to aggravating human rights in the DPRK by way of falling into the trap of threat politics.

Fifth, the international community needs to establish an agreed principle to intervene. It is possible that multiple stakeholders consisting of the UN, the governments concerned, and civil society organizations, collectively intervene in North Korea, but the intervention should be done in a just and peaceful way by a legitimate body. The intervention for human rights should not be performed for a political purpose of any kind. The impact of both intention and actual interventions should be fully examined in advance and from all angles. Last, we suggest that the intervention be based on the principle of equity for every state. It would be impossible to exclude political-power effects if the interventions are discriminately taken reflecting the interests of particular states.

Last, we recognize that the human rights of those who fled from North Korea have been severely infringed upon in several ways and these violations are currently the subject of international criticism. Most escapees from North Korea are now exposed to a massive violation of their human rights. It is the duty of international community to protect their rights in cooperation with civil society actors, neighboring countries, and international organizations. There may be various approaches according to the diverse status of the escapees. Some of them could be identified as refugees satisfying the standards adopted in the UN, while others could be categorized as migrant workers in search of a living. We suggest that the UN respect for varied statuses and seek protections fit to each status group of these people. Furthermore, it is essential that the UN declare that simply encouraging North Koreans to flee their territory may seriously undermine their human rights rather than protect them.

Notes

[1] USCR, *World Refugee Survey 2002-North Korea* (2002.6.6).

[2] The National Human Rights Commission has, for the first time for any South Korean government agency, conducted on-location surveys in China on two separate occasions.

[3] Until 1989, the number of North Koreans relocated in South Korea, on various grounds, stood at around 600; men were predominant, taking up more than 90 percent.

[4] Korea Institute for National Unification (2005), *North Korea Human Rights White Paper 2005*.

[5] Korea Institute for National Unification (2005), *North Korea Human Rights White Paper 2005*.

[6] The Christian Ethics Movement of Korea, a major Christian organization in Korea, in a press conference in July 2004, raised concerns about "planned border crossings" and called for their end. One Mr. Cho Cheon-hyun, a journalist who has frequently written about the issue of North Korean displaced persons, criticized "planned border crossings" (delivering border-crossing North Koreans to South Korea) as having become a money-making venture for some brokers.

[7] On March 18, 2005, a warrant of arrest was issued against a member of the staff in the displaced North Korean program of a major Christian organization. This person is accused of obtaining money from displaced North Koreans for organizing, together with some former displaced North Koreans who have turned to brokering, for passage to South Korea. It is alleged that violence and threats were involved in the process. Thirteen brokers who had links with the accused were arrested on March 16 for taking some 130 million

won granted to the new arrivals by the South Korean government as settlement support. Three of these people were indicted and held in detention, while nine others were indicted without internment. In another case, a broker—who had fled from North Korea in 1998 and found passage to South Korea in 2000—was found to have arranged passage to South Korea for four displaced North Koreans by giving them forged passports in collaboration with a Chinese broker. Upon their arrival in South Korea, the broker was accused of taking some 38 million won the new arrivals had received from the South Korean government for settlement support. The broker is accused of using threats to obtain the money. *NGO Times*, March 21, 2005, http://www.ngotimes.net.

The South Korean government's policy of assisting the settlement of displaced North Koreans in South Korea is seen as a factor that has given rise to "planned border crossings" into South Korea. The South Korean government provides grants of 35.90 million won for settlement of a single person, 45.55 million won for the settlement of a two-person family, 55.11 million won for a three-person family, and 64.66 million won for a family of four persons. The amount of money given as a grant for a single person is a large sum, equivalent to ten year's wages of an average Chinese worker. As a result, money-seeking brokers are known to be involved in most of the "planned border crossings for passage to South Korea." In response to the problems arising from the policy, the South Korean government has changed the payment method from one lump sum payment to monthly payments spread over twenty months. More recently, the settlement support grant was reduced to 20 million won for a single person together with support in kind, such as low-rent housing, vocational training, and job placement assistance.

[8] Some reports claim that forced repatriation by the Chinese authorities increased to 4,000 immediately after the government organized passage to South Korea for some 450 displaced North Koreans from Viet Nam.

[9] Cf. the "Declaration of Conscience" by Oh Young-pil (July 23, 2004).

[10] In fact, over the last five years, no North Korean has settled in the United States as a part of refugee support program. The number of North Koreans granted asylum by the courts is limited: so far, there have been only nine (5 in 2002, 3 in 2003, 1 in 2004). The U.S. government has recently indicated that it will not grant asylum to displaced North Koreans who make their case by entering foreign diplomatic offices in China.

[11] The trustworthiness of the testimony of displaced North Koreans has been an issue of constant concern. The testimony of Lee Soon-ock to the U.S. Congress in 2003, namely, that there have been biological experiments and killing by injection of liquefied metal, has been much contested by other displaced North Koreans. Nevertheless, the U.S. State Department's 2004 *Report on Religion* includes this uncorroborated testimony.

The best-known case of dubious testimony involves Kim Woon-cheol. This case was removed from media spotlight due to another case, involving the family of Chang Ghil-soo. The testimony was later found to be pure fabrication, but it had the irreversible effect of shaping a very negative public opinion. The testimony of Kim Woon-cheol brought to the attention of the international media supposed human rights violations in North Korea, including the state of concentration camps, torture, and executions. Various internationally prestigious media, such as *Le Monde* and *Newsweek*, gave extensive coverage to the testimony, which contributed to widespread alarm. However, the person who gave the testimony turned out to be "false." The person who claimed to be Kim Woon-cheol was in fact Park Choong-il. Park had been moving between China and North Korea since 1997, engaged in various money-making ventures. He was apprehended by the Chinese authorities on five occasions and was repatriated to North Korea. Upon repatriation, he was interned by the North Korean National Defense Ministry. After being released, he crossed the North Korean border again, in April 2001. Upon being described as being similar to a person by the name of Kim Woon-cheol, who was one of seven displaced North Koreans apprehended by Russian border guards and thence repatriated to North Korea, he began to live as Kim. He somehow found his way to South Korea and settled in Pusan. The false testimony about concentration camps was known to have been important in his passage to South Korea. His false testimony came to light when the director of the National Intelligence Service testified before the National Assembly Intelligence Committee on July 17, 2001, that displaced North Koreans Park and Kim were two different persons. The problem was that Park's testimony was one of the keys in raising concern within the international community about the human rights situation in North Korea. The Citizens Coalition for North Korean Human Rights focused its campaign on the claims he made about concentration camps. The reports and documents concerning human rights in North Korea of such bodies and the EU and the UN Commission on Human Rights have yet to correct the testimony of the false Kim Woon-cheol. The false Kim Woon-cheol and the various members of the NGOs who have reproduced this testimony have not made any explanation or apology. The various anti–North Korean organizations in South Korea and some NGOs in Japan profiled this person as Kim Woon-cheol, knowing that Park Choong-il and Kim Woon-cheol are different persons. A recent video tape showing various denunciations of Kim Jong-Il in North Korea, brought to the public's attention since being released on January 18 by an organization called Solidarity for Kidnap Victims and Displaced North Koreans, was soon accused being fabricated. However, it is interesting that the brokers involved in money-making ventures exploiting displaced North Koreans and some NGOs working on the issue of displaced North Koreans are cooperating with each other. The videotape shows slogans denouncing Kim Jong-Il across his picture and carries a voice reading a statement denouncing him. However, a South Korean newspapers, *Sekye Ilbo*, reported on March 1, 2005, that according to the testimony of a displaced North Korean, the videotape is a fabrication made in return for money. The National Intelligence Service had earlier raised "the possibility that the videotape was fabricated given that it contains expressions not used in North Korea and that the filming did not seem to be natural." *NGO Times*, March 14, 2005, http://www.ngotimes.net.

[12] The grave human rights situation in North Korea is, undoubtedly, one of the factors behind the exodus phenomenon. One reason why displaced North Koreans persist in going to China despite much noted human rights abuses may stem not just from their economic motivation but also the grave human rights situation obtaining in North Korea. North Korea, therefore, needs to improve the guarantee of citizenship and political rights of its people and take

positive measures to improve the economic and social rights of its people, which have so far suffered serious retreat. Given, however, the domestic and external conditions faced by North Korea, there are clear limitations, under the current conditions, in terms of the measures the North Korean government can take.

[13] Appendixes 1 and 2 have been edited to improve their readability in English.

A Comparison of U.S. and South Korean National Security Strategies: Implications for Alliance Coordination toward North Korea

Scott Snyder

As the North Korean nuclear crisis unfolds, one of the central pressure points that has come under increasing stress is the political/security alliance between the United States and South Korea. The quality, strength, and depth of U.S.-ROK alliance coordination (both in the political and the military spheres) are key factors that will shape the outcome of the nuclear crisis, especially since the diminution of the alliance is often named as a critical target of North Korea's own strategy as it challenges the United States. It is no secret that there has been a growing divergence in threat perceptions of North Korea between both the U.S. and South Korean publics and their governments, yet the alliance has required continuing coordination in response to rising tensions on the Korean peninsula. As part of the six-party talks, South Korea's negotiating position has been scrutinized by some analysts as one of the potential weak links or the lowest common denominator that is likely to affect the viability of any negotiated outcome in the talks if indeed the six-part talks prove to be the primary vehicle for negotiating North Korea's denuclearization.

A newly emerging challenge is that as the nature of North Korea's deterrence capacity transitions away from a reliance on conventional forces and toward an asymmetrical (i.e., nuclear) threat, the requirements of any joint U.S.-ROK response to achieve effective deterrence and counter-proliferation strategies will also change. Instability deriving from North Korean weakness has become as serious a concern for South Koreans as instability deriving from North Korea's military threat, requiring new forms of coordination in anticipation of a wider range of scenarios that could endanger South Korea's security. At the same time, the Global Posture Review is another factor with implications for the U.S.-ROK security alliance, requiring adjustments in the U.S. force structure on the Korean peninsula. Alliance management is also complicated by the fact that both sides are increasingly hedging against an uncertain future regional security environment in Northeast Asia once the North Korean nuclear crisis is resolved, in some cases appearing to plan for the future by looking past the present North Korean nuclear crisis and the security dilemmas that it entails. As the United States and South Korea look to the future, the two countries increasingly appear to be analyzing current events through very different theoretical lenses regarding the nature of existing threats and the proper means by which to prepare for those threats.

This chapter analyzes some of the above challenges by comparing the national security strategies of the United States (released in September of 2002) and South Korea (released in early 2004) as a fundamental starting point for understanding the contradictions and points of conflict between the two countries. This exercise should provide a clearer view of the nature of the current tensions in the U.S.-ROK security relationship. This analysis should also shed light on both the challenges to near-term policy coordination in response to the North Korean nuclear crisis and the long-term viability of the U.S.-ROK alliance in a post-Cold War, post-North Korean threat environment in Northeast Asia.

The U.S. National Security Strategy (U.S. NSS) and Its Implications for the Korean Peninsula

The American national security strategy has been called "the most important reformulation of U.S. grand strategy in over half a century."[1] As such, it attempts to grapple with the events of 9/11 as a defining historical event and to identify the new threats to American and to global security that those events revealed. The U.S. NSS emphasizes defeating the newly emerging unconventional threats posed by terrorist networks while creating "a balance of power that favors human freedom. . . . The United States will use this moment of opportunity to extend the benefits of freedom across the globe."[2] The report is divided into the following sections, reflecting the main priorities in America's national security strategy: (1) Champion aspirations for human dignity, (2) Strengthen alliances to defeat global terrorism and work to prevent attacks against us and our friends, (3) Work with others to defuse regional conflicts, (4) Prevent our enemies from threatening us, our allies, and our friends, with weapons of mass destruction, (5) Ignite a new era of global economic growth by opening societies and building the infrastructure of democracy, (6) Develop agendas for cooperative action with other main centers of global power, and (7) Transform America's national security institutions to meet the challenges of the 21st century.

The realist and neo-Wilsonian themes of the U.S. NSS are also developed in President Bush's second inauguration and 2005 State of the Union addresses, which emphasize human freedom and freedom from tyranny as universal values and the foremost priorities for which the United States is willing to provide support on behalf of oppressed people around the globe. "The United States must defend liberty and justice because these principles are right and true for all people everywhere."[3] Although much has been made of the fact that President Bush has tempered his rhetoric following his inclusion of North Korea in an "axis of evil" in his 2002 State of the Union address, it is clear that North Korea, although not directly involved in the events of 9/11, has emerged as one of the foremost proliferation concerns and a focal point for the Bush administration's efforts "to keep the world's most dangerous weapons out of the hands of the world's most dangerous people." The linkage between terrorism, tyranny, and proliferation as the nexus of potential threats to America's vital national security interests places North Korea near the top of any administration list of potential threats.

Alliances—based on values and purposes that are shared among fellow democracies are one of the means the U.S. NSS advocates for extending the fight against terrorism and nuclear proliferation to tyrants or nonstate actors around the world. In this view, alliances do not exist as a vehicle for preserving regional stability in and of themselves; they are primarily a means to the end of fighting terrorist threats to the United States and are sources of support in the war against terrorism. The United States and its allies should expect to support governments that are facing terrorist threats beyond their capacities. Implicit in this thinking about alliances is the idea that shared values and commitments to democratic and economic freedom are the motive force that guides national and global interests based on the idea that democracies do not fight against each other. South Korea, along with Taiwan and post-Cold War expansion of democracy in Eastern Europe, is explicitly praised in the U.S. NSS as a model for democratic transformation and expanded human freedom.

As the U.S. NSS describes its relationship to regional conflicts, it articulates two "strategic principles":

1. The United States should invest time and resources in building international relationships and institutions that can help manage local crises when they emerge.
2. The United States should be realistic about its ability to help those who are unwilling or unready to help themselves. Where and when people are ready to do their part, we will be willing to move decisively.[4]

The U.S. NSS does not directly address Northeast Asia as part of the section on regional conflicts. However, one cannot help but imagine that the following section about counter-proliferation is designed to apply specifically to North Korea (and Iran). It cites the emergence of states in the 1990s that "brutalize their own people, have no regard for international law, threaten their neighbors, and callously violate international treaties to which they are a party, are determined to acquire weapons of mass destruction, sponsor terrorism around the globe, and reject basic human values and hate the United States and everything for which it stands."[5] This section also raises a fundamental question about the nature of deterrence in the "second nuclear age."[6] "Deterrence based only upon the threat of retaliation is less likely to work against leaders of rogue states more willing to take risks, gambling with the lives of their people, and the wealth of their nations." Therefore, preemption may be necessary to "forestall or prevent such hostile acts by our adversaries."[7]

The U.S. NSS describes the American commitment to expanding free markets and free trade and redefines the role and purposes of development assistance more directly as a strategic tool for market opening, transparency, and as a reward for internal political reforms and commitments to the rule of law. Finally, the U.S. NSS defines the priority of maintaining "cooperative action with the other main centers of global power." This section reaffirms American alliances but also emphasizes cooperation with "several potential great powers now in the midst of internal transition: Russia, India, and China." The expectation is that such engagement can be used to promote international cooperation on key issues among great powers (including promoting stability on the Korean peninsula through cooperation with China), while also anticipating that these great powers will inevitably be transformed by their own democratic development. Since the U.S. NSS portrays the democratization of the great powers as inevitable, it does not address the apparent conflict that arises from cooperation with great powers despite their differing interests and values because in these cases cooperation is a means by which such great-power transformations will inevitably be achieved.[8]

The National Security Strategy of the Republic of Korea and Its Implications for U.S.-ROK Alliance Cooperation

The national security strategy of the Republic of Korea (ROK NSS), titled *Peace, Prosperity, and National Security*, was released by the ROK National Security Council in early 2004. It builds on themes set forth in President Roh's inaugural address in February of 2003 and in his Liberation Day speech on August 15, 2003. This paper marks the first time that the ROK National Security Council has issued a national security strategy; thus it is a seminal document outlining the national security objectives of the Roh Moo-hyun administration. The ROK NSS has eight sections: (1) New security environment, (2) National security initiatives of the Republic of Korea, (3) Peaceful resolution of the North Korean nuclear issue and establishment of a peace regime on the Korean peninsula, (4) Simultaneous promotion of self-reliant defense and the ROK-U.S. alliance, (5) Leading the path toward common prosperity on the Korean peninsula and Northeast Asian cooperation, (6) Pursuing multidimensional international cooperation, (7) Strengthening domestic security infrastructure, and (8) Toward an era of peace and prosperity in Northeast Asia.

The ROK NSS holds a fundamentally optimistic view of the global security situation and the impact of advances in science and technology deriving from globalization, while admitting that globalization also has the negative consequences of making some laggards less competitive, more vulnerable, and more dependent on foreign assistance. Although the ROK NSS recognizes that 9/11 and the emergence of new global security challenges have had an impact on global security perceptions, the overall tone and assessment is positive: "We can anticipate increasing opportunities for peace and prosperity as progress is made in economic cooperation and multilateral security dialogues among the countries in the region."[9]

Among the challenges addressed by the ROK NSS are the North Korean military threat and nuclear issue, the relocation of U.S. Forces Korea (USFK) and development of the U.S.-ROK alliance, strategic dynamics in Northeast Asia, progress in globalization/information technology and the strengthening of regional cooperation, and the "emergence of diverse security threats." Overall, the ROK NSS takes these challenges in stride as surmountable obstacles that are within the capacity of a newly confident ROK to overcome them through a workmanlike, constructivist approach. Although the ROK NSS addresses regional issues within the broader context set forth by the U.S. NSS—and acknowledges the global spread of human rights and democracy as positive global developments the international context appears more as a cloud on the scene and an obstacle to be delimited and ultimately overcome in the course of constructing a new Northeast Asia with Korea at its center. In contrast with the U.S. NSS, the ROK NSS treats terrorism as an abstraction, lumping it together with the proliferation of WMD, transnational crimes, and "non-military security challenges such as economic, energy, and environmental problems." The implication is that these are problems the rest of the world has that must be recognized and managed, but do not impinge directly on the more pressing concerns related to overcoming the conflict on the Korean peninsula, building Korea as a hub of Northeast Asian economic prosperity and multilateral security, and assuring public safety.

The four principles of the ROK NSS are: (1) pursuit of the "policy of peace and prosperity," (2) conduct of balanced and pragmatic diplomacy, (3) promotion of cooperative self-reliant defense, and (4) development of comprehensive security. The "policy of peace and prosperity" is devoted to opposition to wars of any kind and promotion of the peaceful resolution of all conflicts and issues through dialogue, the pursuit of mutual trust and reciprocity on the basis of mutual recognition, the resolution of all issues concerning the Korean peninsula through international cooperation based on the principle that South and North Korea are the parties directly concerned, and the carrying out of policy initiatives based on public participation.[10] "Balanced and pragmatic diplomacy" emphasizes "cooperative and horizontal" foreign relations and simultaneous strengthening of multilateral security talks and the ROK-U.S. alliance. A "cooperative self-reliant" self-defense combines two seemingly contradictory concepts through simultaneous development of self-reliance and dependence on the U.S.-ROK alliance "to deter any provocation from North Korea." But South Korea "will be equipped with capabilities and systems to play a leading role in repulsing any potential provocation."[11] Cooperative security includes cooperation to address newly emerging transnational threats. Under this framework, the ROK NSS identifies three strategic tasks and two basic tasks, as follows: (1) Peacefully resolving the North Korean nuclear issue and establishment of a peace regime on the Korean peninsula, (2) Simultaneously developing of the ROK-U.S. alliance and self-reliant defense, (3) Leading the path toward common prosperity on the Korean peninsula and Northeast Asia, (4) P) Pursuing multi-dimensional international cooperation, and (5) Strengthening the domestic security infrastructure.

ROK president Roh Moo-hyun stated in his inaugural address that North Korea should not be allowed to have nuclear weapons and that "the North Korean nuclear issue should be resolved peacefully through dialogue. Military tensions in any form should not be escalated." A third principle emphasized in the ROK NSS is "the ROK's proactive role in resolution of the issue,"[12] both through consultations with other parties and by convincing the North Koreans that resolution of the nuclear issue is in its own self-interest. Obviously, if sanctions or military escalation have been ruled out, the only tools available to the ROK government in convincing the DPRK to resolve the issue are persuasion and incentives. The ROK also has in mind the institutionalization of a confidence-building regime and reduction of inter-Korean military tensions as envisioned in the 1992 Basic Agreement between South and North Korea. Finally, the ROK seeks to establish a peace regime on the Korean peninsula as the end state of the resolution of the nuclear issue and the building of confidence through an institutionalized inter-Korean relationship. The ROK NSS emphasizes that "the government will firmly adhere to the principle that South and North Korea are the parties directly concerned," a message to outside parties that their roles are to support and provide guarantees for the establishment of a "peace regime" on the Korean peninsula.[13]

The ROK NSS approach to the U.S.-ROK alliance versus military self-reliance richly captures the contradictions that South Korea now faces as a result of the divergence in South Korean and American views over North Korea, China, and most recently, Japan, not to mention the complexities of responding to a new U.S. global security strategy in which geography and proximity are gradually being superseded by "strategic flexibility," enhanced force projection, and a widening gap in capabilities between the United States and its allies. At the same time, the desire to regain control of South Korea's own security environment, symbolized by the desire to retain full operational control over South Korean forces even in wartime, to develop independent operational planning, and to enhance independent surveillance and reconnaissance collection capabilities is an imperative that derives from increased South Korean nationalism.

The ROK NSS envisions a gradual path toward full inter-Korean reconciliation and cooperation that now represents mainstream thinking among a wide range of South Koreans, but the attractiveness of this vision to Koreans may not be fully appreciated outside of the Korean peninsula. The plan envisages full implementation of the 1992 Basic Agreement and the 2000 North-South Joint Declaration, institutionalization of exchanges in order to achieve "a more practical de facto unification situation," a "stable transformation" of the North Korean economy, and "the resolution of the pending North Korean nuclear issue in tandem with improvement of inter-Korean relations. . . . Inter-Korean economic cooperation is a means of achieving our Policy of Peace and Prosperity as well as a prerequisite for our plan to become a business hub in Northeast Asia" through the establishment of Korea as a logistics and financial center for the region. Finally, the Roh administration seeks to maintain good relationships with the United States and its neighbors in the region (Japan, China, and Russia) and to play a constructive regional security role to prevent the recurrence of major power conflicts on the Korean peninsula. The ROK NSS addresses "terrorism, narcotics, illegal weapons, internationally organized crimes, counterfeiting, and cyberspace crimes" as a function of the need to develop "preventive intelligence activities to address new security threats," and through promotion of information and intelligence sharing.

Squaring the Circle: Challenges in Synchronizing Respective National Security Strategies to Enhance Alliance Coordination toward North Korea

A comparison of the U.S. NSS and ROK NSS reveals fundamental divergences in philosophy, priorities, and approaches toward North Korea, many of which may serve as background or contextual factors that are heightening the difficulty of coordinating a joint approach to North Korea through the six-party talks. Moreover, these divergences project a rocky future for the U.S.-ROK alliance as differing priorities within the alliance increasingly reveal themselves as divergent visions for the future of the Korean peninsula, heightening distrust within the alliance. The conflicts in the respective national security strategies reveal underlying problems in several key areas that help to explain why it has been so difficult to coordinate tactical approaches between the United States and the ROK in the six-party talks. The following differences deserve special consideration.

Contending Theoretical Approaches to Security and International Relations

The U.S. NSS takes a realist, Hobbesian approach to the task of ensuring global security and responding to the terrorist threat. The strategy also shows Wilsonian characteristics, envisioning freedom from tyranny through an American-led order, or at least through the securing of an order in which freedom is the dominant value. The strategy suggests that these ideals must be fought for and can be attained only after terrorist enemies have been overcome. In contrast, the ROK NSS posits an optimistic, constructivist approach to overcoming conflict. Implicit in this strategy is that the challenge is just a matter of constructing the right institutional frameworks for cooperation. If the appropriate structures for cooperation can be created, economic growth will be the route to securing freedom and spreading prosperity through more effective and presumably more transparent rule making.

On a practical level, there is a direct contradiction between the concept of deterrence—much less the focus in the U.S. NSS on the right of preemption to defend against an imminent threat (such as that posed by the proliferation of nuclear materials that may fall into the hands of terrorists)—and the Roh administration's commitment to a peaceful solution to tensions on the Korean peninsula. For many American security analysts, the Roh administration's argument that North Korea will not be allowed to develop nuclear weapons contradicts the principle that the nuclear issue must (at all costs) be resolved peacefully. It also appears to bring the respective U.S. and ROK strategies into conflict, as the Bush administration attempts to reiterate to the North Koreans that all options are on the table while responding to South Korean concerns by providing reassurance to both South and North Korea that the Bush administration has no intention of attacking or invading North Korea. The conflict in the American and South Korean approaches erodes the credibility of both sides as they appeal simultaneously to different constituencies, while sending self-contradictory messages to North Korea. This significant divergence should give the DPRK more confidence in its ability to play on and even heighten tensions between the United States and South Korea through crisis escalation and brinkmanship tactics, and it gives the North a way of gauging its breathing space, since the DPRK must calculate that in the event of a true crisis, either the alliance will force the United States and South Korea together or it will reach the breaking point.

Differing Views on the Likelihood of a Power Transition in East Asia

The U.S. NSS emphasizes America's "position of unparalleled military strength" and states that the United States will "resist aggression from other great powers," while arguing that the great powers are on the same side of the United States, "united by common dangers of terrorist violence and chaos."[14] On the whole, the U.S. NSS projects that the United States will sustain global hegemony and that other great powers including China will inevitably have to accept greater economic openness and democratization. The Pentagon has stated that one of its objectives is to prevent the emergence of a "peer competitor," and the U.S. NSS presumes that the United States will be successful in maintaining global dominance as the ideals of freedom, democracy, and free enterprise eventually prevail throughout the world. By implication, the expectation of the U.S. NSS is that the United States will remain the dominant player in securing stability in East Asia.

In contrast, the ROK NSS, by emphasizing the need for cooperative security structures in Asia, seems to be anticipating an East Asian security environment that is more uncertain, characterized by balancing between the United States and China if not by a shift in dominant influence from the United States to China. The ROK NSS states that "changes in the power paradigm around the Korean peninsula and the fluidity of the interrelationship among the four major powers continue to influence the peace and prosperity of Northeast Asia."[15] The South Korean assumption that the United States may not be the dominant player in Northeast Asia in the future is reflected in South Korean presumptions about the inevitability of expanded Northeast Asian economic and security cooperation, characterized by South Korea's desire to play a central role as a Northeast Asian business hub and by its efforts to promote multilateral security in Northeast Asia. This assumption is also a factor underlying the apparent contradictions in the ROK NSS over an emphasis on self-reliant defense versus expectations for the continuation of the ROK-U.S. alliance.[16]

Contradictions in the Relative Priority of Values and Interests Vis-à-vis North Korea

The U.S. NSS reflects the commonly held assumptions of top Bush administration officials that the freedom that is promoted through democratic governance derives from a commonly held set of shared values and that those shared values are the prerequisite for possible cooperation within America's alliances. The U.S. NSS thus assumes that American allies are partners in the fight to expand freedom and the fight against proliferation of weapons of mass destruction, terrorists and tyranny. Likewise, it is the common values shared by democracies that prevent democracies from fighting with each other. Thus, it is to be expected that alliance partners will band together and share resources in an effort to fight tyranny and to overturn threats to human freedom. As can be seen following 9/11, for the first time alliance partners in NATO and Japan took symbolic and real actions in solidarity with the United States, invoking security clauses to defend the United States from a commonly shared threat and providing logistical support as well as taking on post-conflict stabilization missions in Afghanistan.

Thus, it must be perplexing to the Bush administration that a fellow democracy like the one in South Korea would balk at the vision of expanding freedoms in North Korea or perceive that inter-Korean reconciliation would be more significant to South Korea's national interest than the challenge of spreading democracy to North Korea through absorption. In fact, an irony of the current situation is that President Bush appears to be more supportive of an early Korean unification than his alliance partners in the ROK government.[17] Although the Bush administration has assumed that fellow democracies will be like-minded in their pursuit of expanded democratic freedoms and liberation from tyranny, South Koreans appear to place a higher value on preserving their own security and avoiding instability than on the pursuit of expanded freedom in North Korea on the basis of shared values.

The U.S.-ROK Mutual Defense Treaty has always been a one-way alliance, involving U.S. efforts to provide for the security of the ROK with no reciprocal action envisaged on the part of South Korea. Such a concept reflected the relative roles and contributions of the United States and South Korea as patron and client, respectively, when the alliance was formed, but it hardly is a basis for the shared partnership between two democracies that share the same values under current circumstances. As South Koreans call for *a more equal relationship* and demand greater respect as the United States and South Korea work together in pursuit of common objectives, American critics wonder whether South Koreans are *also prepared to take greater responsibilities* for pursuing those objectives as part of a mutual commitment in the alliance relationship. South Korean willingness to contribute to the reconstruction of Iraq by sending troops to Irbil is a positive example of cooperation in an alliance framework. However, the way in which the issue was handled politically including many delays to achieve political consensus, an apparent absence of political leadership from a president who nevertheless angered some of his core political constituents by cooperating with the United States, and awkward attempts to link South Korean troop dispatch to greater U.S. flexibility in policy toward North Korea turned even this cooperation into a frustrating experience for both sides. Despite alliance cooperation, the way in which the issue was handled on the South Korean side suggested that the request was seen more as an imposition and another burden deriving from the alliance rather than an opportunity to reinforce policy coordination in the service of shared democratic values. Increasingly, American policymakers seem frustrated that Korea's dynamic democracy seems to be hindering alliance cooperation and dramatizing perceived burdens deriving from the alliance rather than reinforcing cooperation based on shared values.

Entrapment Versus Autonomy and the U.S.-ROK Alliance

The U.S. NSS and the ROK NSS show divergent assumptions regarding how to conceptualize the significance and purposes of the alliance. The U.S. NSS shows an American conception of alliances that de-emphasizes contributions to regional stability and rewards contributions to the fight against terror. As technological capabilities arising from the revolution in military affairs have improved in recent years, American security planners have assessed that the strategic importance of forward-basing requirements has diminished, resulting in a major reconceptualization of global security strategy and basing requirements through the Global Posture Review. At the same time, the concept of "coalitions of the willing" seems to have elbowed aside the concept of alliances as the focal point of U.S. strategy in Afghanistan and Iraq. These changes have raised questions about the American commitment to alliances or the significance of alliances in the context of countering a post-Cold War, asymmetric terrorist threat. In addition, the political and practical burdens of failure to cooperate in an alliance context were demonstrated by the failure of Turkey to give permission to U.S. forces to use bases there as part of the invasion of Iraq. Turkey's noncooperation was an unanticipated obstacle in U.S. strategy toward Iraq, but did not hinder the United States from accomplishing its military objectives there. This provides an interesting case study as one considers the limits of U.S.-ROK alliance cooperation in the event of heightened military tensions with the DPRK.

Although the ROK NSS takes great pains to emphasize its formal commitment to the U.S.-ROK alliance, it also raises several themes that may challenge the long-term durability of the alliance or that foreshadow potential near-term contradictions in the respective approaches to North Korea. Although the emphasis on greater equality in the alliance through "cooperative and horizontal" relations or the coexistence of the alliance with a "cooperative self-reliant" defense do not inherently contradict alliance cooperation, the growing practical desire in South Korea to recover wartime operational control and increasing criticisms of the existence of the Combined Forces Command as somehow limiting ROK sovereign control over its military forces are issues that are also directly related to U.S.-ROK alliance coordination in the event of a conflict with North Korea. If the Combined Forces Command itself is truly seen as an obstacle to alliance coordination rather than a facilitator, revised arrangements would be desirable, especially if South Koreans are willing to accept the responsibilities and coordination obligations that accompany an autonomous partnership while retaining responsibility for fulfilling commitments under the alliance.

While the ROK NSS repeatedly emphasizes a "proactive" role in dealing with North Korea as one of the "directly concerned" parties, a risk of the current situation is that as tensions escalate over the North Korean nuclear issue, South Korean options are constrained and major powers such as the United States and the People's Republic of China become more involved in trying to manage the outcome, a prospect that is likely to breed further resentment and blame among South Korean nationalists toward the United States for taking the issue out of the hands of the South Koreans. Such tensions may serve to erode support for the alliance as South Koreans feel entrapped and helpless in managing their own affairs. At the same time, increased desires for equality in the alliance relationship also contributed to a much more lively and contentious debate in South Korea over the U.S. request for South Korea to dispatch troops to Iraq. It was notable that President Roh in the initial stages of the National Assembly debate over whether to send troops presented the question primarily as an alliance issue, breeding feelings of resentment and entrapment among the South Korean public for a perceived inability to refuse such a request from South Korea's alliance partner and security guarantor.

South Koreans are also increasingly sensitive to alliance obligations as entrapments that might jeopardize rather than enhance South Korean security. The question of whether South Korea's alliance with the United States or its involvement with Iraq might increase the likelihood of terrorist attacks against South Korea showed the alliance as potentially bringing less rather than more security to South Koreans. There are critical views among South Korean progressives that the alliance might actually diminish rather than increase South Korea's security in the event of regional conflicts, a theme that has arisen in recent debates over the restructuring of USFK and the questions about "strategic flexibility," or the capacity of U.S. forces to deploy from South Korea in response to a regional contingency rather than being solely focused on a diminishing North Korean threat.

North Korean Threats Deriving from Strength or Weakness?

The U.S. NSS seems to focus on North Korea primarily through the lens of the danger of proliferation of weapons of mass destruction (WMD). The U.S. NSS intertwines the dangers of proliferation with the chronic human rights violations that exist in North Korea's totalitarian dictatorship and designates such regimes as the most dangerous potential breeding grounds for terror. The U.S. NSS objective of promoting human freedom underscores the challenge inherent in a regime like that of North Korea. The assertion among some Bush administration officials that regime transformation is a necessary prerequisite for ultimately resolving the dangers that accompany nonproliferation suggests the gravity of the danger that the Bush administration perceives as it considers the proliferation threat posed by the DPRK.

At the same time, it is interesting to consider whether there is room for redemption in the Bush administration's approach to dealing with North Korea. In other words, would the Bush administration really accept a North Korea that agreed to follow a "Libya model" and was willing to give up its nuclear program in return for a relaxed relationship and gradual integration with the international community? Could the Bush administration conceive of normalizing diplomatic relations with North Korea in the same way that it has with Libya, despite the fact that Col. Moammar Qhaddafi remains in charge? Judging by the speech of former Bush administration State Department director for policy planning Mitchell Reiss, the answer appears to be "no." Rather, Reiss's outline of what the DPRK would have to do to receive the same benefits conferred upon Libya includes action to deal with human rights, missile sales, and other illicit activities such as drug-running and counterfeiting of American currencies. Although these are very serious issues that need to be addressed, the implication of the speech is that what is really on offer to North Korea is what might be called the "Libyan model plus."[18]

Although the ROK NSS does not address directly the prospects for or a prospective response to North Korean instability, the focus on inter-Korean reconciliation in the ROK NSS underscores the desired strategy and outcome for North Korea: a gradual versus sudden transformation and integration with South Korea and the outside world. This desire for gradual change is most clearly marked by the connection between the desire for a peaceful resolution of the North Korean nuclear issue, gradual inter-Korean reconciliation and integration, and the establishment of the Korean peninsula as a hub for promoting peace and regional economic

161

prosperity. The desire to avoid conflict or destabilization in North Korea that might lead to sudden change is clearly a top priority for South Korean policy reflected in President Roh's inauguration speech, a view that directly conflicts with rhetorical demonization of the North Korean leadership by President Bush or the persistent perceptions among South Koreans that Americans are dwelling on the importance of "sticks" versus "carrots" as part of a counter-proliferation strategy for North Korea.

Despite the existence of its own secret plans for responding to a North Korean contingency, the ROK National Security Council most recently publicly demonstrated its discomfort with the idea of U.S.-ROK alliance coordination to respond to the contingencies associated with instability or political collapse within the DPRK by halting plans between the ROK Ministry of National Defense and the Pentagon to develop Concept Plan 5029, which deals with a combined response to potential North Korean instability, into a formal operations plan. The ROK NSC based its opposition to the development of the plan on the idea that some aspects of the proposed joint planning might impinge on the sovereignty of the ROK. However, recent conversations with South Korean government officials revealed two closely related primary issues of concern with the idea of developing an Operations Plan 5029. First, the U.S. concept plan that had been prepared for discussion went beyond security issues to also deal with political issues, including presuming that the objective in the event of North Korean instability would be to absorb North Korea rather than re-stabilize and maintain it as a separate state. Second, because the plan dealt with political issues rather than simply a military response, the focus of the USFK concept plan was perceived as too narrow, raising questions about the need for a political understanding and context within which joint planning might occur, rather than pursuing joint military planning alone to respond to a contingency that would primarily require settlement of political issues.[19]

Conclusion: The Future of the U.S.-ROK Alliance and the Dilemma of North Korea's Diminished Conventional and Enhanced Nuclear Threat

The practical challenge that could serve as a catalyst for exposing serious contradictions in the U.S.-ROK security alliance is the fact that the North Korean threat is simultaneously weakening in the conventional realm while it is strengthening as an asymmetric threat with the acquisition of a nuclear capability. Although U.S.-ROK alliance coordination remains sufficient to respond to a diminished North Korean conventional threat while reconfiguring the U.S. troop presence on the Korean peninsula, the emerging political and philosophical challenges outlined above that arise from changes in the nature of the North Korean threat may be the bigger challenge to the future of the alliance in the mid- to long-term. In the context of possible tectonic shifts in the regional security order, enhanced bilateral tensions in the Sino-Japanese and Japan-ROK relationships, and doubts about how the influence of a rising China may change the fundamental basis for managing regional security in the future, the philosophical and practical differences between the United States and South Korea could well represent potentially irreparable cracks in the alliance.

As the ROK NSS suggests, a "cooperative self-reliant" South Korean defense envisions preparation for the day when the ROK military would have sufficient capability to independently deter potential military threats to the Korean peninsula. USFK Commander General Leon LaPorte characterized the DPRK military as "resource constrained" in congressional testimony, noting that North Korean pilots receive only 1215 hours per year of training and that the DPRK rarely conducts military exercises above the brigade level. PACOM Admiral William Fallon characterized that level of training as "not appropriate for any kind of readiness level."[20] Recent South Korean analysis of the comparative military capabilities of the ROK and DPRK implies that South Korean conventional military capabilities have improved to a degree that South Korea alone might be able to defeat any North Korean military aggression.[21]

On the other hand, there is an urgent need to coordinate a joint assessment of North Korea's nuclear capabilities and to engage in joint security and political coordination to carefully adjust respective U.S. and ROK strategies to a situation in which the DPRK is a declared nuclear weapons state. Although some may argue that it is premature to give up hope that negotiations can bring the DPRK to give up its nuclear weapons program, prudence requires that the appropriate adjustments be made to alliance strategies and operational plans to cope with the scenario that the DPRK might potentially use nuclear weapons as an act of desperation in the event that the Kim Jong-Il regime cannot find a solution to its own regime survival difficulties. Recent reports on the difficulties in coordinating operations planning underscore the critical need for a shared understanding of how to prevent the imminent threat of a North Korean last-ditch nuclear detonation from becoming a reality.

As North Korea's conventional weapons capability diminishes, the U.S. presence —and the purposes of the alliance are likely to come under greater scrutiny and question from several different directions. In this sense, the erosion of North Korea's conventional military threat may indeed be the biggest threat to the U.S.-ROK security alliance, especially in the absence of a supplementary rationale for the alliance beyond deterrence of the North Korean threat. The ongoing efforts of the Security Policy Initiative (SPI) to develop a strategic rationale for the U.S.-ROK security alliance that encompasses a role in regional stability are long overdue, but may not be sufficient to assure a common approach without direct involvement from the top leaders and a more comprehensive approach that extends beyond the security sphere alone.

Despite continued uncertainty regarding the strategic environment in Northeast Asia in the mid- to long-term and the security dilemmas it is likely to pose for South Korea in a post-North Korean threat environment, it is easy to imagine that a combination of base closures and enhanced scrutiny in the United States along with heightened nationalism and longstanding South Korean public frustration with the "unequal" nature of the U.S.-ROK security alliance may limit long-term prospects for continued U.S.-ROK alliance cooperation. This prospect makes the need for enhanced frank dialogue and careful scrutiny of the underlying philosophies and national security strategies of the United States and South Korea, respectively, all the more important. It will be necessary to carefully consider and directly address the underlying philosophical contradictions between the American and South Korean national security strategies if the alliance is to survive; otherwise, both sides should be frank about the limits of cooperation and adjust their expectations accordingly through a process that fundamentally redefines and appropriately spells out the potential and limits of U.S.-ROK defense cooperation. These sensitive issues should not be allowed to become obstacles to the sustenance of an otherwise thriving comprehensive partnership.

Notes

[1] John Lewis Gaddis, "A Grand Strategy of Transformation," *Foreign Policy* 133 (2002): 50–57, as quoted in Felix Sebastian Berenskoetter, "Mapping the Mind Gap: A Comparison of U.S. and European Security Strategies," *Security Dialogue* 36, no.1: 71–92.

[2] *National Security Strategy of the United States of America*, http://www.whitehouse.gov/nsc/print/nssall.html, accessed on May 4, 2005.

[3] *National Security Strategy of the United States of America.*

[4] *National Security Strategy of the United States of America.*

[5] *National Security Strategy of the United States of America.*

[6] Paul J. Bracken, *Fire in the East: The Rise of Asian Military Power and the Second Nuclear Age* (New York: HarperCollins, 1999).

[7] *National Security Strategy of the United States of America.*

[8] For additional analysis of the U.S. national security strategy and its implications for the Korean peninsula, see Wade L. Huntley, "Goliath's Game: U.S. Policy toward North Korea in Strategic Context," paper presented at a workshop on "America in Question: Korean Democracy and the Challenge of Nonproliferation on the Korean Peninsula," Seoul, May 10–11, 2005.

[9] National Security Strategy of the Republic of Korea, p. 14.

[10] National Security Strategy of the Republic of Korea, p. 24.

[11] National Security Strategy of the Republic of Korea, p. 27.

[12] National Security Strategy of the Republic of Korea, p. 33.

[13] National Security Strategy of the Republic of Korea, p. 37.

[14] *National Security Strategy of the United States of America.*

[15] National Security Strategy of the Republic of Korea, pp. 13–14.

[16] I am indebted to Professor Daniel Okimoto for his observations on the contradictory assumptions about a future power transition from the United States to the PRC that are implicit in the two national security strategies.

[17] President Bush Visits Demilitarized Zone, Remarks at Dorasan Train Station, February 20, 2002, http://www.whitehouse.gov/news/releases/2002/02/20020220-2.html, accessed on May 15, 2005.

[18] Mitchell B. Reiss, director of policy planning, "North Korea's Legacy of Missed Opportunities," remarks to the Heritage Foundation, Washington, DC, March 12, 2004, http://www.state.gov/s/p/rem/30363.htm, accessed on May 16, 2005.

[19] Author conversations with ROK government officials in Seoul, May 9–12, 2005.

[20] Hearing of the Senate Armed Services Committee, Fiscal year 2006 Defense Department budget, Federal News Services Transcript, March 8, 2005.

[21] "ROK Monthly Notes Five Truths about DPRK's Long-Range Artillery Pieces," *Sindong-a*, December 1, 2004: 98105, translated in FBIS #: KPP20041202000084. See also Taik-young Hamm's contribution in this volume (chapter 9) for an additional comprehensive assessment of the relative military strengths and weaknesses.

NORTH KOREA: ECONOMIC FOUNDATIONS OF MILITARY CAPABIILITY AND THE INTER-KOREAN BALANCE

Taik-young Hamm

Analyses of the security and military affairs of North Korea (DPRK, or the Democratic People's Republic of Korea) have focused on its aggressiveness, its military superiority over the South, and recently, its nuclear weapons program. As late as 2004, the Republic of Korea (ROK, or South Korea) government emphasized the military superiority of the North, even though the North's gross domestic product does not exceed the military spending of the South. A large number of would-be experts on national security and North Korea continue to repeat the claim that the North is militarily superior.

The official ROK position can be summarized as follows: the North has maintained military superiority, owing to its earlier defense industrialization and much heavier defense burden.[1] The DPRK has been alleged to maintain aggressive policies without paying any attention to its economy, the security environment in East Asia, or the changing inter-Korean balance of power. Arming the ROK has been justified as an effort to catch up with the DPRK in order to achieve self-reliant deterrence and defense capabilities. The Reagan administration in the 1980s maintained the same argument by repeatedly delaying the target year when the ROK was supposed to have caught up.[2] The external causation or arms race explanation has been the official rationale for arming the ROK. On the other hand, the arming of the DPRK has been explained by internal factors: the aggressiveness of the regime, with its unending ambition to unify Korea under communism and the bureaucratic-organizational inertia of its military-industrial complex. Its own perception of threats has not been properly addressed. The "myth" of the North Korean threat continues even though the regime has been in a continuing economic crisis ever since the early 1990s. Against the military modernization of the South or the superior combined ROK-US war-fighting capability, weapons of mass destruction (WMD) have been alleged to be the perfect solution. Viewed from this perspective, North Korean military superiority is a *constant*.

This chapter challenges the official/mainstream position, utilizing more accurate data, methods, and interpretations.[3] First, it examines the component variables of military capability. Second, it evaluates various indicators of the military capabilities of the two Koreas according to their validity, reliability, and utility. So-called "bean counts" and combat value, or "firepower scores" are rejected in favor of *military capital stock* as the most proper indicator of the military capability of the two Koreas. Third, it introduces more valid and reliable time-series data of military expenditures and military capital stock, as official ROK, DPRK, and U.S. data are unacceptable. Most ROK and U.S. estimations of DPRK defense expenditures have been based on a constant share of the DPRK total budget or GDP, guaranteeing a 100 percent statistical explanation! Fourth, based on an analysis of the inter-Korean military balance in terms of *military capital stock*, it analyzes North Korea's threat perception and the development of its WMD programs.

Understanding Military Capability: War Potential Versus Standing Army

The Korean peninsula has remained one of the most highly militarized and tension-ridden regions of the world. Out of 70 million Koreans, North and South, today there are about 1.8 million soldiers on active duty, plus 33,000 American soldiers, more than 100,000 paramilitary forces on each side (police/internal security units) and several million reservists. North Korea alone maintains an army of more than 1.1 million soldiers, the fourth largest number in the world after China, the United States, and India, outranking even Russia.[4] North Korea is the most highly militarized state in the world, with 5 percent of its population serving in the army.[5] In recent years, its official defense budget has been about 1,516 percent of the total government budget. The real defense burden is estimated to be at least 1,315 percent of its GDP, assuming its defense burden is more than 2.53.0 times as large as the 5 percent force ratio.[6] Furthermore, about 6,570 percent of the Korean People's Army (KPA) ground forces are forward deployed, within 100 kilometers of the demilitarized zone (DMZ).[7] In this situation, an armed conflict would quickly escalate to a brutal, large-scale war. Assessing what is required in the way of deterrent and defensive capabilities is a critical task indeed.

However, the military balance in Korea has been the subject of both confusion as well as debate. The confusion and controversy have been reinforced by the "propaganda debate, conducted mainly in the media" rather than "the real debate among serious analysts, conducted largely in scholarly publications."[8] The first mistake in the analysis of military capability would be to focus on "forces-in-being" rather than "war potential." Studies have shown that overall national capability is the most important variable determining the outcome of major wars.[9]

A 1985 Rand study points out that "the larger, more dynamic, and more technically advanced South Korean economy provides the South with an impressive pool of assets."[10] Nevertheless, the South Korean Ministry of National Defense (MND) still emphasizes the superiority of the North: "While the ROK is far superior in war-fighting potential, the two Koreas are relatively equal in mobilization capabilities, and North Korea possesses a predominant superiority in standing armies."[11] The fear of a KPA blitzkrieg attack is further aggravated by the geographic location of Seoul, only 40 kilometers by air from the DMZ. A strategic retreat to trade space for time would mean the fall of Seoul and hence the end of the war.

Be that as it may, North Korea is definitely over-armed in terms of its resource base, demographic and economic. If we accept bean counts or firepower scores as military capability, Russia today should be still be respected as a superpower. However, it is China with its economic potential that the United States sees as its future rival. Even in better days, the "tooth-to-tail ratio" of the KPA was too high to properly operate and maintain its troops. It is increasingly doubtful that the poverty-stricken North has the ability to carry out a large-scale or extended campaign against the South. It should be also noted that the forward deployment of the KPA is not a good indicator of aggressiveness. The ROK Army is more forward deployed: to defend Seoul, all 21 active army divisions, one marine division, and the U.S. Second Division have been deployed within 100 kilometers of the DMZ.[12]

Bean Counts and Weapon System Scores

Another mistake in assessing military capability is to rely on so-called bean counts based on simple numbers derived from the order-of-battle. This involves a comparison of numbers of the visible components of military might: manpower and the number of tanks, artillery tubes, ships, aircraft, missiles, and so on. However, numbers are not power. Military capability, even in the narrow sense of the term, is the combat potential of a state's active and ready-reserve armed forces. It is the sum total of the combined effects of human (manpower), material (equipment and supplies), and organizational (effectiveness) resources that a state brings to bear on war.[13] Manpower and material resources are readily visible and thus sometimes described as "quantitative" as opposed to organizational components, which are usually dubbed "qualitative." However, human and material resources have their own qualitative dimensions as well. Organizational capacity includes strategy, tactics, supplies, and "unit cohesion," the last of which encompasses discipline, leadership, and so-called command, control, communication, and intelligence (C3I, or, if one includes computers, C4I). History shows that organizational effectiveness is more important than the sheer number of troops and equipment, by several hundred percent.[14]

The bean-counting methodology is widely used in the "media debate." Especially since 1978–79, when the U.S. Army and intelligence agencies discovered the growth of the KPA that had been undetected in the 1970s, probably all ROK and U.S. official documents and a great number of articles, media reports, and monographs have repeated the same theme: the KPA's numerical superiority. In 1979, the DPRK military superiority over the ROK was reported to be 1.1:1 in manpower, 2.1:1 in tanks, 2.3:1 in artillery, and 2.3:1 in armored personnel carriers, while the ratios in 1977 were 0.9:1, 1.5:1, 1.9:1, and 1.9:1, respectively. The ratio of naval vessels was alleged to have been 4:1, while that of combat aircraft was 2:1.[15] After more than 25 years of heavy investment by the ROK, these ratios have not changed substantially.

A more sophisticated variation of the theme is firepower scores. For instance, the "combat capability coefficient" (CCC) is the Korean version of the Armored Division Equivalent (ADE), or the Division Equivalents Firepower (DEF) that followed the ADE, developed by the U.S. Army Concepts Analysis Agency.[16] The ADE methodology is based on standard measures of a unit's total capabilities in firepower, mobility, and protection, that is, the Weapons Effectiveness Index, and Weighted Unit Value (WEI/WUV) methodology.[17] A given unit's capability is the "sum total" of its WUV scores: the number of each weapon category times WEI (say, a typical Soviet tank is 1.02 times as effective as the M-60A1 tank, the category's standard) times weight (64 for a tank; 1.0 for a rifle). The comparison of WEI/WUV scores of a given unit will provide its ADE index against the 1976 standard U.S. armored division (by definition, 1.0 ADE).[18] The DEF that followed the WEI/WUV-II and III "varies little from the ADE methodology."[19] The same can be said for the Equivalent Division (ED) or CCC comparison in the Korean balance assessment.

Owing to the arms buildup programs called Yulgok Projects, the CCC of the South increased from 50.3 percent of the North's in 1973 to 65 percent in 1988 (or 70 percent if we add the U.S. forces in Korea), 71 percent in 1992, and 75 percent in 1997, which is not much different from the above quoted bean counts.[20] A report of the Korea Institute of Defense Analysis (KIDA) shows that the South was still inferior in 2004, after a decade of economic crisis in the North and consequent disparity in the arms race, in a modified version of the CCC that includes training/morale and information force multipliers: 80 percent in ground forces, 90 percent in the navy, and 103 percent in the air force.[21]

Certainly, bean counts or weapon/firepower scores have their merit, namely, simplicity and straightforwardness. Almost any numerical assessment of military capability is a variation of bean counts or at least uses them as the baseline. Certainly, quantifying the qualitative dimensions must be based on numerous subjective judgments, assumptions, and estimates, thereby losing parsimony and persuasiveness. However, a bean-counting methodology provides a poor snapshot of military capability, and a distorted one at that.

First, bean counting does not give due credit to the quality of weapons, which is also true of the ADE and the DEF methodologies that are believed to include some qualitative factors in their "judgmental" firepower scores. The CCC firepower scores adopted by the ROK do not appear to fully appreciate the "quality multipliers," considering the inferiority of Russian-made or -designed weapon systems. Almost every new generation of Soviet weapons has failed to solve various critical problems that plagued those they were intended to replace.[22] The "performance" inferiority of weapons is not the only problem that plagued Soviet-type armed forces. The "quality" or "reliability" of Russian-made high-tech weapons is much lower than that of Western models.[23] If we add "human engineering" factors such as crew comfort and survivability, the ROK would get more favorable exchange ratios. Overall, the so-called revolution in military affairs (RMA) has greatly increased the effectiveness and lethality of information-based weapons and related military technology. Compared with the WUV scores in the past that granted only a 2,040 percent superiority to modern Western weapons over the obsolescent Soviet-vintage systems, a new model called the technique for assessing comparative force modernization (TASCFORM) in the 1990s accepts a two- to fourfold superiority.[24] Likewise, the weapons scores for a war game model of the Rand Corporation that replaces the WEI/WUV method recognizes a wider superiority margin of new, advanced weapons systems.[25] Contrary to common belief, for instance, the South leads the North in the weapon scores of tanks, owing to its qualitative edge. It is South Korea that has the latest model of Russian tank, the T-80U, imported under a loan repayment deal, which is almost as good as its K-1s, a scaled-down version of the U.S. M-1. The best North Korean tank is the 1960s-vintage T-62, which is at least two generations behind the T-80U.[26] The superiority of the North in firepower scores is mainly due to its larger number of artillery tubes, especially low-cost multiple rocket launchers (MRLs), but its numerical superiority is more than matched by the 35 times more accurate and lethal artillery of the Allies.[27]

Second, bean counts and firepower scores do not fully cover all quantitative components, leaving some important numbers untapped. The ADE firepower score "does not take into account such factors as ammunition availability, logistical support, training, communications, and morale."[28] Firepower scores represent the number of artillery tubes rather than total rounds of ammunition fired. In the Korean War, "the

UNC advantage in artillery lay in better fire control equipment and techniques and in the supply of ammunition."[29] In the naval balance, the comparison of numbers is ridiculous. The KPA Navy was alleged to enjoy a 500:130 numerical superiority in 2004 in surface combatants and submarines combined, although most of its surface combatants are small patrol craft/boats under one hundred tons.[30] Total tonnage or ship-days would be a better naval indicator. The same is true for aircraft: it is the number of sorties rather than the simple number of aircraft that counts. Furthermore, like the Soviets, the KPA "seldom retire[s] old models of weapons and tend[s] to maintain a large number of equipment stock."[31] For instance, many obsolete or obsolescent T-34/54/55 tanks, W- and R-class submarines, MIG-15/17/19 fighters, IL-28 bombers, AN-2 transport biplanes, SA-2 SAMs, and so on may not be operationally ready. In short, weapon/firepower scores are not the stock but flow of firepower, that is, firepower at a given time point. To adopt an analogy to power generation, the firepower scores are MW, not the MWH. The KPA cannot effectively operate and maintain its obsolete/obsolescent weapons and large number of troops with its weak logistic infrastructure. More important, Pyongyang is simply unable to carry out a large or extended campaign because of its almost bankrupt economy.

Last but not least, bean counting is not a "dynamic" but "static" approach." We should introduce organizational and operational "force multipliers" for a reasonable balance assessment. "Organizational effectiveness" has an inverse relationship with the "friction in war."[32] Bean counting cannot deal with the process through which various categories of units and weapons are brought to bear in actual combat. The historical evidence is that there was a rough parity between the two opposing armies in the second half of the Korean War. However, we should note that, as it is the case for weapons quality, the West enjoyed a substantial advantage in organizational effectiveness over the Soviet-type armies, which spent much less on operations and maintenance (O&M). Stories of poor training and operational readiness of the Red Army are legion.[33] The KPA is not an exception. Large-scale maneuver exercises are very rare and there are very few daily aircraft sorties. Living conditions of the KPA soldiers have also deteriorated. Even the Pentagon admits that South Korea would appear to enjoy "outright superiority" in static indices of firepower scores once the effects of superior training, equipment maintenance, logistics, C4I, and other support infrastructure are factored in.[34]

Dynamic Analysis: War Games

Dynamic analyses put firepower scores and the above-mentioned multiplier parameters into a certain conceptual model to generate combat outcomes most commonly expressed in terms of casualties and/or changes in the front line. The problem in a dynamic assessment is how to quantify the effects of "operational factors" (offense vs. defense, or surprise) and "environmental factors" (climate, weather, geography, terrain, etc.), or the combination of both, in combat analysis. Usually the defender receives some premium or a force multiplier. As von Clausewitz argues, "defense is the stronger form of waging war" since "it is easier to hold ground than take it."[35] The conventional rule of thumb is that an attacker needs more than a 3:1 superiority in the main axis of attack for a successful breakthrough.[36] However, in a typical war game, the defender usually receives a force multiplier 1.3~1.4 (hasty defense) or 1.5~1.7 (prepared defense), which would be again multiplied by 1.4~1.5 if the terrain were rugged.[37] Situational Force Scoring (SFS) includes the effects of posture and terrain on the combat values of weapons and units in the calculus of equivalent divisions (EDs).[38]

The rugged/mountainous terrain of Korea confers an advantage on defense. It precludes a large-scale armored/mechanized attack.[39] Pessimists who really believe in a KPA blitzkrieg do not seem to have drawn lessons from the Korean War. The terrain definitely favors area defense oriented around key positions, and the decisive military arm is most likely to be infantry backed by artillery.[40] A large-scale KPA combined arms attack would lead to a series of savage battles, but the very high force-to-space ratio and poor road networks north of the DMZ would impede a rapid deployment of KPA armored/mechanized columns. Even if they made a breakthrough, they would be quickly channeled into killing zones. They would be unable to commit a sizable Soviet-style operational maneuver group to the exploitation phase, due to the lack of mobile air defense and logistical support. The KPA does not have mobile air defense systems such as the SA-6 SAMs that Syria and Egypt used to a considerable success in the 1973 war. Also, "the KPA, like the Soviet Army, reflects heavy investment in initial combat power at the expense of the logistic support capabilities required to sustain a prolonged conflict. A force so organized . . . might suffer a logistic breakdown."[41]

On the other hand, a "surprise attack" can partly compensate for the inferiority of the attacker, although the advantage of surprise diminishes rather quickly.[42] Most analyses of the Korean military balance put a heavy emphasis on "early warning." However, a successful KPA surprise attack is simply a worst-case scenario, considering the readiness of the ROK-U.S. forces and their early warning capabilities.[43] Nevertheless, classified reports of inter-Korean war games utilizing, among others, the

JICM of the Rand Corporation have been leaked to the press from time to time, and usually they are the most pessimistic: without the U.S. troop presence, Seoul would be taken by the North within 10 to 14 days.[44] This prediction is based on a worst-case scenario that includes two least probable assumptions: that the KPA will actual launch a surprise attack and that it will engage in all-out chemical warfare.[45] Although it may be desirable that the ROK-U.S. Combined Forces Command (CFC) presupposes in its operational plans the massive use of chemical agents by the North from the very beginning of an attack, the North's capabilities and intentions, as well as the probability of such an all-out attack, are quite overrated.

Korean war games utilizing simpler dynamic models such as the basic Lanchester "square law" simultaneous equations, the KuglerPosen "attrition-FEBA expansion model," or the Apstein "adaptive dynamic model" show that the ROK can defend itself.[46] The more we move away from simple bean counts, the more powerful the ROK conventional war-fighting capability becomes. In particular, information capability is crucial.[47] Models to better simulate another Korean war involve an additional order of assumptions, judgments, and calculations, thereby losing parsimony and even persuasiveness.

Since dynamic analysis depends too much on artificially generated parameters, we need a more simple and straightforward indicator that is far superior to bean counts or firepower scores.

Defense Expenditures

The *stock*, not *flow*, of defense expenditure (DE) is the "sum total of factor cost" invested in the human, material, and organizational components of military capability. It can successfully capture the qualitative dimension, that is, the quality of weapons, support systems, and organizational effectiveness. One of the conceptual problems is that defense spending may not mean the same thing in the two Koreas. Particularly, we have to deal with the "hidden spending" of the North and the "unreported spending" of the South in the official statistics.

The U.S. estimated the "real" Soviet DE, either in U.S. dollars or rubles, since the so-called 1976 "Team B" report of the Central Intelligence Agency (CIA) to be about twice as high as that of previous reports, which was mainly due to re-evaluations of the productivity/price of Soviet defense industries.[48] In 1989 Gorbachev revealed that the Soviet defense budget, announced to be 20.2 billion rubles in 1988, would be 77.3 billion rubles or about 9 percent of GNP.[49] Like the unreasonably low Soviet defense budget until 1988, the ROK-U.S. governments have suspected that the official DPRK figures since 1972 exclude hidden spending. *The Military Balance* and the *SIPRI Yearbook* have adopted the official DPRK data, alternating between the "commercial/trade rate" and the "basic rate," which values its won 22.2 times higher.

The DPRK budget figures since 1953 show three distinct categories for different periods. For instance, the original defense budget in 1960 was 3.1 percent of the government budget and 2.612.0 percent in 1961–66, while it was later admitted to be 19.0 percent and 19.8 percent, respectively. The defense budget was not announced for the 1962–66 period, but it can be derived through calculations of increases in other expenditures.[50] It jumped to 30.9 percent during the next five years (1967–71) after the decision by the party for the "Simultaneous Development of Economic and Defense Construction" in October 1966. Then the official DPRK figures dropped from a peak of 30.9 percent in 1967–71 to 17.0 percent in 1972. The ROK estimation of the "real" DPRK military spending, at least 30.9 percent, is based on the official DPRK budget of 1967–71. A CIA report in 1978 suggests the DPRK defense burden to be 1,520 percent of GNP.[51] The *World Military Expenditures and Arms Transfers (WMEAT)* data, inconsistent and unstable over time, estimated the DPRK's defense spending at 20 percent of GNP in 1978–91 and 25 percent thereafter.

Another question is whether military power is a linear function of monetary value. The "more-bang-for-the-buck" argument has been oft-repeated in Korean balance analyses. The MND maintains that the KPA personnel, O&M, and procurement costs are low, owing to the characteristics of the socialist economy, namely, lower per capita income and lower production costs. Surely Soviet- and DPRK-made weapons are cheaper.[52] However, their alleged price effectiveness would diminish rapidly if we move to the more expensive, high-tech category, that is, aircraft and missiles. Their cost-effectiveness in performance and quality is lower than expected in exchange ratios in actual combat.[53] These ratios would outweigh any price difference. Many elaborately built Soviet air defense systems failed in Egypt, Syria, and Iraq. Also, duels between comparable forces, such as in Afghanistan and Angola, have shown that the Soviet-type air force/air defense system has been a great failure thus far. Their lagged technology, coupled with poor combat management, caused the Soviets to put a tremendous drain on their defense budget. Total Soviet spending on strategic air defense was estimated at $500 billion in the mid-1980s, "yet it has produced very little net result."[54] The Gulf War again demonstrated the effectiveness of the U.S. doctrine of "air superiority."[55] In a nutshell, it is not the unit price but the overall effectiveness of weapon systems or the entire force structure that should be counted in the cost-effectiveness of military investment.

According to the MND assessment of the South-North arms race, the ROK has been in the process of catching up. The total firepower scores of the ROK compared with those of the DPRK were 75 percent at the end of 1996–97 and its military capital stock was over 92 percent of that of the North, while the cost-effectiveness of the two was almost on a par in 1988 (see Table 1, page 180).[56] However, the ROK military capital stock in the 1970s is unreasonably low, yielding much more bang for the buck! The three time-series of the MND, Sang-Woo Rhee, and the Rand Corporation are misleading.[57] The MND and Professor Rhee used "gross investment," that is, military capital stock without depreciation. More important, all three sources omitted the U.S. military aid to Seoul that was almost entirely responsible for the ROK stock until the early 1970s. This "grant" aid, not to mention FMS credit, amounted to $5.25 billion in the 1954–74 period.[58] Likewise, the capability assessment of the USFK, 5 percent of the KPA or only one-thirteenth of the ROK (5 percent against 65 percent) is problematic. In fact, the MND assessment of the USFK stock in the early 1990s was $15.9 billion, or roughly 60 percent of the total ROK stock in 1988.[59] The sophisticated C4I and early-warning systems of the USFK are not included in the assessment, which indicates the inadequacy of sheer firepower scores.

The third problem is whether the "total" defense budget or the spending on military "investment," that is, procurement, R&D, and construction, is a better measure. Investment usually covers the material component of military capability. The factor cost of inputs for organizational effectiveness, that is O&M expenses (for both "unit" and "equipment" in the ROK definition) should be included in investment. It can be said that O&M spending is an investment in "organizational capital." It has been pointed out that the KPA has had a very low O&M/stock ratio. The MND also complains about the decline in O&M/stock ratio of the ROK armed forces.[60] We will use both the cumulative "total DE" and the cumulative "investment plus O&M."

Estimating ROK-DPRK Military Capital Stock

Estimated defense expenditures of the two Koreas vary by a considerable margin from one source to another. The problem with the ROK military expenditures is the exclusion of the U.S. aid, which exceeded the ROK military budget at least until 1970. Kyong-hun Lee and Young-sun Ha have made it possible to identify the "total" DE, that is the defense budget and net military aid, of the ROK (see Appendix, Figure 1).[61]

As for the "real" DE of the DPRK, estimates of the North Korean DE by the United States and the ROK are based upon a simple but questionable assumption, a perfect example of "a procedure guaranteed to 'support' hypotheses like those of bureaucratic inertia."[62] The ROK authorities have estimated the North Korean DE as 30.9 percent of the government budget (or "over 30 percent" since 1987), of which investment makes up 48 percent. Pyongyang may have begun to conceal some of its DE in other budget items to demonstrate its commitment to peace during the North–South Korean talks in 1972–73. "Analysts now conclude that even though military expenditures did decline somewhat as a proportion of the total budget after 1971, the drop was by no means as large as portrayed in official statistics."[63] However, it is unrealistic to argue that the regime has consistently spent 30.030 percent of its total budget or 2,025 percent of its GNP on defense for several decades. A factor-cost estimation for 1971–75 by the Korean Central Intelligence Agency (KCIA) suggests lower figures than other estimates, although the figures were subsequently raised in the 1978–82 estimates.[64]

There are several reasons why the official ROK estimation should not be accepted. First, it tends to overestimate "defense burden," since the growth rate of the total DPRK budget has been higher than that of its NI (or GNP). Second, the North cannot have doubled its manpower and at the same time spent 48 percent of its DE on investment during 1974–90 with a low DE growth rate (3.5 percent per annum compared to 8.7 percent in the South).[65] The ROK has spent only 33 percent of its DE on investment with a more or less constant manpower level. Third, the crash buildup of the KPA air force/air defense capabilities with Soviet aid in the second half of the 1980s, which cost $23 billion and must have created a hump in the DE trend curve, is not recognized. Fourth, consequently, it is highly probable that military aid, either Chinese grants or Soviet loans, has not been included in the DPRK defense budget since 1972. Finally, there is evidence suggesting a reduced defense burden in 1972. The industrial growth of the North was much higher in the Six Year Plan period (197177) than in the previous decade, which must have a negative impact upon the defense burden on its capital scarce economy.

For better estimates of the DPRK's defense spending, we may make two assumptions, namely the "price superiority of military goods" and the "exclusion of military aid" from the official defense budget since 1972. But it is next to impossible to obtain a reliable estimation of the overall price advantage of military goods, although we may obtain rough annual arms import data from the Arms Control and Disarmament Agency (ACDA) reports.[66] The estimated range of the DPRK's defense expenditures since 1972 is derived from the following methods: (1) the *addition of military aid* (arms imports) and/or (2) *multiplying the official national defense budget by a factor of 1.5*. The parameter of 1.5 is derived from the reasonable assumption that the real DE/total budget ratio in 1972 was roughly identical to the 1961–70 average (25.4 percent) rather than the 1967–71 peak of 30.9 percent (17 percent x 1.5 = 25.5 percent). For the 1972–76 period, the first alternative would yield the minimum estimate of the DPRK's DE, while the second indicates the maximum. The ceiling of the estimated DE would be pushed upward after 1976:

military aid *plus* 1.5 times of the official defense budget. Finally, for the period since 1991, the ceiling would be the official defense budget plus 8.5 percent of the TGE (also derived from the 1972 estimate: 0.5 × 17 percent = 8.5 percent). Finally, we adopt a time-series of purchasing power parity (PPP) of the DPRK won, derived from differential rates of inflation of the won and the U.S. dollar.[67]

Based on these estimates, the North-South *military capital stock* can be compared. We will use both the "cumulative DE (CDE)," and the "cumulative investment and O&M," with 8 percent/year *depreciation* suggested by the Rand report (for the former, 10 percent). We do not make a comparison of the capital stock since a reasonably acceptable estimation for the DPRK's military investment is not available and, more important, O&M plus investment is a superior measure of military capability. Many Soviet-type armies including the KPA stockpiled too many weapons (without retiring obsolete systems) to properly operate and maintain them. The calculation is based on the equation, $S_t = E_t + (1-a)S_{t1}$, where S and E represent stock and flow respectively and a designates the depreciation ratio.

Figure 3 in the Appendix is a comparison of annual and cumulative DE of the two Koreas in constant 1987 U.S. dollars, with 10 percent depreciation per annum. The cumulative DE of the ROK is derived from the postwar (195459) DE in Figure 1 in the Appendix, with a misallocation or corruption factor added. The DPRK cumulative DE is derived from the same figure. It is assumed that the cumulative DE of the North is 75 percent of that of the South in 1959, a rather generous assumption considering the military aid and manpower at that time. The cumulative investment and O&M spending of the North in 1959 is assumed to be 80 percent of that of the South. At any rate, the ROK's superiority was eroded thereafter by a rapid DPRK catch-up when the North began to outspend the South in 1964. The DPRK achieved a slight lead in cumulative DE in 1968 and expanded it until the early 1970s. Owing to its First Force Improvement Plan (FIP I: 1974–81), the ROK began to outspend the DPRK in 1976. Its cumulative DE exceeded that of the DPRK in 1977–79, depending on the estimated range of the latter, or in 1981, even if we adopt the official ROK estimates revised with the depreciation factor. In the late 1990s, the ROK superiority was more than 2.5-to-1.

The comparison of the *cumulative investment plus O&M spending* is based on the total DE minus expenditures on personnel. In the case of the DPRK, personnel costs are estimated as a function of per capita GNP and the ratio of manpower to the total population. We may underestimate personnel costs of the KPA enlisted men who "receive food, clothing, and housing superior to those available to the average peasant."[68] The ROK investment stock is derived from the estimated stock in 1953 and the postwar investment that includes the ROK's spending on investment and U.S. military aid for procurement.[69] The ROK stock in 1960 may appear overestimated if we compare the cumulative investment plus O&M, but the latter is based on only postwar spending. Overall, the ROK stock is less favorably estimated.

Figure 4 in the Appendix shows a picture of the North-South military balance similar to that of the cumulative DE comparison. The North began to outspend the South in non-personnel DE as well as total DE in 1964 and maintained an annual spending lead until 197576. Consequently, the DPRK became superior in cumulative non-personnel DE in 1968–69, which it maintained until 1980. The DPRK's superiority was a qualitative, rather than quantitative one: automatic assault rifles (AK-47) and naval/air capabilities that could have been matched by quick U.S. reinforcements. Like the cumulative total DE comparison, the ROK regained superiority in the 1980s and gradually has expanded the gap. Due to the decline and halt of Soviet and Chinese aid (see Figure 2 in the Appendix) and the North's negative economic growth, the DPRK investment can hardly make up the depreciation in the 1990s.

Table 1 on page 180 compares the author's findings against various claims that the DPRK is militarily superior. The claims are not warranted. First of all, the ROK estimation exaggerates the DPRK spending on defense. The second factor is U.S. military aid to the South. Third is the depreciation factor, which is not included in the official ROK data. Even the ROK estimation would produce a clear, if somewhat less pronounced, ROK superiority from the early 1980s if depreciation were included. One may argue that the DPRK inventories should be less depreciated, but the O&M spending on numerous underground military facilities of the North should be depreciated equally or more.[70]

North Korean Threat Perception and Asymmetric Capabilities

The past five decades after the Korean War have witnessed a prolonged arms race between the two divided states: a simultaneous race, diachronic seesaw games, status quo, and unilateral buildups. The North has tried since the late 1970s to maintain a balance by its own means. It adopted a *labor-intensive* buildup in the 1980s. Its manpower has more than doubled since the mid-1970s. In particular, the KPA has increased the more economical but effective light infantry and special forces (sniper, airborne, and reconnaissance), now totaling 88,000 men in 2,225 brigades.[71] Faced with the ROK-U.S. conventional superiority in the 1990s, the North has adopted an *asymmetric force* approach that includes WMD and missiles.

The one-sided South Korean conventional arms modernization in the 1990s and 2000s may have been an effort to offset what it has perceived to be a major force imbalance. However, it is widely admitted in official

ROK and U.S. documents that the South is qualitatively superior by a wide margin. There has been much talk of the perception of the threat from North Korea, but "North Korea's threat perception" should be equally dealt with. In fact, North Korea has been threatened with U.S. nuclear retaliation since at least 1955, while neither Moscow nor Beijing has officially confirmed a nuclear umbrella for Pyongyang. The most probable future war scenario on the peninsula is not a surprise attack by the North but a U.S. preemptive attack on the nuclear facilities in Yongbyon followed by retaliatory attacks by North Korea.

Table 1. ROK-DPRK Military Capital Stock Compared

(Unit: South/North **percent**)

	MND (I)[a]	Rhee (II)	Rand (III)	Official ROK (IV)[b]	Hamm (V)	Hamm (VI)
Expenditures Military Aid Depreciation (per annum)	Investment Excluded No —	Investment Excluded No —	Investment Excluded Yes 8%	Total Included Yes 10%	Total Included Yes 10%	Investment +O&M Included Yes 8%
1960	—	46.7	—	133.3	133.3	125.0
1965	—	11.5	—	129.7	123.7	133.9
1970	—	7.3	13	01.2	91.7	89.3
1973	— (50.8)[c]	—	13	90.6	87.8- 84.5- 87.8	72.6- 78.0- 81.8
1975	3.3	13.6	13	82.2	90.5- 81.8- 90.5	67.8- 74.0- 84.1
1976	10.4	19.9	18	85.0	98.6- 86.1- 98.6	70.7- 77.1- 91.4
1978	—	34.4	37	94.8	95.3-100.0-122.0	81.4- 86.9-112.2
1980	35.8	47.4	58	100.4	109.6-113.6-144.8	93.8- 98.6-136.3
1981	— (54.2)	54.3	68	104.5	116.0-119.6-154.9	98.8-103.3-146.7
1983	—	68.0	94	110.9	123.9-126.8-168.2	105.4-109.2-162.4
1984	49.8	74.2	—	113.1	126.4-129.0-173.3	107.7-111.2-169.1
1986	— (60.4)	—	—	115.2	128.3-130.4-177.3	109.7-112.6-175.6
1988	67.2 (65)	—	—	123.5	138.8-140.5-191.3	119.2-121.7-192.2
1989	71	—	—	131.2	149.9-151.5-206.6	128.7-131.1-210.2
1991	80	—	—	144.2	173.7-175.1-235.5	148.3-149.4-237.8
1992	82.4 (71)	—	—	149.6	184.8-188.0-249.3	154.9-158.0-248.4
1994	82.9	—	—	161.8	208.1-221.5-287.6	168.6-179.7-274.7
1996	91.9	--	--	180.2	251.0-272.4-346.0	189.6-209.1-310.1
1997	-- (75)	--	--	--	269.7-295.8-370.9	200.8-222.8-327.

Source: Adapted from Taik-young Hamm, *Arming the Two Koreas: State, Capital and Military Power* (London: Routledge, 1999).

[a] Figures in parentheses are ROK/DPRK Combat Capability Coefficients.

[b] Official ROK data with 10 percent depreciation.

[c] Divided into about 60 percent in ground force capability and about 40 percent in air/naval capabilities.

The drama of North Korea's nuclear weapons program and Nodong and Daepodong missiles reflects the weakness, not strength, of the self-proclaimed "powerful socialist nation."[72] In the late 1980s, the collapse of the existing (or once existed) socialist regimes in the Soviet Union and Eastern Europe reinforced North Korea's already deep-rooted "siege mentality." The dramatic economic growth, democratization, and aggressive *Nordpolitik* of the South further accelerated Pyongyang's fear of being isolated. After the collapse of the Berlin Wall, North Korean media began to criticize the alleged "unification by absorption" policy of the South. The Gulf War demonstrated many weaknesses in Soviet-type weapon systems, while South Korea continued to build up its capabilities with more sophisticated equipment. To make matters worse, Moscow and Beijing established diplomatic relations with the ROK without the "cross-recognition" of the DPRK by the United States or Japan. The two former socialist allies cut their already shrinking aid to Pyongyang and demanded hard currency payments at market prices in bilateral trade.

The ailing North Korean economy, which showed virtually no growth in the 1980s, was badly hit. Pyongyang officially reported the failure of its Third Seven-Year Plan (1987–93). During the 1990s, its economy showed continuous negative growth. The government budget and national income (or GDP) in the late 1990s declined to less than one half of what it had been in early 1990s, even in nominal terms.[73] The North had neither internal resources nor foreign aid available for its economic recovery. Furthermore, the sudden death of the "Great Leader" in July 1994 raised the challenge of leadership succession. Political and economic troubles of the North reached such an extent that its government budget, usually announced in April by the Supreme People's Assembly, was not announced at all from 1995 to 1998. Again, the state budget was not announced in 2003 and 2004 except for the vague expression of percentage of annual growth. The so-called "military-first policy" declared in 1998 implies that the authority and role of the civilian sector of the Korean Workers Party has been considerably weakened. In the midst of the crisis that threatened its very survival, North Korean leaders could not attempt a serious reform or open door policy. The July 1 economic reform measures in 2002, including elements of farmers markets and price liberalization, have not produced substantial growth or prospects for major change.

Faced with the unprecedented crisis, Pyongyang pursued its nuclear option in the 1990s. The nuclear project might have appeared as a dual-edged sword to solve its energy shortage and to gain a great leap forward in the arms race against the ROK-U.S. allies. The North Koreans reportedly approached Moscow for their own nuclear bomb project as early as 1963. Ever since U.S. satellites found that Pyongyang was building a larger reactor and a so-called "radioactive laboratory" (a plutonium reprocessing plant) at Yongbyon in the late 1980s, the North Korean nuclear program has "replaced MIGs, forward deployment, commandos, tunnels, dams, and the million-man army as the number-one concern."[74] The reprocessing plant, if completed, could reprocess enough plutonium (from the spent fuel of the larger reactor) to fabricate several bombs a year. Worse still, North Korea has been suspected of reprocessing enough plutonium to fabricate one to six bombs from the spent fuel of its small, gas-cooled graphite reactor.

During the nuclear crisis, the two Koreas and the U.S. made threats and counterthreats. In April 1991, the ROK minister of national defense Lee Jong-koo suggested that an "Entebbe-style" preemptive strike (or an Osirak-style air raid?) could be an option for Seoul. In the climax of the nuclear crisis in June 1994, the Clinton administration almost decided to carry out a military option.[75] It is in this period that the ROK-U.S. Air/Land Battle scenario, the OPLAN 5027, was disclosed to the public. The plan called not only for counterattacks but also the virtual elimination of the North Korean state itself. Being who they are, North Koreans responded with a counterthreat: if a war breaks out, "Seoul would become a sea of fire."

Although it may not have pursued a nuclear program as a "bargaining chip," North Korea soon recognized the utility of its own version of a "neither confirm nor deny" policy. The North Korean brinkmanship diplomacy finally produced the U.S.-DPRK Agreed Framework in 1994. However, both Washington and Pyongyang violated the framework in the second North Korean nuclear crisis after the Kelly visit to Pyongyang in October 2002. For Pyongyang, President George W. Bush and his associates appeared to demand surrender, not negotiation. The unilateral foreign policy approach of the Bush administration, the declaration of the right of preemptive attacks on states armed with WMD and harboring terrorists, the desire to bring about regime change/transformation in Pyongyang, and remarks about an "axis of evil" and an "outpost of tyranny" have strongly reinforced North Koreans' desire to develop nuclear weapons for the survival of the state and regime.[76] It is highly probable that North Korea is simultaneously pursuing two options, namely, nuclear weapons qua weapons and as a bargaining chip. The U.S. accusation of the secret highly enriched uranium (HEU; recently, just uranium enrichment) program has yet to be validated.[77] North Koreans may have a pilot enrichment project, but their skill or infrastructure to produce several dozen kilograms of weapon-grade uranium to fabricate a Hiroshima-type bomb is quite limited. However, the plutonium path is a more serious case. Unlike the previous informal claims in 2003 and 2004 that it has nuclear weapons, the declaration of being a nuclear power by the DPRK Foreign Ministry on February 2005 is too serious to interpret as another "brinkmanship tactic" of Pyongyang. It is highly unlikely that North Korea would use the bomb in a war against the South or the Allies. Its bombs may be too big to be delivered by missiles or light bombers, too unreliable, or too few to be risked. The use of any nuclear weapon would lead to retaliatory nuclear attacks by the United States. Nevertheless, the uncertainty regarding the nuclear device/weapons is a strong deterrent.

More credible North Korean deterrents are its ballistic missiles. Pyongyang developed modified Scud SSMs and the Nodong 1, an extended-range version of the Scud, through reverse engineering. As was the case with its nuclear program, the missile development program served two purposes. North Korea exported missiles in earnest to Middle Eastern states. The Kumchang-ri incident and missile talks indicate North Korean efforts to achieve limited political and economic objectives as well as military gains. The missile launch and the declaration of the "powerful socialist nation" had domestic motives as well: to encourage the depressed people of the North and to augment the legitimacy of the regime. Kim Jong-Il consolidated his leadership as the chairman of the National Defense Commission as well as the general secretary of the party in the fall of 1998. More important, the Daepodong missile, a multistage rocket that flew over Japan in 1998, demonstrated a symbolic threat to Japan and the United States and brought Washington back to the conference table. Contrary to the widespread fear of the ballistic missiles in the South, they are too inaccurate (with a CEP of 13 km) to use against military targets; it would take dozens, if not hundreds, of these missiles to deactivate a South Korean air base. Yet North Koreans have been trying to extend the range of their ballistic missiles at the expense of accuracy. [78] As the German V-1 and V-2 were called "vengeance weapons," North Korea's ballistic missiles are terror weapons against civilian targets—an excellent deterrence weapon against the South.

North Korea has been also accused of stockpiling thousands of tons of chemical weapons, the "poor man's atomic bomb." The MND has maintained since the late 1980s that North Korea has not only the first generation of chemical agents such as phosgene and mustard gas, but also various blister, nerve, blood, choking, and tear gases. It organized the Anti-CBW Command in 1999, taking the threats of chemical and biological warfare seriously. However, Washington tends to believe that there may be limits to the North's production capacity.[79] Both Seoul and Washington have yet to identify the types of chemical ammunition, means of delivery, and the units assigned to offensive chemical warfare. There are also strategic, tactical, and technical constraints on the KPA's chemical warfare capability. It is technically challenging to deliver and effectively disperse chemical agents by missiles. Chemical attacks by front-line artillery units would be quite limited for fear of the counter-battery fire on their chemical rounds stockpiles or the hazard to their attacking ground troops. Chemical attacks on strategic targets would reduce the war-fighting capability of the South by delaying the arrival of reinforcements and supplies, but they would not change the basic capability imbalance. The front-line KPA long-range artillery threats to Seoul are considerable, but the number of SP guns and large-caliber multiple rocket launchers (MRLs) and total rounds that may be fired are quite overrated.[80] A widespread use of chemical rounds against Seoul would bring about international condemnation and probably nuclear attacks by Washington. Like nuclear bombs, chemical weapons are "weapons of desperation."[81]

Today, there exists an *asymmetric balance* between the two Koreas in spite of the ROK superiority in military capital stock. It is a balance between the ROK(-U.S.) superiority in war-fighting capabilities against low-cost DPRK deterrents. The North possesses both conventional deterrents, hundreds of long-range artillery (including 170 mm SP guns and large-caliber multiple rocket launchers) that can hit Seoul as well as nonconventional deterrentsthe alleged WMD capability. It has become next to impossible that the North could occupy Seoul in a surprise attack. Yet the psychological and political impact of the uncertainty about long-range artillery and missiles attacks by the North on the fragile, vulnerable metropolis and its 11 million inhabitants is and will remain a strong deterrent. Against military threats from Washington, North Korea will keep Seoul hostage.

Conclusion

Several findings can be drawn regarding the inter-Korean military balance. On the methods of balance assessment, first of all, "forces-in-being" does not faithfully reflect the military capability of the two Koreas as it does not include mobilization. Second, "bean counts" or the derivative firepower scores do not fully represent the capabilities of forces-in-being. Qualitative factors of weapons, organizational effectiveness, and manpower, as well as the stock of firepower, should be included. Third, capital stock is the best single measure of military capability as it represents the financial inputs for human, material, and organizational components. Measured by military capital stock as well as firepower scores with force multipliers, the South is much superior to the North. The ROK could have achieved better bean counting ratios "if it had opted for less expensive weapon systems that could still match or outperform those of the North."[82]

The empirical findings are no less obvious. First, the official ROK and DPRK defense budgets (and ROK-U.S. estimates thereof) are not reliable measures of defense expenditure as they omit foreign military aid and some hidden spending. Second, the balance assessment by the

ROK-U.S. side has been distorted, favoring the North. The ROK was superior to the DPRK until the mid-1960s, lost the edge in the following 10 to 15 years, and then regained it and has expanded the gap since the early 1980s.

The arms model has an intrinsic appeal especially in the Korean case. To oversimplify, there have been periods of simultaneous buildups, diachronic seesaw games, status quo, and one-sided races. The one-sided ROK race especially in the 1980s and 1990s has been justified by a misperception or (intentional distortion) of the DPRK military capability, which would lead us to the bureaucratic-organizational inertia explanation. Of course, it is economic growth that fundamentally restrains or promotes arms buildups. North Korea has tried since the late 1970s to maintain a balance in its own race: the labor-intensive approach and the asymmetric arms race. An arms race does not have to conform to the Richardsonian model of a symmetric "annual tit-for-tat."[83] Finally, there is another external variable of the Korean arms race: the alliance factor. The decision for an arms buildup by the North in 1962 and the consequent self-reliant defense policy were not a response to the South or to internal pressures. They were an attempt to compensate for Moscow's reduced commitment. Likewise, a series of arms buildup decisions by the South in the 1970s were responses to reduced U.S. aid and troop withdrawals. In short, the two Koreas are trapped in a security dilemma. Neither the North nor the South can buy more security through an arms race, as there exists a *balance of threat* or *asymmetric balance*. The North will respond to the buildup of the South with much cheaper WMD. As the limitations and danger of the "porcupine strategy" of the North attests, the "law of diminishing returns" applies to military investment. The two Koreas possess such strengths and vulnerabilities that a "mutually assured destruction" is highly probable.

To conclude, the North Korean nuclear crisis and the solution to the Korean military rivalry require a multilateral "common security" approach through economic cooperation as well as arms control and disarmament in the region. South Korea and the United States should *negotiate* defense burden sharing and phased withdrawals of the USFK in accordance with the development of inter-Korean relations. The role of the United States is no longer to maintain a balance; it has a preponderance of power in the inter-Korean conflict. At the same time, the United States is a hegemonic stabilizer in the Far East. Its "hegemonic" presence in East Asia, in both the conventional and the Gramscian sense of the term,[84] will continue in the foreseeable future. Korea, unified or not, will need to maintain a strong alliance with Washington. However, the two allies should develop a more equal partnership in every aspect of the alliance system, including the fate of the USFK. In spite of some conflicts in the security relationship as well as over trade issues, the two allies should be able to find a better alternative. Enlightened U.S. hegemony combined with the democratization, growing pluralism, and market economy of South Korea will facilitate mutual understanding and adjustment between the two allies. Furthermore, Korea should avoid a counterproductive and almost suicidal arms race against any major power in East Asia: China, Japan, Russia, and the United States.

Appendix

Figure 1: Defense Spending (Budget + Net Aid)

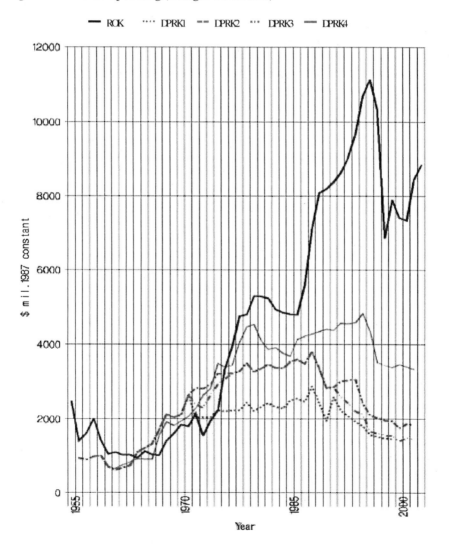

Figure 2: Arms Imports (Including Aid)

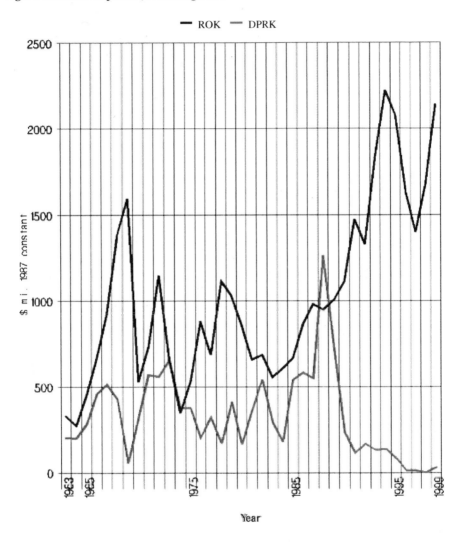

Source: U.S. ACDA

Figure 3: Military Capital Stock (Cumulative Defense Spending)

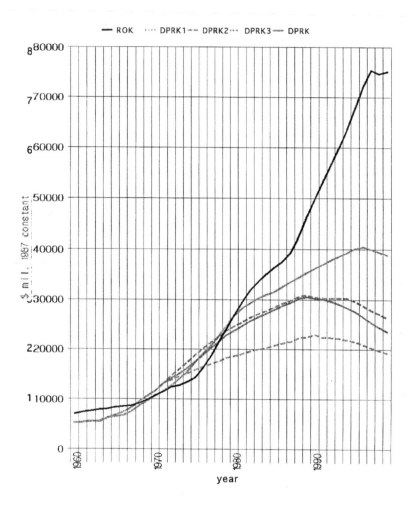

Figure 4: Military Capital Stock (Cumulative O&M + Investment)

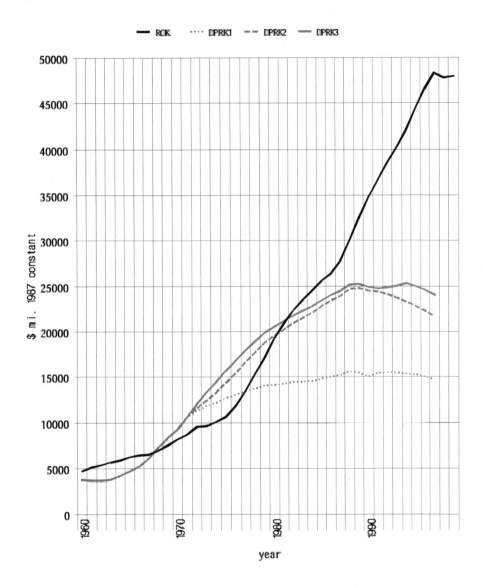

Notes

[1] See, for instance, ROK Ministry of National Defense, *Defense White Paper,* annual editions since the first publication in 1988.

[2] U.S. House of Representatives, Committee on Foreign Affairs, *Foreign Assistance Legislation for FY 1984–1985*, pt. 5: Hearings and Markup (Washington, DC: U.S. GPO, 1983), pp. xxxii, 360–61; *for FY 1985,* pp. 144–45; *for FY 1990–1991,* pp.117–19. U.S. intelligence reports submitted to the president and Congress in the 1970s showed a rough inter-Korean military parity in 1970. See U.S. Senate, Committee on Foreign Relations, *U.S. Troop Withdrawal from the Republic of Korea,* report by Humphrey and Glenn (Washington, DC: U.S. GPO, 1978), p. 27.

[3] Cf. Taik-young Hamm, *Arming the Two Koreas: State, Capital and Military Power* (London: Routledge, 1999); idem, "Military Capability of North and South Korea," *Korean Journal of International Relations* (in Korean) 37, no. 1 (1997): 27–60.

[4] KPA manpower in 2004 was estimated to be 1.1061.170 million. (Pyongyang itself does not provide data on its military manpower). ROK Ministry of Defense, *Defense White Paper 2004*; International Institute for Strategic Studies, *The Military Balance 2004–2005* (London: Oxford University Press, 2004).

[5] Another nation that shows a comparable force ratio is Eritrea, while that of South Korea is 1.4 percent. International Institute for Strategic Studies, *The Military Balance 2004–2005.* Cf. Department of State, Bureau of Verification and Compliance, *World Military Expenditures and Arms Transfers 1999–2000* (Washington, DC: U.S. GPO, 2002), p. 8.

[6] So far in this century, the defense burden of the ROK has been 2.8 percent of its GDP, or about twice as great as its force ratio (1.4 percent). The per-soldier personnel cost to the South has been almost identical to its per capita GDP during the last two decades. We can estimate that the per-soldier personnel cost to the North may be 1.5 times as large as its per capita GDP, since the living conditions of the military are relatively better than those of the average civilian. See Hamm, *Arming the Two Koreas,* chap. 5.

[7] ROK Ministry of Defense, *Defense White Paper,* various annual editions. Also see, Guy R. Arrigoni, "National Security," in Andreas Matles Savada, ed., *North Korea: A Country Study,* Department of the Army Area Handbook Series, 4th ed. (Washington, DC: U.S. GPO, 1994), pp. 221, 226.

[8] Quoted from John J. Mearscheimer, "Correspondence: Reassessing Net Assessment," *International Security* 13, no. 4 (1989): 128.

[9] Klaus Knorr, *The War Potential of Nations* (Princeton, NJ: Princeton University Press, 1956); A. F .K. Organski and Jacek Kugler, *The War Ledger* (Chicago: University of Chicago Press, 1980).

[10] Charles Wolf Jr., et al., *The Changing Balance: South and North Korean Capabilities for Long-Term Military Competition* (Santa Monica, CA: Rand, 1985), pp. 35–42. Liberals in Seoul point out the ROK's superiority in resource mobilization and the quality of weapon systems. Cf. Young-Hee Lee, "A Comparative Study of War-Fighting Capabilities of North and South Korea," *Society and Thought* (in Korean) 1 (1988): 140–66.

[11] ROK Ministry of Defense, *Defense White Paper 1989* (Korean edition), p. 185. The MND also maintains "the outcome of any future war on the Korean peninsula would be determined after only a few days of engagement." ROK Ministry of Defense, *Defense White Paper, 1993–1994*, p. 85.

[12] Rodney P. Katz, "National Security," in Savada, *North Korea: A Country Study*, pp. 281–82.

[13] Taik-young Hamm, "An Analysis of North-South Korean Arms Race and Military Balance," in Taik-young Hamm et al., eds., *The North-South Korean Arms Race and Arms Control* (in Korean; Seoul: Institute for Far Eastern Studies, Kyungnam University, 1992), pp. 6–7.

[14] Trevor N. Dupuy, *Numbers, Predictions and War* (London: Macdonald & Jane's, 1979). Cf. Allan R. Millett, Williamson Murray, and Kenneth H. Watman, "The Effectiveness of Military Organizations," in Allan R. Millett and Williamson Murray, eds., *Military Effectiveness, Volume I: The First World War* (Boston: Allen & Unwin, 1988), pp. 1–30.

[15] U.S. House of Representatives, Committee on Armed Services, *Impact on Intelligence Reassessment of Withdrawal of U.S. Troops from Korea*, Report by Investigations Subcommittee (Washington, DC: U.S. GPO, 1979), pp. 2, 5.

[16] ROK Ministry of Defense, *Defense White Paper 1988*, pp. 151–52.

[17] U.S. Congressional Budget Office (CBO), *Assessing the NATO/Warsaw Pact Military Balance* (Washington, DC: CBO, 1977), p. 56.

[18] For instance, a U.S. mechanized infantry division is 0.94 ADE, a U.S. infantry division 0.87 ADE, a West German armored division 0.72 ADE, a standard Soviet motorized rifle division 0.68 ADE, a tank division 0.66 ADE (standard) to 0.90 ADE (in East Germany), and so forth. William P. Mako, U.S. *Ground Forces and the Defense of Central Europe* (Washington, DC: Brookings Institution, 1983), pp. 105–25.

[19] Barry R. Posen, "Is NATO Decisively Outnumbered?" *International Security* 12, no. 4 (1988): 190.

[20] See annual editions of ROK Ministry of Defense, *Defense White Paper*.

[21] *JoongAng Ilbo*, August 30, 2004.

[22] Cf. David C. Isby, *Weapons and Tactics of the Soviet Army*, new ed. (London: Jane's 1988); Anthony H. Cordesman and Abraham R. Wagner, *The Lessons of Modern War*, 3 vols. (Boulder, CO: Westview, 1990); Steven Zaloga, *Soviet Air Defence Missiles: Design, Development and Tactics* (Couldson, UK: Jane's, 1989).

[23] Isby, *Weapons and Tactics of the Soviet Army*; Malcolm Chalmers and Lutz Unterseher, "Is There a Tank Gap? Comparing NATO and Warsaw Pact Tank Fleets," *International Security* 13, no. 1 (1988): 549; and James F. Dunnigan, *How to Make War*, 3rd ed. (New York: Quill, 1993).

[24] Michael O'Hanlon, *The Art of War in the Age of Peace: U.S. Military Posture for the Post-Cold War World* (Westport, CT: Praeger, 1992), pp. 66–67.

[25] Rand, "JICM Weapons Categories and Scores," unpublished draft, July 6, 2004.

[26] For the tank inventories and weapon scores of the two Koreas, see Taik-young Hamm, "North Korea's Military Capability and Military Threats Revisited," *North Korean Studies Review* (in Korean) 7, no. 3 (2005): 71–72.

[27] Michael O'Hanlon, "Stopping a North Korean Invasion: Why Defending South Korea Is Easier Than the Pentagon Thinks," *International Security* 22, no. 4 (1998): 161.

[28] Barry R. Posen, "Measuring the European Conventional Balance," *International Security* 9, no. 3 (1984–85): 58.

[29] Walter G. Hermes, *United States Army in the Korean War: Truce Tent and Fighting Front* (Washington, DC: U.S. GPO, 1966), p. 510.

[30] ROK Ministry of Defense, *Defense White Paper 2004*, p. 251. The U.S. Defense Intelligence Agency (DIA) rates KPAN as "a coastal defense force" and reports that "most naval vessels are small patrol-sized craft unable to operate over 50 nautical miles from the coast." U.S. DIA, *North Korea: The Foundations for Military Strength* (Washington, D.C.: Defense Intelligence Agency, 1991), p. 44.

[31] Arrigoni, "National Security," p. 222. Also see, ROK Ministry of Defense, *Defense White Paper* 1989, p. 181; and *Defense White Paper 1992–1993*, p. 69.

[32] Carl von Clausewitz, *On War*, Michael Howard and Peter Paret, eds. & trans. (Princeton, NJ: Princeton University Press, 1976), p. 119.

[33] See, for instance, Isby, *Weapons and Tactics of the Soviet Army*; and John J. Mearscheimer, "Why the Soviets Can't Win Quickly in Central Europe," *International Security* 7, no. 1 (1982): 3–39.

[34] GlobalSecurity.org, "OPLAN 5027 Major Theater War West: Phase 2 ROK Defense,"http://globalsecurity.org/military/ops/oplan-5027-2.htm.

[35] von Clausewitz, *On War*, pp. 358–59.

[36] John J. Mearscheimer, "Assessing the Conventional Balance: The 3:1 Rule and Its Critics," *International Security* 12, no. 4 (1988): 54–89.

[37] U.S. CBO, *Assessing the NATO/Warsaw Pact Military Balance*, pp. 59–61; Dupuy, *Numbers, Predictions and War*, pp. 228–31.

[38] Patrick Allen, *Situational Force Scoring: Accounting for Combined Arms Effects in Aggregate Combat Models* (Santa Monica, CA: Rand, 1992). For instance, the capability of an infantry unit against an armored unit is greater in a defensive posture or rugged/mountainous terrain.

[39] U.S. Senate, Committee on Foreign Relations, *U.S. Troop Withdrawal from the Republic of Korea: An Update, 1979* (Washington, DC: U.S. GPO, 1979), p. 8; and U.S. Congressional Budget Office, *Force Planning and Budgetary Implications of U.S. Withdrawal from Korea* (Washington, DC: Congressional Budget Office, 1978), pp. 36–37.

[40] Stuart E. Johnson and Joseph A. Yager, *The Military Equation in Northeast Asia* (Washington, DC: Brookings Institution, 1978), p. 57. The KPA and the Chinese Volunteers did not deploy any sizable armored/mechanized forces at the front during the latter half of the Korean War. Hermes, *United States Army in the Korean War*, p. 80.

[41] Ralph N. Clough, *Deterrence and Defense in Korea: The Role of U.S. Forces* (Washington, DC: Brookings Institution, 1976), p. 11.

[42] Dupuy, *Numbers, Predictions and War*, p. 231.

[43] Lt. Gen. Howell Estes III, commander of U.S. Seventh Air Force in Korea, said, "We have a very sophisticated indications and warning system. . . . I am very comfortable with our indications and warning over here." *Armed Forces Journal International* (March 1993): p. 40.

[44] For the manual of the JICM model, see Barry A. Wilson and Daniel B. Fox, *Ground Combat in the JICM* (Santa Monica, CA: Rand, 1995).

[45] *Hankook Ilbo*, October 5, 2004. Cf. Hamm, "North Korea's Military Capability and Military Threats Revisited," pp. 69, 72.

[46] Nick Beldecos and Eric Heginbotham, "The Conventional Military Balance in Korea," *Breakthroughs* (Spring 1995):, 18; O'Hanlon, "Stopping a North Korean Invasion," pp. 155–61; Jae-Jung Suh, "Blitzkrieg or Sitzkrieg? Assessing a Second Korean War," *Pacifica Review* 12, no. 2 (1999): 151–76.

[47] The Lanchester square law, the starting point of many models, defines combat power as the number (of troops) squared times effectiveness in the "aimed fire" situation (with perfect information and mobility). To oversimplify, combat power is the product of firepower, mobility, and information. See John W.R. Lepingwell, "The Law of Combat? Lanchester Reexamined," *International Security* 12, no. 1 (1987): 89–139.

[48] U.S. Central Intelligence Agency, *Estimated Soviet Defense Spending in Rubles, 1970–1975* (n.p.: Central Intelligence Agency, 1976). Cf. Franklyn Holzman, "Politics and Guesswork: CIA and DIA Estimates of Soviet Defense Spending," *International Security* 14, no. 2 (1989): 101–31.

[49] The previous figures were explained as O&M spending, or "what we could call the budget of the Ministry of Defense." *Jane's Defence Weekly*, June 10, 1989; *SIPRI Yearbook 1990*, p. 163.

[50] *Rodong Shinmun* [Workers' Daily], November 10, 1970; *Korea Central Yearbook*, various years; ROK Central Intelligence Agency (KCIA), *Comparison of North-South Korean Economic Capabilities*, vol. 3 (in Korean; Seoul: KCIA, 1974), pp. 461–622. Cf. Dal-Hee Lee, "North Korea's Economy and Military Spending," in Joseph S. H. Chung et al., eds., *The Development of the North Korean Economy* (in Korean; Seoul: IFES, Kyungnam University, 1990), pp. 198–202.

[51] U.S. Central Intelligence Agency, *Korea: The Economic Race between the North and the South* (Washington, DC: Central Intelligence Agency, 1978), p. 6.

[52] The MND shows that a MIG-29 fighter ($22 million) or a T-62 tank (roughly $220,000 in the 1991–92 exchange rate) is cheaper than an F-16 ($35–43 million) or a K-1 tank (roughly $2.3–2.8 million) respectively. ROK Ministry of National Defense, *Questions and Answers Regarding the Nation's Defense Spending* (in Korean; Seoul: Ministry of National Defense, 1994), p. 42.

[53] Cf. Benjamin Franklin Cooling, ed., *Case Studies in the Achievement of Air Superiority* (Washington, DC: Center for Air Force History, 1994); Cordesman and Wagner, *The Lessons of Modern War*, vols. 1 and 2; Steven Zaloga, *Soviet Air Defence Missiles: Design, Development and Tactics* (Couldson, UK: Jane's, 1989).

[54] Herbert York, *Does Strategic Defense Breed Offense?* (Lanham, MD: University Press of America, 1987), p. 24. The U.S. Department of Defense estimation in 1987 was $400 billion. U.S. Department of Defense, *Soviet Military Power 1987* (Washington, DC: U.S. GPO, 1987), p. 45.

[55] Cf. U.S. Department of the Air Force, *Gulf War Air Power Survey, Volume II: Effects and Effectiveness* (Washington, DC: U.S. GPO, 1993). The Coalition vs. Iraqi fixed-wing sorties were 92,517:610, or roughly 150:1 (Pt. 2, pp. 106–7), losses/sortie rates were 0.055–0.077 percent vs. 7.6 percent (p. 115), and the air-to-air exchange ratio was 33:0 or 1 (p. 113).

[56] ROK Ministry of National Defense, *Questions and Answers Regarding the Nation's Defense Spending*, pp. 37, 40–41.

[57] Ibid.; ROK Ministry of National Defense, *Defense White Paper*; Wolf et al., *The Changing Balance*, pp. 45–49; Sang-Woo Rhee, *The Security Environment of Korea*, vol. 2 (in Korean; Seoul: Sogang University Press, 1986), p. 734.

[58] Hamm, "An Analysis of the North-South Korean Arms Race and Military Balance," pp. 27–28.

[59] ROK Ministry of National Defense, *Defense White Paper 1989* (Korean edition), p. 167; and *Defense White Paper 1992–1993* (Korean edition), p. 140. The USFK stock includes $4.5 billion of weapons and equipment, $3.3 billion of other equipment and supplies, $4.6 billion of ammunition stockpiles, $3.5 billion of early warning systems, while the O&M is $2 billion per year. Myung-Gil Kang, "Defense Spending of Korea," in Jong-chun Baek and Min-yong Lee, eds., *Korean National Defense Today* (in Korean; Seoul: Ministry of National Defense, 1994), p. 265.

[60] ROK Ministry of National Defense, *Defense White Paper 1993–1994*, pp. 189–90; ROK Ministry of National Defense, *Questions and Answers Regarding the Nation's Defense Spending*, pp. 69–70.

[61] Kyong-hun Lee, "National Defense and the State Budget," in Chong-ki Park and Kyu-ok Lee, eds., *State Budget and Policy Objectives* (in Korean; Seoul: KDI, 1982), pp. 139–75; Young-sun Ha, *War and Peace on the Korean Peninsula* (in Korean; Seoul: Chongkye Institute, 1989).

[62] Bruce Russett, "International Interactions and Processes: The Internal vs. External Debate Revisited," in Ada Finifter, ed., *Political Science: The State of the Discipline* (Washington, DC: American Political Science Association, 1983), p. 545.

[63] Ralph N. Clough, *Embattled Korea: The Rivalry for International Support* (Boulder, CO: Westview, 1987), p. 102.

[64] For KCIA estimates, see, Choon-sam Park, "Assessing the Size of North Korean Military Spending," *National Defense Proceedings* (in Korean) 15 (1991): 88–99.

[65] ROK Ministry of National Defense, *Defense White Paper 1991–1992*, p. 136.

[66] For U.S. military aid and FMS credits, see U.S. Defense Security Assistance Agency, *Military Assistance and Foreign Military Sales Facts* (Washington, DC: Defense Security Assistance Agency, various years).

[67] Hamm, *Arming the Two Koreas*, pp. 91–104.

[68] Larry Niksch, "North Korea," in Richard A. Gabriel, ed., *Fighting Armies, Nonaligned, Third World and Other Ground Armies* (London: Greenwood, 1983), p. 111.

[69] U.S. House of Representatives, Committee on Appropriations, *Foreign Assistance and Related Agencies Appropriations for 1970, Hearings: Pt. I* (Washington, DC: U.S. GPO, 1969), pp. 701–3; for 1972, p. 203; for 1973, p. 721; for 1974, pp. 1138, 1151–52.

[70] The underground construction of industrial and military facilities is "at the very least . . . three or four times more expensive than similar above-ground construction and much more time consuming." Central Intelligence Agency, *Korea: The Economic Race between the North and the South*, pp. 6–7.

[71] International Institute for Strategic Studies, *The Military Balance 2004–2005*, p. 178. Cf. Joseph Bermudez, Jr., *North Korean Special Forces*, 2nd ed. (Annapolis, MD: Naval Institute Press, 1998). However, the capability of these forces, with the exception of surprise, is lower than might be expected due to their limited firepower, logistics, and means of transportation/infiltration. Also, the number is exaggerated: for instance, the 25,000-man strong ROK Marines, equivalent to the KPA navy sniper brigades, are not counted as special forces. Consequently, the mission of North Korean special forces is countering the ROK special forces operations in the North, supporting the regular troops, and internal security. U.S. DIA, *North Korea: The Foundations for Military Strength Update 1975*, pp. 21–22.

[72] Taik-young Hamm, "North-South Korean Reconciliation and the Security on the Korean Peninsula," *Asian Perspective* 25, no.2 (2001): 140–43.

[73] *Korea Central Yearbook*, various years. Cf. *Vantage Point: Developments in North Korea*, monthly issues.

[74] Stephen D. Goose, "The Comparative Military Capabilities of North Korean and South Korean Forces," in Doug Bandow and Ted Nolan Carpenter, eds., *The U.S.–South Korean Alliance: Time for a Change* (New Brunswick, NJ: Transaction Publishers, 1992), p. 55.

[75] Don Oberdorfer, *The Two Koreas: A Contemporary History* (Reading, MA: Addison-Wesley, 1997), pp. 323–30.

[76] Cf. Chung-In Moon and Jong-Yun Bae, "The Bush Doctrine and the North Korean Nuclear Crisis," *Asian Perspective* 27, no.4 (2003): 18–33.

[77] Selig Harrison, "Did North Korea Cheat?" *Foreign Affairs* (January–February 2005): 99–109.

[78] Jae-Jung Suh, "Assessing the Military Balance in Korea," *Asian Perspective* 28, no. 4 (2004): 73–76.

[79] International Institute for Strategic Studies, *North Korea's Weapons Programmes: A Net Assessment* (New York: Palgrave Macmillan, 2004), pp. 53–54.

[80] Hamm, "North Korea's Military Capability and Military Threats Revisited," pp. 69–71.

[81] O'Hanlon, "Stopping a North Korean Invasion," p. 162.

[82] Hamm, "An Analysis of the North–South Korean Arms Race and Military Balance," p. 7.

[83] Anderton, "Arms Race Modeling: Problems and Prospects," pp. 346–67. Also, it would be a mistake to analyze arms races or arms control exclusively as a "prisoners' dilemma" game. See Matthew Evangelista, "Cooperation Theory and Disarmament Negotiations in the 1950s," *World Politics* 42, no. 4 (1990): 502–28.

[84] Antonio Gramsci, *Selections from the Prison Notebooks* (New York: International Publishers, 1971). Americans would prefer the term "leadership."

ON DEALING WITH A HARD CASE: NORTH KOREA

Henry S. Rowen

This paper draws eight key conclusions:

1. There is little likelihood that the North will actually give up nuclear weapons.

2. There is also little chance that it will accept inspections extensive enough for us to be confident of compliance with an agreement to give them up.

3. The United States is blocked from making a preventive attack unless there is strong evidence that the North is facilitating a nuclear attack on us. The main danger—the North selling nuclear weapons or critical components—is high enough to concentrate our minds on preventing this.

4. South Korea, and probably China, will continue to support the Kim Jong-Il regime.

5. Nevertheless, the regime's vulnerability to a coup or internal upheaval is not negligible.

6. We should be more active on the plight of the North Korean people.

7. Economic aid has pernicious effects in contrast to certain kinds of trade and investment that have positive ones. There may now be an opportunity for developing commerce with the aim of fostering conditions for political change

8. The possibility of unification, which now seems remote, might not be.

The Changes in 2002

In 2002 something important happened in North Korea (its nuclear weapons programs aside). The government greatly increased prices and wages and allowed private markets to expand. According to the International Crisis Group (ICG), "the North is undergoing the most profound economic changes since the founding of the state 57 years ago."[1] Marcus Noland has written: "Make no mistake about it: North Korea has moved from the realm of elite to the realm of mass politics. Unlike the diplomatic initiatives of the past several years, these developments will affect the entire population, not just a few elites."[2]

According to the International Crisis Group, official prices and wages were increased to close to black-market levels: food, fuel, and electricity prices rose by 26 times on average and the price of rice by 550 times; public transport fares increased by up to 20 times; and wage levels were raised by an average of 13 times. Different categories of workers received increases based on the importance and skill of their work, with soldiers, miners, and scientists receiving larger increases than office workers. Teams on cooperative farms were to be paid allowances based on what they produced, not on the number of hours worked. The North Korean won was devalued from 2.15 to the U.S. dollar to 150 to the dollar. This was not a one-time increase in prices; there has been an average doubling in prices over the past year, with the black market rate reportedly reaching 2,400 won to the dollar in March 2005.[3]

Removing constraints on market transactions and entrepreneurship offers the promise of increased output. However, this large a move is bound to create big winners and losers. Presumably, anyone who controls resources will come out ahead: farmers, some market middlemen, powerful elites able to turn power into money. Pyongyang now has more foreign cars, "300 expensive restaurants," and a Chinese-run department store selling foreign goods.[4] "Everyone was talking about money, money, money," said a Beijing-based North Korea expert who visited Pyongyang recently, and with whom I spoke. "I never saw it before."[5] Likely losers are those on fixed salaries, notably mid- and low-level bureaucrats.

These market-oriented actions run counter to a basic tenet of the regime: suppressing capitalist influences long seen as lethal to it. While the North experienced deep privations, including mass starvation, and held fast to a statism that kept its production meager and repelled foreign investors, South Korea's income rose to over ten times per capita that of the North and China's economy took off.

The early Chinese experience may have relevance for North Korea now. The "big bang" event, the privatizing of agricultural production, began bottom up in a set of villages in late 1978 and Deng Xiaoping and his colleagues had the wisdom to let it expand throughout the country and then to extend the reforms. However, there is no assurance now that North Korea will follow up with further reforms; indeed it has reversed at least one: cell phones were allowed in Pyongyang briefly in 2003–4 and then were forbidden. But it, like China, might have unleashed difficult-to-control forces.

Increased Access to Information

Although reliable data do not exist on this, there has also seems to have been a marked increase in North Koreans' access to information, much of this via the now more porous border with China. One indicator is the presence of videocassettes. According to Andrei Lankov, "They are within the reach of the average family. "They watch, almost exclusively, smuggled and copied South Korean movies and drama. Only a few weeks after airing here [in South Korea], they will go throughout North Korea." The images are of a modern Seoul—the high-rise buildings, huge traffic jams, late-model cars. Kim Jong-Il has created a special prosecutor's office to arrest people who deal in South Korean goods, largely videotapes, or who use South Korean expressions or slang, according to South Korean analysts.[6]

The Kim Family Business Model

Why has the North persisted in its poverty-assuring policies while living next to South Korea that began to take off 35 years ago and to China that began switching to capitalism and openness 25 years ago with spectacular results? One reason is that the Democratic People's Republic of Korea began life under Soviet Union influence and that model had a lasting effect. Another has to be a keen sense of vulnerability. Kim Il-Sung saw China's liberalization as apostasy; he and his son, Kim Jong-Il, saw their rule as more fragile than China's, less able to tolerate private enterprises and foreign influences. Both China and South Korea became dangerous models and the South's economic progress also led to its growing military strength. The price has been high, but Kim Jong-Il no doubt takes satisfaction in still being in power while the former rulers in Moscow, Bucharest, etc. are gone.

Given its endowment of minerals and a people with a tradition of working hard, the North should be able to support itself as the region did when under Japanese control. But the export of licit goods yields only $1 billion a year, about $50 per person. Various illicit and troubling activities, such as the sale of narcotics and weapons and the counterfeiting of foreign currencies, yield around $1 billion, while South Korean and Chinese subventions supply another $0.5 billion more. As Nicholas Eberstadt points out, an important component of the Kim business model is to live off military power by exporting weapons, so far mostly ballistic missiles, and by extortion based on this power—which now includes a nuclear threat.[7] This has been a good living only for the inner core, but it has risks. They evidently have looked less bad than the alternatives.

In this model, foreign subventions loom large. The North got an estimated $2.5 billion in aid from the South during Kim Dae-Jung's rule, more than $1 billion from the United States in 1995–2003, and probably about $2 billion from China, and several hundred million dollars each from Japan and the European Union. One motivation for this support is humanitarian. Economic output virtually collapsed in most of the 1990s with the ending of Soviet aid, the reduction of China's aid, and bad weather in the mid-1990s. But for such sums to still be sent to a seriously trouble-making state can mainly be understood as payments intended to ward off something worse. An example is the 1994 Agreed Framework with the United States in which the North agreed to stop the extraction of readily fissionable materials from its nuclear fuel rods usable in nuclear weapons in exchange for supplies of food and fuel and other benefits.

The resulting situation is that a country with a tiny economy poses threats dire enough to get others to pay to keep it from destroying others—and itself. These payments are small to the givers, but help keep the regime in business.

The Pernicious Effect of Aid

Aid, whether supplied from humanitarian motives or as payments to keep the North from creating havoc, reduces pressure for economic reforms. A classic instance of a dysfunctional transfer was the large (perhaps as much as $500 million—at the time secret) gift in the year 2000 by South Korean president Kim Dae-Jung to Kim Jong-Il. Absent such aid, the pressure to allow markets to work would become stronger, indeed irresistible, because the alternative is to become progressively weaker than other nations. To have resisted economic liberalization and to have so far survived is a bravura performance, but the risks are high. If the aid were to stop, and worse, economic sanctions applied, the game would be over.

The negative effects of aid are increased by its flow to the core supporters of the regime who live tolerably well while the bulk of the population lives on the margin of survival—or dies.

In contrast, open trade with the outside world would promote internal changes both directly and indirectly and direct investment by foreigners would do even more. These would help the economy to grow and, in time, create a middle class. This is what has happened in much of East Asia and the argument for this is now being made by the government of South Korea to justify its help to the North. Such trade would foster the end of a totalitarian regime, which is a sound reason for the Kim dynasty to avoid it and for others who want to see freedom for North Koreans to favor it.

However, for trade and investment to have beneficial effects they cannot be a cover for gifts, which is what much of current South Korean and Chinese transactions could be.

The Military Balance

Nuclear weapons aside (a large exception), the North's security situation has progressively worsened. Its million-man army, poorly trained and equipped, has become less formidable. The South, together with the United States, would quickly win Korean War II. (The South alone could do it but not as quickly.) That certainly is a war to be avoided, not least because of the vulnerability of Seoul to an artillery barrage from across the DMZ, but the ruler in Pyongyang has good cause to be nervous about the military balance. One can imagine that the generals tell Kim Jong-Il that their security position is dire without the deterrent effect of nuclear weapons.

The North says it has nuclear weapons while representatives of some other governments (notably China) have expressed doubt about this. This has led to the North increasingly trying to show that it really does have them. There is no good reason to doubt this—and perhaps it will detonate one to settle the question. According to Don Oberdorfer: "The North Koreans have always wanted nuclear weapons. The United States threatened to use nuclear weapons against them during the Korean War, although this was never done. When the Chinese exploded their first nuclear device in 1964, Kim Il-Sung sent word to Mao Tse-tung, the leader of China, asking his 'brother' to share the secrets of nuclear weapons. Mao refused."[8] The North went on to develop nuclear technology and in time nuclear weapons.

These weapons have three functions: One is to deter an attack on the North, the second is to elicit aid, and, looking ahead, the third is to enable the North to dominate the peninsula after the American forces leave. They seem to have become so central to the regime's survival it is hard to imagine it giving them up. Moreover, the countrywide inspection requirements that the United States would insist on as part of an agreement to eliminate them—a large challenge—seem most unlikely to be met by such a secretive regime. As for the third function, dominating the peninsula after the Americans leave, their number *are* going down and ROK-U.S. relations are worsening.

For those who like to keep score, a widely expressed view is that North Korea is winning because it keeps building nuclear weapons while the talks go on (or for long periods have not). That view's premise, that weapons-making could have been stopped through negotiations, is dubious (which is not an argument against trying to find out). Meanwhile, in the absence of the large injection of resources expected from a deal, domestic conditions in the North have become so precarious that the risky economic policy changes had to be taken. This situation might be better characterized as lose-lose than win-lose.

Regime Vulnerability

The self-isolation of the regime reflects a deep sense of vulnerability. If the Kims have seen their rule as fragile, why should outsiders disagree? In any case, as the East European and Soviet regimes fell there were many predictions that the Kim family dynasty would soon follow, a view bolstered by the famines of the mid-1990s.[9] The regime having survived those traumas, this view has recently fallen out of favor. However, there are three main reasons for thinking that it may be increasing. One is the greater knowledge by people of the outside world. The long border with China is porous both to goods and the (mostly illegal) movement of people. The second is the aforementioned disruptive change in prices and wages together with ongoing high inflation. The third is the fading role of ideology; communism long ago was displaced by *juche* (the doctrine that combines nationalism, self-reliance, and Kim family worship). The Korean Workers Party has declined in importance and evidence from émigrés suggests that *juche* is eroding. What is left is the military. It apparently absorbs 20–25 percent of the national income while the national slogan is "military first."[10] There is a similarity with China and a difference: in both, communism has faded, but the Chinese Communist Party has a claim to authority in delivering fast-growing incomes while the Kim family has declining incomes to show.

In such a situation the end can come quickly. Kim Jong-Il is 62 and preparations for his successor, presumably one of his sons, seem not far advanced. One can guess about bottom-up versus top-down mechanisms for such an end, but there is too little theory and data to go on. Conjectures multiply: disaffection within a unit of the palace guard, assassination by someone with a grievance, local disturbances that become nationwide. Or might China, at last fed up with the dangers posed by the North, decide that change is needed at the top and act accordingly? The communist party, such as it is, need not go; indeed a change at the top might save it for a while. As Eberstadt puts it, the place needs a better class of dictator.[11]

China

What can we guess about the Chinese government's view of the North's regime? There should no longer be any question that it has much leverage over it through its aid, the lifeline it offers against sanctions on the North, and its long common border. But what does it want? Its line is that it wants to avoid chaos and American troops on the Yalu. And it surely does not want to see the collapse of yet another communist regime. Does it believe that the North having nuclear weapons, on balance, is tolerable? (After all, it is tolerating them.) Does the effect of the North's nuclear program on Japanese politics register as inconsequential in Beijing?

Perhaps it believes the Japan is going to get nuclear weapons anyway. Does it take enough comfort in the widening difference between South Korea and the United States to want to keep the North's nuclear weapons in play? Is it biding its time before demonstrating that it, and only it, can make the North come to a position acceptable to the United States and Japan? Would a nuclear test stir China to action? I do not know the answers, but if the North's nuclear weapons program is a problem for China, it has not been enough of one to warrant actions that are within its capacities.

If the Chinese government decides that Kim Jong-Il costs more than he is worth, it could work for his replacement. An obvious step is his replacement by a Deng Xiaoping or Park Chung Hee type of growth-focused economic rationalizer.

South Korea

The South wants to avoid a war, a collapse in the North that could bring millions of people across the DMZ, and paying to bring the North up to its economic level. On the one hand, Seoul is vulnerable to artillery emplaced north of the DMZ and on the other, many (most?) South Koreans seem unworried about the North's nuclear weapons. According to President Roh: "The North Korean threat has decreased far more than ever before. This is because neither does North Korea have modern high-tech weapons nor does it have economic capability to stage a war."[12]

One might assume that the South's government can be patient in the belief that sooner or later conditions will arise for unification, preferably step-by-step, in which its economic dominance would lead to its political system prevailing. And the unified country presumably would inherit the North's nuclear weapons. In any case, President Roh Moo-hyun's government helps the North, but in a less secretive way than did that of Kim Dae-Jung. It promotes commerce using subsidies to get firms to go to such a difficult place.

Such activity centers on the (limited) opening of the city of Kaesong, which is close to the DMZ. According to Roh: "Inter-Korean relations will get better, and economic cooperation projects [will] gradually reduce tension on the Korean peninsula. The Kaesong industrial complex, where 13 Southern firms are currently manufacturing goods, is expected to employ some 4,000 North Koreans when in full-fledged operation, improving the situation in the long term." South Korean companies pay the North's government the workers' wages, of which they get only a small part. The North tries to get the benefits of trade and investment while limiting corrupting contact with Southerners. It would be far better if the South insisted that its companies pay the workers directly, that it continue with the Mount Kumgang arrangement for South Korean tourists only if restrictions on their contacts with Northerners be relaxed, and much more.

A puzzling—and distressing—aspect of South Korean policy is its indifference to the awful plight of North Korea's many thousands of refugees across the border in China. Only a small proportion have been allowed in. This callousness can mainly be attributed to a desire not to destabilize the Kim Jong-Il regime.

Helping the North has divided South Korea, with younger people taking a more positive view of it than their elders. That attitude is in the ascendancy and has affected relations with the United States, which have markedly worsened in the past six years.

Japan

Japan's relations with the two Koreas have several facets, only two of which are touched on here. One is the alarm created by the North's missile and nuclear programs. These, along with growing worries about the rise of China, are nudging Japan toward arming itself more. North Korean having nuclear weapons probably will not be sufficient to tip Japan into getting them, but that fact along with increasing concern about China might do it. The other is the expectation that if a deal is reached with the North, Japan will be a large source of aid to it. Here, the argument above on the perverse incentives of aid apply.

The United States

The Agreed Framework of 1994 having fallen apart (a much debated topic) the North's withdrawal from the Nuclear Nonproliferation Treaty, the United States suspending supplies of fuel (and recently food), the construction of two nuclear reactors, and the North's announcement on February 10, 2005, that it has nuclear weapons, have changed the landscape. Today, these weapons presumably can be delivered not only nearby but also at a great distance. (Ballistic missiles are not the only way to do this.) And there is the possibility of components—or entire weapons—being sold to whoever is willing to pay. This should be the main concern of outsiders, and not only Americans. Is the Chinese government not concerned about nuclear explosives of North Korean origin coming into the possession of some Uighurs or the Russians about the Chechens getting them?

The United States proposes a freeze on all of Pyongyang's nuclear programs, followed by their complete dismantlement, in exchange for security assurances as well as energy assistance to be provided by China, South Korea, and Japan. The weapons are to be removed in a way called CVID: complete verifiable irreversible disarmament. The "irreversible" bit aside (what could that mean?), the position of complete and verifiable disarmament is understandable: the North has an impressive list of violated agreements. President Bush has said he is willing to make a declaration of non-hostile intent toward the North and might have the United States participate in supplying various goods as we did under the 1994 Agreed Framework. Meanwhile, the United States has been urging others to agree to the inspection of North Korean international traffic to check for nuclear materials in accordance with the Proliferation Security Initiative and to track its criminal channels that might be used for nuclear smuggling.

Before declaring that it has nuclear weapons and pulling out of the six-party talks, North Korea had a "reward-for-freeze" position in which it promised to freeze (not dismantle) its nuclear facilities if the United States took "corresponding measures," including removing Pyongyang from its list of terrorist-sponsoring countries, lifting economic sanctions, and participating in the initial provision of energy assistance.

One can imagine, in principle, convergence on an agreed position starting from these positions but there are formidable obstacles to having a stable agreement. From the American side, the North's record of violating agreements implies not giving it any slack, especially regarding monitoring of compliance. From the North's side, its economic and military weakness must make it most reluctant to give up its main asset: nuclear weapons.

In this light, what do those who have urged the United States to engage in bilateral talks with the North hope will come out of them? (Anyway, we have had them.) Clearly, it is that the United States weaken its position. The hoped for result would be something like the Agreed Framework of 1994 but with the crucial difference that the North has declared that it has nuclear weapons and we presumably will not know how many and where. It would likely be the illusion of a settlement in which the North appears to be backing off having weapons in exchange for economic benefits. Such an illusion might be maintained for some years if the economic benefits received are big enough to cause the North to abandon visible weapons activities and to stay its threats. However, it has been so dependent on threats that one wonders how long this would last. And there would still be the temptation to sell nuclear weapons components, and maybe more, to those willing to pay.

It is a shameful fact that the United States, famous for openness to refugees from around the world, has not accepted a single North Korean refugee. Presumably, this is because the United States does not wish to offend the South Koreans and the Chinese who, in turn, do not want to disturb the North Koreans. If so, it is a poor reason. For us to accept some North Koreans who manage to leave the country would not only be right for humanitarian reasons but could send a strong signal to the people in the North that the American people care about their plight and are doing something about it. It would also put useful pressure on South Korea and China.

As for the American military posture in Korea, our ground forces are being moved away from the DMZ and, more significantly, in June 2004 an agreement was reached on removing 12,500 troops out of the total of 37,000 by 2008. Although there has been no signaling of an intention to take the rest out, and there are strong arguments against doing this, it is not hard to imagine congressional pressure that this be done if ROK-U.S. relations continue to worsen. The argument would be "We cannot stay where we are not wanted." The present trajectory is not a promising one.

Hopes that we might have had that China will solve our North Korea problem have not been realized. Nor have any hopes that economic sanctions would be agreed upon by the key countries. What about military actions?

Military Action

According to former secretary of defense William Perry, "We narrowly avoided a military conflict with North Korea over its nuclear program. The DPRK nuclear facility at Yongbyon was about to begin reprocessing nuclear fuel, which would have yielded enough plutonium to make about a half-dozen nuclear bombs."[13] A deterrent to our acting then was the vulnerability of Seoul but at least we were confident of the location of the North's fissionable materials and could destroy them. Today, Seoul remains vulnerable, the South Korean government is opposed to any attack, and we presumably have no basis for confidence on knowing where these materials are.

So a preventive attack seems ruled out. But it would not be preventive if a reprisal were made after a North Korean weapon is detonated in Washington. (However, it could be intended to prevent another attack.) But suppose there is evidence of North Korea selling nuclear weapons or critical parts of them to terrorists? This category of threat was pioneered by A. Q. Khan, and Kim Jong-Il might build on his business model. He is already in the weapons export business and has threatened to sell nuclear weapons to al-Qaeda. The old model of deterrence was addressed at direct attack by states; this development requires deterring and preventing indirect—but potentially highly lethal—ones. What are we to do in such a case?

There seems to be only one answer, and not an easy one: it is to pose dire threats to anyone in the supply chain of delivering nuclear weapons that might be used against the United States and be ready to act.

Unification

Presumably, a unified Korea it is in the interest of (almost all) Koreans, but people in the North do not have a vote. South Koreans express worries about chaos in the North and these concerns are held to justify propping up the North, lack of hospitality toward refugees, and opposition to American policies seen as trying to bring down Kim Jong-Il. Nonetheless, a peacefully unified and democratic Korea is in the American interest because it would remove a highly dangerous situation.

How it might happen matters greatly. Both the South Koreans and Chinese want to avoid disorder in the North that might send millions of refugees both south and north. And everyone should want to avoid the North's nuclear weapons from falling out of government control. There is a high premium on unification being peaceful.

How does China view the prospect of a unified, democratic Korea? Without enthusiasm, one should assume. But much might depend on how it happens. If, through a sequence with no immediate overthrow of a communist regime, and with U.S. troops out of the peninsula in the end (a likely outcome), the prospect from Beijing might not look too bad. It would anticipate a mutually beneficial relationship but a decidedly unequal one, with China dominant. It might expect three main factors to be at work: strong Korean nationalism, an advanced Korean economy as a valued trading partner, and continued coolness toward Japan (a proposition contingent on how China behaves toward Korea). How troubled might China be about having a democratic Korea on the Yalu? At a guess, Chinese self-confidence would carry the day, leading them to regard such a neighbor as a manageable circumstance.

The United States has forces on the ground because of the attack by North Korea in 1950 and the continued threat from the North. Our presence there also contributes to Japan's security. We would not need ground forces in a unified Korea. Whether a unified Korea and the United States would want to have a security relationship is a separate—and currently unknowable—question.

It might seem remote, but there should be wide agreement that such a regime is doomed and the questions are when and how it goes? The end might be closer than is widely assumed. This argues for planning for the contingency of unification. The benefits of (peaceful) unification greatly outweigh its costs but ut the transition costs could be large. Here I only assert that these costs will be lowered if examined in advance and addressed collectively as far as possible by the governments of the countries that would be most affected.

Conclusions

The above leads to the conclusions stated at the beginning.

There is little likelihood that the North will give up nuclear weapons and there is also a low probability that it will accept inspection rights adequate to give us confidence that it has none. Giving up nuclear weapons would mean giving up the core of the regime's power. It would see itself vulnerable to a change in U.S. policy toward it. It would be seen to be vulnerable and be deprived of its major instrument for producing essential resources. And conceding extensive inspection would mean abandoning a core element of the regime's character, extensive secrecy. That said, these are not arguments against trying to reach a deal or even reaching one. However, if achieved, it might not endure long.

There is an important related issue: What happens with North Korea affects the larger proliferation phenomenon? It used nuclear materials supplied under the NPT to make bombs, and should be brought to account for this at the UN Security Council. The IAEA filed a noncompliance report with it in February 2003. Nations that violate treaties can be held accountable for their violations even if they later withdraw from the treaties. The prospect that China and perhaps Russia would veto such a move is not an adequate argument against our doing this. It would not be a bad thing to make them defend the DPRK in that forum.

The United States is blocked from making a preventive attack unless there is good enough evidence that the DPRK is fostering a nuclear attack on us. The hard question—what is "good enough evidence"?—is not addressed here. But the North does have to be put seriously on notice that selling nuclear technology risks its destruction.

South Korea, and probably China, will continue to support the Kim Jong-Il regime. The argument that the present situation is nudging Japan toward getting nuclear weapons and might lead the South to do so has not moved China, but maybe the possibility of an "Islamic" bomb supplied by North Korea would do so. Regarding the South, it is hard to imagine what might cause the Roh government to change its stance toward the North.

The regime's vulnerability to internal change is probably growing. North Korea's neighbors and the United States should be preparing for basic changes there, possibly violent ones. Among the events to prepare for is loss of control by the government of its nuclear weapons, aka "loose nukes."

The danger of the North selling nuclear weapons, or critical components, is high enough to concentrate our minds on preventing this. It implies having the option of using force despite the difficulties.

Economic aid has pernicious effects in contrast to certain kinds of trade and investment that have positive ones. There may now be *an opportunity for developing commerce with the aim of fostering conditions for political change.* Governments should move from making gifts to insisting on direct commercial transactions. Realistically, most such activities would have to be subsidized, but that component should be kept small.

Whether or not negotiations lead to some kind of agreement, promoting political change in the North and eventual unification with the South should be our principal goal. Given the infeasibility of effective enough economic sanctions as the route to political change, the only alternative seems to be through a strategy of engagement with the North centered on promoting a market economy. This is the stated South Korean view. Also, an aim of H.R. 4011, the North Korean Human Rights Act of 2004, is the "promotion of a market economy inside North Korea." Therefore, we should not object to a "pro-commerce" policy with the North as distinct from a "gift" policy. Sooner or later economic progress and openness would bring an end to the regime (as it will eventually to China's).

The North will try to limit the exposure of its people to corrupting influences, but it will not succeed. The elite will see irresistible opportunities for enrichment and the gap between it and everyone else is likely to keep growing until it becomes intolerable to the deprived and perhaps to many in the elite.

Notes

I thank Philip Yun and the participants in the May 2005 conference on North Korea, held at the Walter H. Shorenstein Asia-Pacific Research Center, for helpful comments.

[1] "Can the Iron Fist Accept the Invisible Hand?" International Crisis Group, *Asia Report No. 96,* April 25, 2005.

[2] Marcus Noland, *Korea after Kim Jong-Il,* Policy Analyses in International Economics 71, (Washington, DC: Institute for International Economics, January 2004).

[3] Ibid.

[4] Ibid.

[5] *Christian Science Monitor* online, June 2, 2005.

[6] James Brooke, New York Times News Service, March 19, 2005. Lankov was a Russian exchange student at Kim Il-sung University in 1985 who now teaches at Kookmin University in the South.

[7] Nicholas Eberstadt, *Policy Review,* March 2005.

[8] Don Oberdorfer, "Dealing with the North Korean Nuclear Threat," Foreign Policy Research Institute email, June 8, 2005.

[9] Ibid.

[10] Taik-young Hamm, *Arming the Two Koreas: State, Capital and Military Power* (London: Routledge, 1999).

[11] Nicholas Eberstadt, *Weekly Standard,* November 29, 2004.

[12] President Roh interview with *Die Welt*, April 14, 2005.

[13] Testimony of Dr. William Perry, U.S. North Korea policy coordinator and Special Advisor to the President and the Secretary of State, Testimony before the Senate Foreign Relations Committee, Subcommittee on East Asian and Pacific Affairs Washington, DC, October 12, 1999.

THE NORTH KOREAN NUCLEAR WEAPONS PROGRAM: WHY REGIME CHANGE THROUGH COERCION WON'T WORK

Philip W. Yun

For much of the George W. Bush presidency, the United States has engaged in a war of words with North Korea and has little to show for its efforts. Like a broken record, the United States repeatedly calls for the "complete, verifiable, irreversible dismantlement" of North Korea's nuclear weapons-related activity; North Korea reiterates its long-standing demand for the United States to end its hostile policy. Meanwhile, the security situation on the Korean peninsula since 2002 has become markedly worse. Pyongyang's weaponizable nuclear stockpile, at one time estimated to be one, possibly two, bombs' worth of material, is now at a probable six to eight and growing; its Yongbyon 5 MW(e) nuclear facility is once again operational, capable of producing enough fissile material for one nuclear weapon per year; international inspectors placed on the ground in North Korea in 1994 to monitor the location of nuclear-related material are no longer in the country; and despite the diplomatic niceties, China and South Korea are uneasy with the U.S. approach.[1] Pyongyang declared early in 2005 that it has manufactured a nuclear weapon; in addition to the usual worries about North Korea testing a nuclear device or breaking its moratorium on the testing of long-range missiles, there are more concrete concerns that the North has reloaded its Yongbyon reactor and could move ahead with the construction of much larger reactors at Yongbyon and Taechon.[2]

As a way to deal with North Korea's nuclear ambition, many in the Bush administration maintain that unrelenting pressure is the best approach—the rationale for this stance is that such pressure will result in the North's collapse, a change in its regime, or compliance.[3] While these "superhawks" do not yet control policy, they certainly are in a position to influence it greatly and at various times have had the ear of President Bush.[4] This is troubling because I believe these individuals gravely misread the situation—not necessarily with respect to North Korea's intent, but with respect to North Korea's reaction to a policy of coercion or threats as a means to effect regime change. Indeed, when we apply the extensive research, experience, and theory regarding coercive diplomacy (specifically the seminal work of Alexander L. George) to the North Korean situation, it becomes clear that this policy path will eventually leave the United States with the even more undesirable choices of either accepting a North Korea as a permanent nuclear weapons state or risking a second Korean War.

Why the Focus on Regime Change and Coercive Measures?

The Bush administration's approach has been a curious mix of avoidance, inattention, and attitude. In its first year, the administration was occupied with an internal policy review during which contacts between U.S. and North Korean officials were virtually nonexistent. At the end of this policy review, the United States in effect abandoned the two separate tracks of negotiations established by the Clinton administration—one on nuclear weapons, the other on long-range missiles. September 11 focused the administration on Afghanistan and then Iraq and commandeered the attention of most, if not all, of the U.S. government's senior officials. To the extent the administration gave thought to North Korea at all, its approach was rhetorical—North Korea was one of the Axis of Evil and Kim Jong-Il, a petty tyrant.[5] In late 2002, U.S. concerns over a clandestine highly enriched uranium (HEU) project created an escalating tit-for-tat exchange, resulting in the current standoff between the two countries. Refusing to reward "bad behavior," the United States meticulously avoided official bilateral meetings and subsequently committed in 2003 to a six-party multilateral format. For two years, the six-party talks produced nothing of substance. However, in September 2005, the talks unexpectedly yielded modest results in the form of a set of general principles to guide future discussions. Yet the parties left the most difficult task to follow-on negotiations—that of turning the loosely configured general principles into concrete steps that would lead to a North Korea free of nuclear weapons.

Stepping back and surveying the options, there are limited alternatives that the U.S. administration can take to roll back North Korea's nuclear weapons program. They are (1) acquiesce; (2) use military force; (3) "buy our objectives"; (4) negotiate; and (5) instigate regime change, that is, bring about new leadership by ousting Kim Jong-Il. When carefully examined, each of these presents serious problems, and most have fatal flaws.

The strategy of acquiescence—letting North Korea become a nuclear weapons state—poses substantial security risks. A nuclear North Korea increases the threat that its nuclear material could fall into the hands of terrorists, either by sale or by accident.[6] It significantly increases North Korean military capabilities and is deemed a threat to U.S. and allied civilians and military personnel in South Korea and Japan. In addition,

North Korean activity, if left unchecked, is antithetical to American global nonproliferation efforts. An active North Korean nuclear weapons program has the potential to trigger a nuclear arms race in Asia—the fear being that South Korea, Japan, and possibly Taiwan, might pursue a nuclear option.

The use of military might to compel North Korea's compliance is a policy of last resort and not likely to be used any time soon, and for good reason—the use of military power in this part of the world could very well lead to war on the Korean peninsula. While it is all but certain that the ROK and the United States would prevail in such a conflict, the costs would be horrendous—hundreds of thousands if not millions of casualties and the destruction of Seoul, one of the most vibrant and populated cities in the world. Moreover, there is no way to calculate the loss of standing the United States would suffer in the region as a result of its role in the conflict.

Buying our objectives is also undesirable and unrealistic.[7] North Korea is extremely poor. Its economy is in dire straits, and it can barely feed its own people. In the past it has offered to give up its nuclear and missile activities for food, energy, and other benefits. However, there is a distinct possibility that such a deal would encourage further blackmail as well as set a precedent for other potential proliferation-prone countries elsewhere. Moreover, this alternative is highly unlikely to gain any kind of political support from a Congress that would be responsible for allocating any money.[8]

Given the problem with these alternatives, the Bush administration appears to have adopted either negotiation or regime change as its preferred course to end the North's nuclear program. While the six-party negotiations are currently preferred by the administration, I believe that the current political context in both countries undercuts the chances for success. The United States declares its desire for a settlement is genuine. However, other participants see the six-party talks as a way for the United States to minimize direct negotiations or contacts with the North.[9] Whether negotiations remain in a six-party or bilateral format, no meaningful progress will result so long as the mindset and approach of both the Bush administration and the North Korean leadership remain as they are.

One reason for this stalemate is a fundamental gap in how key American and North Korean decision makers perceive each other—each feels threatened by the other and characterizes its own actions as a response to acts of the other. The vast majority of Americans have little sympathy for North Korea's fear of attack. Though we abhor the North's political regime, we equally abhor the idea that the United States would initiate hostilities unless provoked. To the North Korean leadership and populace, however, that fear is real and growing. In addition to citing the

U.S. attack of Iraq, North Korean officials selectively point to Mr. Bush's "Axis of Evil" speech, the administration's "preemption doctrine," and Secretary of State Condoleezza Rice's "outpost of tyranny" comments as evidence of aggressive American intentions. Just as Americans are unable to grasp North Korea's unease, the same can be said of North Koreans with respect to the U.S. perception of threat. North Korean officials often express astonishment that the most powerful country in the world would feel endangered by the "defensive" actions of a tiny state thousands of miles away.[10] While many understand intellectually the impact of 9/11 on the U.S. psyche, it appears that those in the North are confounded by legitimate U.S. concerns; they dismiss our statements as a cynical justification to overthrow governments we do not like. Many in South Korea and elsewhere share this perception of American subterfuge.[11]

Another reason why negotiation faces serious hurdles is a conflict of working assumptions. Superhawks in the United States believe Kim Jong-Il is determined to keep his nuclear weapons program and that any "deal" would be meaningless.[12] While they are not yet in command of policy, these superhawks are able to restrain those trying to assess the viability of a negotiated settlement. In short, the United States is willing to return to the table, but has insisted on the North's compliance with U.S. demands first, thus constraining the negotiating team's ability to advance anything meaningful or to probe new ground that might produce a compromise.[13] North Korea appears to have a firm belief that the Bush administration long ago decided to focus on regime change as the only viable way to deal with the nuclear weapons issue.[14] Under these circumstances then, it makes no sense, according to North Korean logic, for Pyongyang to give up its nuclear capability; if Pyongyang unilaterally acceded to U.S. demands, the Bush administration would have a free hand to impose its "solution." Therefore, North Korea has required that the United States give security assurances and economic benefits first, before giving up its weapons program.[15] At one level, the dispute is procedural—who goes first. However, this process issue reveals a more significant structural problem, the deep-seated and abiding mistrust each has of the other. As a result, in the current environment, there is likely to be little movement by either side to tangibly address longstanding concerns.

Recent events seem to confirm this assessment. On March 31, 2005, the North Korean government issued a statement that in effect declared the Bush administration's focus on North Korea's unilateral disarmament to be unacceptable and stated that the DPRK would only engage in arms control discussions or disarmament talks for the entire peninsula.[16] For the United States to agree to such a formulation would signal de jure U.S. acceptance of North Korea's nuclear weapons status—something that the administration is unwilling to do. In September 2005, following the announcement that the six parties had agreed to a set of general principles, North Korea insisted that light-water reactors be a part of any future accord, stating that it would not give up its nuclear weapons program until these reactors were supplied.[17] Yet this demand is precisely what the Bush administration had stated on previous occasions that it would as a matter of principle never agree to support.[18]

If negotiations then fail, the administration will move to the last alternative—regime change. Superhawks by then will have won, arguing that North Korea does not intend to give up its nuclear weapons and that the failed negotiations prove the point. Since the current regime will not depart willingly, and given that the United States is unlikely to use military force, how will it then accomplish this objective?

The most probable strategy will be to increasingly pressure North Korea in the hopes that it will eventually comply with U.S. demands or that the regime will collapse.[19] Indeed, Bush administration officials already have cryptically referred to using "other means" to get North Korea to the bargaining table and to be ready to deal on U.S. terms.[20] Implicit in this approach is the threat of force or step-by-step escalation of coercion or punishments. Indeed, this approach of steady and mounting pressure should be familiar to many, since this has been a strategy used in the past by the United States in Vietnam and elsewhere and more recently by the Clinton and the Bush administrations with respect to Iraq. However, as will be shown, this policy will ultimately be unsuccessful and leave the United States with the most unpalatable of policy choices.

A Descriptive Model: North Korean Reaction to U.S. Policy and the Level of Threat

To illustrate the success (or failure) of a given U.S. policy, I create a simple model based on how U.S. action toward North Korea increases or decreases the perceived level of threat—generated by North Korea—to U.S. interests. This model is conceptual, yet it usefully encompasses the realties of a North Korea that is regularly producing fissile material.

If past North Korean behavior is any indication of future action, we can assume North Korea will react to American pressure.[21] If we chart, then, North Korean action over a period of time in response to Bush's policy decisions and assign a value to North Korean action in terms of how the United States perceives such actions as threat to U.S. national security, we can produce a rough picture of the general level—and trend—of threat from a U.S. perspective. Such an exercise would be similar to charting the price of stock of a particular company. If we make a reasonable guess as to what such a chart might look like, it would probably be some variation of Figure11.1.

For the purposes of this chapter, it is not necessary to assign absolute values to any given North Korean action, but simply to have an idea as to the relative nature of each action; that is, how a specific North Korean act compares to its previous acts.

Figure 11.1: North Korean Action over Time (as a function of the level of threat perceived by the United States)

North Korean Activity

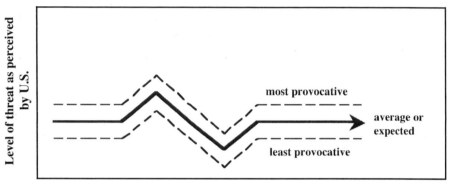

The dotted lines (----) in Figure 11.1 represent upper and lower boundaries, with the bold line representing the average or expected level of threat during any point in time. I draw these upper and lower bounds to take into account three kinds of uncertainty. First, various policymakers could have a different perceptions of threat resulting from a specific North Korean action. In other words, superhawks may see a North Korean act as more threatening than other policymakers; the upper bound depicts this possible gap. Second, a specific North Korean act may have a slightly different value as time goes on and therefore may shift up or down. For example, an act that was deemed provocative today may be or appear to be more or less provocative tomorrow due to a change in world circumstances or additional information. Finally, the current intelligence upon which certain judgments of threat are based may be inaccurate or inadequate. Indeed, recently publicized assessments of U.S. intelligence capabilities—or lack thereof with regard to North Korea—highlight this problem.[22]

Unlike the price of a company's stock, however, the general trend of the level of threat in this construct can be confidently predicted: it will continue to rise (see Figure 11.2). The reason we can make this conclusion is because the 5 MW(e) research nuclear reactor at Yongbyon is by all accounts fully operational and exists for the principal purpose of producing weapons-grade plutonium.[23] By current estimates, it is capable of producing approximately 6 kg of weapons-grade plutonium per year, roughly equal to one nuclear weapon's worth of fissile material.[24]

There are also U.S. concerns about a clandestine highly enriched uranium (HEU) program and the construction of larger reactors, to increase its capability. This means the perceived threat to U.S. interests will steadily increase. It is certainly possible that North Korea may engage in other actions to increase the level of threat—a spike here and there is likely given the nature of the regime; but without a major shift in North Korean policy, the level of threat can never go lower than an upward-moving base line.

Figure 11.2: North Korean Action (incorporating activity at the Yongbyon Nuclear Facility)

North Korean Activity

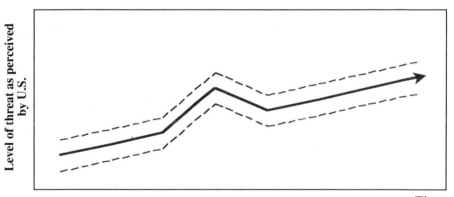

Time

Adding Red Lines to the Model

To insure that our model more accurately reflects reality, it is necessary to show that there exists a threshold level of threat as perceived by the United States that is too great for the United States to bear. To do this, I introduce the often-mentioned concept of a "red line."[25] Indeed, this concept of a threshold that, when crossed, causes a forceful U.S. response is consistent with at least one past U.S. action toward North Korea.

According to former U.S. secretary of defense William J. Perry, the U.S. government was prepared in 1994 to take forceful, but unspecified, action to prevent North Korea from reprocessing the 8,000 spent fuel rods that had been removed from the Yongbyon nuclear facility. The plutonium in those rods could have produced an estimated five to six nuclear weapons, a significant jump in the North's military capability.[26] The implication of this particular "red line" was clear. The Clinton administration felt that North Korea's crossing of this line was enough of a threat to the United States that the administration was willing to risk the possibility of a devastating war to prevent it.[27]

For the purposes of this chapter, I use "red line" to denote a level of threat that cannot be tolerated by the United States. A North Korean act that crosses the "red line" is considered to be enough of a risk to U.S. national security that the U.S. government would feel itself justified to use military force in response. The crossing of a red line does not mean military action *will* occur. However, it does mean that the military option that was in the past deemed an "option of last resort" has a new status as *one* (of a few) "primary" options.[28]

Using the line set in 1994—the only one with respect to North Korea publicly declared a red line by the United States—as a primary reference point, any one of the following North Korean acts could arguably be deemed as crossing a red line—one that the United States would seek to prevent: (1) a test of a long-range missile;[29] (2) a test of a nuclear device;[30] (3) the establishment of an operational highly enriched uranium (HEU) facility;[31] (4) the sale of fissile material or a nuclear device to a third party;[32] or (5) the buildup of a fissile material or a nuclear weapons stockpile of an unspecified number or the $X + 1$ line.[33]

In terms of the model, this concept of a red line is represented by the solid horizontal line in Figure 11.3 and is similarly depicted as having an upper and lower boundary.[34] This red line could represent any of the potential red lines outlined above, and its inclusion allows us to see how North Korean action relates to threat as perceived by the United States and to existing notions of threat deemed intolerable by the United States. I have also placed an upward-running base line, which represents the increasing threat from the ongoing production of plutonium at Yongbyon; the slope of this line could be steeper if we take into account concerns about North Korea's HEU program. In addition to a future red line, I have inserted for comparative purposes the 1994 "red line" that the North presumably crossed in 2003 when it purportedly reprocessed 8,000 spent fuel rods once in storage at Yongbyon.

Figure 11.3 shows how North Korean activity could go "too far." It is critical to recognize that if the Bush administration allows Yongbyon to continue its operations and if North Korea continues its nuclear weapons development, the upward trajectory of North Korean action will be a path that crosses a red line at some point (see Line 1, Figure 11.3). How soon this occurs is in the hands of both North Korea and the United States. North Korea must make a conscious decision to undertake an act that crosses any one of the red lines set forth in Figure 11.3; but, at least with respect to the $X + 1$ red line, the United States has the ability to set what that yet-undetermined number is.

Because North Korean action could reach a level of threat that is deemed intolerable, a prudent approach for any U.S. administration would be to take steps that attempt to prevent the threat level from even approaching that red line. In terms of the model constructed, the Bush administration should do what it can to bring the threat level down to an acceptable level (see Line 2, Figure 11.3). But after negotiations have proved unfruitful, the U.S. government will move to a strategy of coercive diplomacy or compellance.

Figure 11.3: North Korean Action: Adding the 1994 Red Line and a Future Red Line

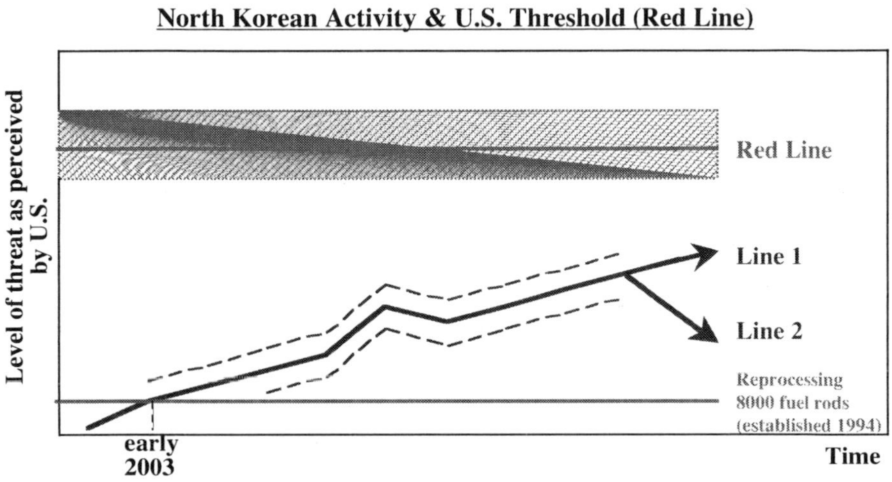

North Korean Activity & U.S. Threshold (Red Line)

(Line 1 represents the status quo, and at some point in the future will touch the red line. Line 2 represents desired effects of coercive diplomacy)

Integrating Alexander L. George's Theoretical Work on Coercive Diplomacy

I argued earlier in this chapter that the Bush administration will most likely pursue a policy toward North Korea based on regime change; I also advanced a conceptual model intended to measure the likely success of a given policy and some of the hidden perils. I now evaluate what the likely outcome of a Bush policy based on coercion will be. To do this, I turn to the groundbreaking work of Alexander L. George on international conflict and the use of coercive diplomacy and the work of others building on George's foundation.[35]

George defines coercive diplomacy as a "defensive strategy that is employed to deal with the efforts of an adversary to change a status quo situation in his own favor."[36] Coercive diplomacy—or compellance—"employs threats of force or quite limited increments of force to persuade the opponent to call off or undo the encroachment in which he is engaged—to induce him, for example to halt provocation or to give up territory he has seized."[37] George points out that coercive

219

diplomacy differs from pure military coercion because the point of coercive diplomacy is to avoid the actual use of military force.[38]

Over the course of two decades, George, with the help of colleagues, systematically examined a number of international conflicts and determined that certain factors are more influential than others when looking at whether coercive diplomacy as a strategy used by one state against another will succeed or fail. *The Limits of Coercive Diplomacy,* coedited by George, presents seven case studies of U.S. attempts at coercive diplomacy.[39] In a subsequent study completed in 2003, Robert J. Art and Patrick M. Cronin apply the analytic framework established to eight additional cases.[40]

These writings distinguish three types of coercive diplomacy—Type A, Type B, and Type C—according to the objectives pursued. Specifically, George and his coauthor William E. Simons assert the following:

> In Type A, the coercing state attempts to persuade the opponent merely to stop the aggressive action short of its goal. In Type B, the coercing state goes further, demanding that the opponent undo its action. Even more extreme is Type C coercive diplomacy, in which an attempt is made to stop the opponent's unacceptable policies and behavior by demanding that it make changes in its government.[41]

Based on these 15 cases, the authors conclude that coercive diplomacy is difficult to make work for a variety of reasons.[42] However, if coercive diplomacy is to be used, they identify eight conditions that favor its use.[43] But of those eight, George and Simons find that three related to the opponent's perceptions are most significant—asymmetry of motivation, unacceptability of escalation, and sense of urgency.[44] Bruce Jentleson in his study of the Reagan administration's policy toward Nicaragua and Type C coercive diplomacy refines and adds to the key George/Simon factors.[45] For the purposes of this chapter, I have made further adaptations to the George and Jentleson formulation and look at the following: the opponent's perception concerning the asymmetry of motivation, unacceptability of escalation, domestic and international support, and sense of urgency.[46]

Asymmetry of Motivation

Coercive measures are more likely to succeed if the coercing party is more highly motivated than the coerced. George highlights the idea that perceptions are critical—the coerced party must believe that the coercing party is more highly motivated to achieve the objective than the coerced party is in resisting it.[47] Therefore, it is theoretically possible for the coercing party to take action to create a perception that it is more highly motivated that the coerced party. However, George also points out that there are some cases where "the relative motivation of the two sides tends to be fixed by the nature of the conflict and may not be subject to manipulation."[48] Bruce Jentleson in his study of the Reagan administration's policies toward Nicaragua argues that that Type C coercive diplomacy cases are exactly that: "the motivation of an adversary to resist efforts to overthrow him is fixed—and fixed at a rather high intensity—by the very nature of the conflict."[49]

Unacceptability of Escalation

The impact of coercive measures is greater if "the initial actions and communications directed against the adversary arouse his fear of an escalation to circumstances less acceptable than those promised by accession to the coercing power's demands."[50] In other words, the coercing party has a better chance of success if the coerced party is made to fear the reprisal or punishment resulting from resisting the coercer's threats. However, it is best if the potential costs to be inflicted upon the coerced party are used in a "controlled, discriminating manner" because the use of pressure is more conducive to influencing behavior rather than "imposing one's will upon [the coerced party]."[51] The question therefore centers on the credibility of the threat, its potency as well as the general susceptibility of the coerced party to intimidation. If the coercing party's threats are not credible or its actions are seen as weak or if the coerced party is not easily intimidated, then there is a good chance the coerced party will deem the coercer's threat a bluff.[52] In this circumstance, the coercer may have no other choice but either escalate if it wants to be taken seriously or back down.

Domestic and International Support

It seems axiomatic, but domestic and international support are critical to any U.S. decision to use coercive diplomacy.[53] As the lead up to the two Gulf Wars attests, the U.S. government places a high importance on mobilizing support at home and abroad. Strong domestic support gives any administration greater latitude in shaping and executing policy; weak domestic support eventually makes a policy unsustainable. In the same way, obtaining moral authority through strong international support can be critical to success. Strong international and domestic support also is a key to establishing credibility of a threat of force or escalation. At the same time, it must be noted that regime change is generally not favored as a government policy within the United States and internationally.[54] Bruce Jentleson has argued that in the "post post-Vietnam" period, public opinion is more supportive of the use of military force when it is used to enforce restraint, rather than to bring about regime change.[55]

Likewise, he points out that that principles of nonaggression, national sovereignty, and noninterference in a country's internal affairs are ignored with great difficulty.[56]

Sense of Urgency

If the state using coercive measures genuinely experiences a sense of urgency, then it is likely to impart this sense of urgency to the coerced party—which then becomes a source of pressure of its own.[57] However, this factor is most applicable to cases where an explicit or implicit ultimatum is used for coercive effect and is less salient in cases where coercive measures are used in less dramatic fashion, such as a "try and see approach" or a "gradual turning of the screw."[58] Without this sense of urgency, the coercer must find other ways to convey a credible sense of need to secure its demands.[59]

Why Regime Change through Coercion Is Likely to Fail

Should the six-party talks break down, the Bush administration's predicament with regard to North Korea fits neatly within the theoretical framework pioneered by George. First, North Korea has sought for some time to change the status quo by acquiring an active and operational nuclear weapons program. As a way to protect the status quo, the Bush administration seeks to prevent this from occurring and is likely to use pressure as well as implicit or explicit threats of force. Second, the Bush administration presumably will engage in Type C coercive diplomacy, believing that any accommodation with Kim Jong-Il could not be verified or trusted; the Bush policy would thus be to change the government of North Korea as the only practical way to ensure it does not upset the status quo and become a nuclear weapons state.[60]

Applying the George and Jentleson criteria, a U.S. policy employing coercive diplomacy will be more likely to succeed if the United States can answer "yes" to the following questions: (1) Does the opponent believe that the coercer's motivation is higher than his own? (2) Does the opponent believe that the threatened punishment is credible and potent enough to necessitate compliance with the demand? (3) Does the opponent believe the coercer has support internationally and domestically? (4) Does the opponent believe that it is time sensitive to respond to the coercer?[61]

In attempting to find answers to these questions, we are immediately faced with the common dilemma of asymmetry of information. Specifically, we do not know with certainty how Kim Jong-Il and his leadership cadre perceive the United States. The decision making process in North Korea is difficult to read and has been the source of endless speculation for many years. Nonetheless, we may be able to glean a sense of North Korean views from official and unofficial news sources, opinions of experienced North Korean watchers, and most important, actions of the North Korean government and the historical and contemporary context in which such actions are taken. I have also had many conversations with key policymakers in North Korea, and I have a general sense of Pyongyang's priorities. We must also not confine our frame of reference to particulars of the current situation; thus I take into account when relevant the long history of the North Korean involvement with the United States.

On the basis of this methodology and noting George and Simons's warning how heavily context-dependent the use of coercive diplomacy is, I argue that it is highly doubtful that the U.S. use of pressure or threats to compel North Korean compliance will succeed.[62]

Does North Korea believe the U.S. motivation is higher than its own? Very unlikely. It is reasonable to assume that the North Korean leadership believes the United States seeks regime change. Under these circumstances, it is hard to argue that the resolve of the United States is higher than that of North Korea—or at least that North Korea's ruling clique perceives otherwise.

The stated U.S. objective is the complete and permanent end to North's nuclear weapons program. But, according to Pyongyang, the true U.S. goal is to end Kim Jong-Il's rule—and as George notes, it is the coercing party's perception that is most relevant.[63] Recent official statements of the North Korean government are very clear on this point.[64] Most prominent is a rare DPRK Foreign Ministry memorandum, dated March 2, 2005. In explaining its reasons for suspending its participation in the six-party talks, the North Korean government declared the following:

> The DPRK-U.S. nuclear issue is a product of the Bush administration's extreme hostile policy, and the basic key to its resolution lies in the United States changing its hostile policy to a policy of peaceful DPRK-U.S. coexistence. As it did during the first term, the second-term Bush administration established it as a policy not to coexist with us and overthrow the system chosen by our people. . . .
>
> The United States' true intention is that it will never peacefully coexist with us and that it will pursue overthrowing of our system through disarmament is deeply rooted and has not changed even once. We cannot find anywhere in the remarks made by the United States' official figures the expression of coexistence with us or change in the hostile policy.[65]

While we cannot rely entirely on such public statements as a valid indicator of North Korean perceptions, an examination of events over the past two years, culminating in the above Foreign Ministry statement, reinforces the case that at least to the North Koreans the U.S. policy is one of regime change, even though the United States has stressed the very opposite.

In October 2000, the United States and the DRPK signed a joint communiqué in which the United States accepted the existence of the Kim Jong-Il regime as a basis to move forward on resolving U.S. concerns about North Korean missile and nuclear weapons activity. The United States acknowledgment was extremely important to the North because it conferred a degree of international legitimacy to North Korea and was the beginning of a process to allay the North's overall security concerns. Between January 2001 and October 2002, Pyongyang in essence was waiting for some indication that the Bush administration would continue the policies set by the Clinton administration.[66] Instead of a policy reaffirmation, President Bush made a number of personal attacks against Kim Jong-Il, named North Korea as one of the "Axis of Evil," and included North Korea as a nuclear preemption target. He did not respond to Kim Jong-Il's personal letter of November 2002, in which Kim indicated his willingness to resolve the nuclear issue.[67] In 2003, the administration went to war with Iraq, hardening the impression that North Korea might be next, and the following year Congress passed the North Korean Human Rights Act, which Pyongyang has interpreted as concrete evidence of U.S. intent to overthrow the DPRK.[68]

While former of secretary of state Colin Powell has stated a number of times, particularly toward the end of his tenure, that the United States has "no hostile intent" toward North Korea,[69] President Bush has made no such statement. From Pyongyang's perspective, Powell's remarks—which may have sufficed in a period of less strained relations—may have been overshadowed by other U.S. actions, which include, among other things, the U.S. Proliferation Security Initiative, and congressional funding of the National Endowment for Democracy for activities in South Korea to promote change in the North.[70] Powell's successor, Condoleezza Rice, appears to be charting a new policy course, but in some ways she has added to the confusion by being both hardline (calling North Korea an outpost of tyranny early in 2005) and more conciliatory (recognizing the North's sovereignty during her first trip to Asia).[71]

Finally, there are many influential Americans, in and out of government, who have been advocates—or identified by the media as such—of regime change.[72] Though he has not specifically mentioned regime change, U.N. Ambassador John Bolton, when he was Undersecretary of State, was highly critical of North Korea and Kim Jong-Il.[73] The media also reported widely on a secret memorandum circulated by Donald Rumsfeld proposing regime change.[74] Also significant is a remark attributed to Vice President Dick Cheney regarding talks with North Korea stating that "we don't negotiate with evil, we defeat it."[75] The news media are at times wrong, but North Korea carefully tracks reported remarks made by administration officials regardless of their accuracy.[76]

If North Korea believes the true U.S. goal is to end the Kim Jong-Il regime, then we have a classic Type C coercive diplomacy case. What is at stake for North Korea is not just its nuclear weapons program, but the very survival of those who lead the country. It is hard to believe that Kim Jong-Il would see anyone in the Bush administration as having a greater incentive than he and the country's power elite. As Bruce Jentleson points out in examining the Reagan administration's unsuccessful attempt to coerce the Sandinista regime, "for the leaders like the Sandinista Directorate, there is no stronger motivation than preservation of personal power and the accompanying perquisites. This is not a motivation easily shaken by coercive diplomacy."[77]

In this regard, the Bush administration needs to fully appreciate the commitment of the North Korean regime to survival. Alexander George points out that faulty images of the opponent usually result in poor policies and other miscalculations and that "[i]n the absence of adequate information, one side often arrives at such images by assuming the opponent has a similar value system and reasoning process...."[78]

As an example of this, George highlights how Lyndon Johnson and his advisors never understood the underlying reasons for North Vietnamese action during the war.

> Although Johnson made an effort to visualize himself in his opponent's shoes for bargaining purposes and apparently recognized the relative advantage experienced by Ho Chi Minh in early March 1965, he did not fully appreciate Ho's strength of motivation and moral conviction. ... This misjudgment was also evident in the confidence expressed by his top advisors—which Johnson apparently accepted—that once the leaders in Hanoi realized they could not win in South Vietnam, then the threat of destruction to the industries and economic infrastructure around Haiphong and Hanoi would have a truly coercive effect.[79]

The existence of North Korea is predicated on the North Korean ideology of self-reliance, known as *juche*.[80] This doctrine espouses that there is no higher calling for North Koreans than the preservation of the state from outside domination (which also at one time included the "liberation" of South Korea). According to its national myth, North Korea is a weak country surrounded by powerful neighbors that seek to destroy it; its people are thus in a perpetual psychological state of war, a pressure they have endured for over 50 years. The preservation of the state has become their raison d'être. While the Bush administration may be quick to dismiss Kim Jong-Il and his cadre as corrupt and capricious,

North Korean history and ideology indicate it would be ill-advised to underestimate their determination to preserve their state at all costs.

Does North Korea believe a U.S. threat of punishment is credible and potent enough to escalate to a point that is unacceptable to North Korea? Probably not. North Korea may have doubts about U.S. resolve and thus credibility; North Korea clearly believes it can withstand coercive measures, which in theory may be seen as strengthening the regime; moreover, it is likely North Korea feels it has its own credible threat. While this may seem to be a contradiction—that Pyongyang both believes that the United States wishes to destroy the government, yet does not believe that U.S. threats are credible—it is not. The consistency in these two beliefs lies in understanding that North Korea believes that the United States *wants* to eliminate the Kim Jong-Il regime, but further believes that the United States does not have the resolve to do so; nonetheless North Korea is happy to use such threats against its sovereignty to galvanize its population and to bolster its stated position of needing nuclear weapons.

Since 2002 North Korea has taken a number of actions to revive, what had been since 1994, its dormant fissile material production program. It withdrew from the NPT, kicked out international inspectors and monitoring equipment, restarted the 5 MW(e) reactor at Yongbyon, and most significantly reprocessed the 8,000 spent fuel rods in storage. Many regional and political military experts agree that North Korea during this period has significantly increased its nuclear weapons capability, crossing what were considered "red lines" in 1994.

Time and time again senior officials in the Bush administration and South Korea's Roh administration have stated that a nuclear North Korea is unacceptable, and both presidents are on record as stating that they will not "tolerate" nuclear weapons in North Korea.[81] Speaking in South Korea, President Bush declared, "We will maintain our presence here [South Korea]. And as I told the Congress and the world in my State of the Union messages, we will not permit the world's most dangerous regimes to threaten us or our friends or our allies with weapons of mass destruction."[82]

But other than tough talk and a refusal to deal with North Korea directly, the Bush and Roh administrations have done very little.[83] This presents a huge problem for the credibility of U.S. resolve and reflects on any subsequent U.S. threat, increasing the likelihood of miscalculation because previous threats were deemed to be bluffs. The North Koreans know that what was once a "red line" in 1994 was crossed with impunity.[84] In 2003, North Korea withdrew from the Nonproliferation Treaty virtually without penalty, and it continues to enjoy trade and aid from South Korea and China.[85] Some could argue that the U.S. war in Iraq should sufficiently demonstrate U.S. resolve to the North Koreans;

however, one could also point out that of the three cases involving nuclear weapons programs cited by the administration—Iraq, Iran, and North Korea—the administration decided to deal with the country that was the least pressing and the weakest, which still leaves open the question of U.S. commitment.[86]

In addition to the issue of U.S. credibility, North Korea has proved its remarkable ability to endure incredible hardship and misery. By touting the *juche* ideology, limiting access to information, and enforcing a draconian reward-punishment system, the North Korean leadership uses extreme methods to extract great sacrifice from a compliant public.[87] For example, one million or more people have been estimated to have died during the early to mid-1990s from famine and famine-related causes, yet the regime continues unchallenged; its citizens appear to accept these casualties as the price of survival in a hostile world.

There is also doubt as to whether coercive measures of any kind would be effective. Robert J. Art, referring to the work of Thomas Schelling, alludes to the counterproductive effects of coercion since they tend to "engage the passions of the target state . . . and cause the government [of the target state] to mobilize domestic support . . . [and] perversely make the government more popular after it becomes subject to coercive action than it was before."[88] Jon B. Alterman's study of the United States and Iraq in the period 1990–98 reinforces this view. Examining the dynamics of economic sanctions on the Iraqi leadership, Alterman observes that long-term sanctions may have been seen by Saddam Hussein as promoting his interests because the shortages caused by the sanctions gave him a greater ability to reward and punish individuals and to profit from black markets.[89] Indeed, there are many who argue for reasons similar to those advanced by Alterman—citing the lack of success in Burma, Iraq, and Cuba—that sanctions will make the North Korean government stronger, not weaker.[90]

One also must remember that North Korea has prepared itself as best it can for war. It has one of the largest standing armies in the world, thousands of artillery tubes capable of causing great damage to Seoul, a formidable array of short-range and intermediate-range missiles and possibly nuclear weapons. Yet its military infrastructure—like its nonmilitary infrastructure—is deteriorating.[91] Though reasonable people can disagree, North Korea's military doctrine is one of deterrence, relying on a "porcupine strategy": if you attack, you will get hurt. For example, while many cite the purpose of the North's forward deployment of artillery along the DMZ as offensive, classic deterrence strategy also reasons it could be defensive.[92] In a conflict, a U.S. victory would be at great cost, notwithstanding any decline in North Korea's current manpower or conventional forces.[93] The cost associated with the outbreak of a war would be multiplied if North Korea does have or at some point acquires an operational nuclear device. Against this backdrop, it is difficult to make the case that the current leadership would allow itself to be intimidated by the United States. In fact, it is just as likely that the opposite would occur.

William M. Drennan in his thoughtful examination of the Korean nuclear crisis in 1994 shows instances where North Korea employed its own coercive strategy, using brinksmanship tactics, deadlines, and threats of force. He is quick to point out that the North's approach "had worked too well, apparently blinding North Korea to the fact that it was about to cross the real 'red line' that the United States had—preventing North Korea from acquiring additional nuclear weapons capability."[94] His analysis comports with my own experiences as a State Department official in dealing with North Korea. During my hundreds of hours of negotiations with the DPRK, it was clear that my interlocutors felt that weakness invited repeated intimidation—so a "push" usually led to a harder "push in return."[95]

This prospect that North Korea sees itself as having the ability to escalate and respond to U.S. coercive measures—as it did in 1994 and in subsequent years—poses another significant problem for U.S. credibility and for the likely success of coercive measures themselves. Referring to U.S. efforts to deal with Slobodan Milosevic in the Balkans, Robert Art observes the following:

> Serbian military figures visited Iraq to see if they could learn how to thwart U.S. airpower. One device the Serbians hit upon was not to fire most of their surface-to-air missiles (SAMs) but instead to hold them back. This forced NATO pilots to fly at high altitudes over Kosovo and impeded their ability to knock out Serbian armor placed there. Thus, believing that he had the means to ride out an air war, Milosevic did not back down under NATO's threats.[96]

Indeed, in examining why coercive diplomacy is so difficult, Robert Art states that "the target's belief that it has effective counter-coercion techniques . . . makes it highly likely, if not guaranteed, that coercive diplomacy will fail."[97] The concern here is that North Korea understands how effective it was in 1994 and that it remains confident of its ability to deal with whatever path the United States takes.

Does North Korea believe that the United States has domestic and international support for a policy of coercive diplomacy? Unlikely. At present, the Bush administration does not have a strong basis for support domestically and internationally and is unlikely to garner such support in the future as long as its policy goal is perceived to be regime change. In the United States, domestic support is weak not so much because the public disfavors a particular Bush policy, but because the public is not focused on the problem. Americans are aware of and concerned about the problem of North Korea's nuclear weapons program, but they appear to have no sense of urgency; certainly very few, if any, groups in the United States are clamoring for action.

To garner support at home for a policy of forcing regime change in North Korea, the Bush administration must deal with the increasing public weariness resulting from U.S. involvement in Iraq. First and foremost, Mr. Bush said Saddam Hussein had weapons of mass destruction and that the Hussein regime had links to Al Qaeda. Yet both proved to be incorrect. In a time of huge budget deficits, lingering concerns about the U.S. economy, and the mounting human and financial cost of the Iraq War, support will be difficult to gain.[98] While it is conceivable that Americans would favor a policy of regime change in North Korea if there were assurances that the cost would be relatively low, it is doubtful that the American public would welcome a policy based on greater military risks and unsubstantiated promises. Since effectiveness of a coercive policy ultimately rests on the willingness of the coercer to use force in a worst-case scenario, the effect of any U.S. pressure or threat to escalate is muted.

Moreover, there are other high-priority issues that occupy the Bush administration at this time. Senior policymakers are focused on getting out of Iraq, maintaining pressure in Afghanistan, and securing progress with Iran. Domestically, challenges, such as economic/tax reform, the appointment of a Supreme Court Justice, sagging approval ratings and the 2006 mid-term election to name a few, are sure to take a great deal of the administration's senior staff time. The situation the Bush administration faces is not unlike the circumstance Lyndon Johnson faced in the early years of the Vietnam War. When faced with a number of policy options to pressure the North Vietnamese government to stop supporting the Communist forces in South Vietnam, Johnson was extremely sensitive to the impact any escalation in Vietnam would have on his Great Society agenda.[99]

With regard to the international community, North Korea's nuclear problem is not only a concern for the United States, it also is one for South Korea, China, Japan, and Russia. The focus of major power struggles for over a hundred years, the Korean peninsula touches upon the security interests of these neighboring countries, a fact that limits the range of U.S. options.

While all in the region agree that a North Korea with nuclear weapons is not in anyone's interest, there is a clear disagreement as to priorities.[100] For the United States, preventing a nuclear North Korea is a top priority. For South Korea, the priority is to prevent a war and deal with the primary threat to South Korea, which it sees as coming from an imprudent United States moving prematurely against North Korea.[101] China, in contrast, has multiple policy goals—a nuclear-free Korean peninsula, avoiding a North Korean collapse, and avoiding outbreak of hostilities; and its priority among these three is not at all clear.[102] Japan's priorities fit well with those of the United States, since it too views North Korea as a primary threat; the country is home to major U.S. bases and thus a potential target in the event of hostilities. Russia has been less a player in this part of the world, but due to a common border, it is focused on regional stability and preserving its economic relationship with South Korea in particular and the region in general.[103] In addition to differing priorities, there is a disagreement as to the perceived overall U.S. objective—South Korea and China do not endorse or support regime change in North Korea, and Russia is uncomfortable with the U.S. approach.[104]

These gaps translate into differences in strategy among the five parties, and ultimately affect the ability of the United States to effectively execute a policy of coercive diplomacy. The United States and for the time being Japan prefer pressure, but China and South Korea support a more positive engagement.[105] Chinese and South Korean government officials in public and private have voiced concerns that the United States has not made a good-faith effort to determine if a negotiated resolution of the North Korean nuclear issue is possible.[106] China, South Korea, and Russia see the six-party process as a forum created by the United States as a way to avoid dealing with North Korea bilaterally and as a way of avoiding having to deal with the nuclear issue. Barring provocative North Korea action, it is unlikely that China, South Korea, or Russia will reverse their current positions. None of the countries can be counted on to support a U.S. policy of coercion.[107]

In addition to providing international legitimacy for its policy toward North Korea, the United States requires support from China, South Korea, and Russia for other practical reasons. China is a permanent member of the UN Security Council with veto rights; and if various estimates are believed, it supplies about 70 percent of North Korea's energy and close to 40 percent of its food. Moreover, the two countries share a very long and relatively porous border.[108] South Korea is one of North Korea's most significant economic partners, with a trade volume of about $690 million in 2004 and about $1.16 billion in humanitarian aid since 1995.[109] Russia's trade with North Korea is limited, but Russia too is a permanent member of the UN Security Council. While no one can say with certainty that a combined effort among the United States, China, South Korea, and Russia to curb North Korea's nuclear ambitions would be a success, one can say with confidence that the probability of success is higher if all four countries work together as opposed to the United States going it alone. Collectively imposed economic sanctions would impose greater costs on North Korea; the passage of a UN Security Council resolution would be more likely. In fact, despite the Bush administration's concerted efforts to isolate North Korea from South Korea, China, and

Russia, North Korea is enjoying a surge in trade and has become less isolated than it has been for some time.[110]

This current lack of international cooperation on North Korea is similar to the predicament faced by the Reagan administration when it decided in the mid-1980s to pressure Libya's Col. Muammar Qaddafi to stop aiding terrorist groups. As a first step, the U.S. government initiated economic sanctions. However, for economic sanctions to have any meaningful impact on Qaddafi, the Reagan administration needed its European allies, whose support in the end was tepid at best.[111] Given the ineffectiveness of economic sanctions, the Reagan administration increased its pressure, which resulted in further Libyan escalation, culminating in a full-scale bombing raid by the United States. As Tim Zimmerman concludes:

> Any coercive policy that seeks to achieve pressure on an adversary through political and economic sanctions is likely to suffer from the difficulty of achieving multilateral unity on all but the most pressing issues. There are situations in which the United States so dominates the foreign trade relations of a country or region that unilateral sanctions can result in substantial pressure. However, this was not the case with Libya. As a result, the most ready instrument at the administration's disposal to pressure Qaddafi was almost totally ineffective.[112]

Does North Korea believe that it is time sensitive to respond to the United States? Unknown. No deadlines have yet been set, making this inquiry into urgency less relevant. However, the Bush administration in mid-2005 hinted of penalties if the six-party talks did not begin soon and in earnest; yet it did not asserted anything resembling a time line for compliance.[113] Still, there is a good chance that the United States may set some sort of deadline in the future, if the talks stall again or if in the unlikely event North Korea tests a nuclear weapon. Under these this circumstance, the key inquiry again returns to North Korea's view of the circumstances, and the issue turns back to credibility. As we argued earlier, if the United States does not react in the face of provocative North Korean action, the credibility of the United States will become problematic.

Application of the Model to U.S. Coercive Diplomacy: A Terrible Choice or Inadvertent Risk of War?

In terms of the model outlined earlier, U.S. efforts at coercive diplomacy will have three possible outcomes (see Figure 11.4). They can (1) make matters worse and cause the threat level to increase (Line 1, Figure 11.4);

(2) have little to no effect (Line 2); or (3) make things better and cause the threat level to decrease (Line3).

Figure 11.4: North Korea Action: Possible Effects of Coercive Diplomacy

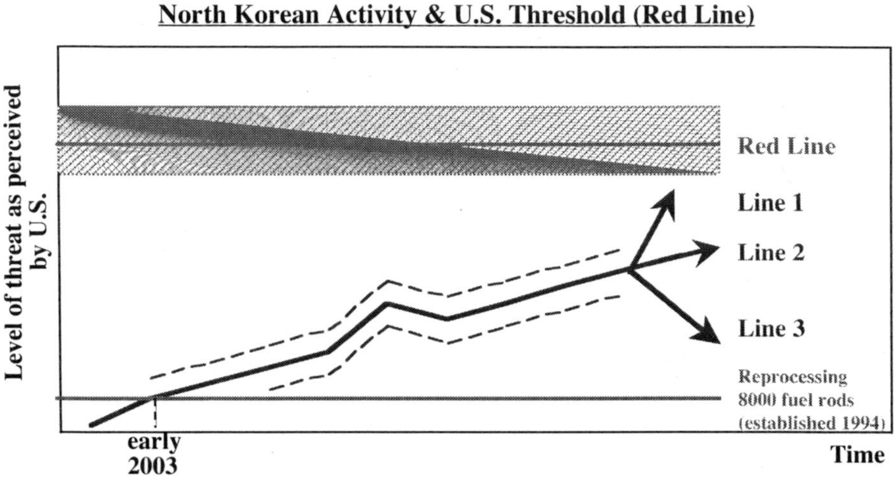

North Korean Activity & U.S. Threshold (Red Line)

Line 1 shows North Korean escalation; Line 2 shows no effect; and Line 3 shows reduction of threat.

With respect to the Line 3 in Figure 11.4 (reduction of threat), the existing body of research on coercive diplomacy in past confrontations and its application prospectively to the current confrontation between the United States and North Korea in this chapter show that it is highly unlikely that the use of pressure in pursuit of regime change will succeed. This is the case in part, not because there is a problem so much with regard to the use of pressure, but because the objective of regime change—and its likely effects on the motivation of the North Korean leadership to resist—is highly problematic. Bruce Jentleson's case against the efficacy of Type C coercive diplomacy in general is compelling. [114] There are also issues related to the credibility of the U.S. threat and the perceived effects of such a threat on North Korea by the North Koreans.

In the case of escalation (Line 1, Figure 11.4), the failure of coercive diplomacy means that the level of threat will continue to move upward more rapidly toward a red line. If a red line is reached and passed—whether it is the result of North Korean action or U.S. inaction—the United States will have to make good on its threats or it will have to back down. The United States could create another "red line," but its credibility by then would be destroyed; the United States then would have to use a form of force in an attempt to change North Korean action.

232

Therefore, when the day comes that North Korea crosses a red line, the United States will in the end be faced with the terrible choice of either accepting that particular North Korean act or risking the outbreak of war to prevent it.

Even if North Korea in the course of counter-coercive moves or escalation has no intent of crossing a red line (Line 2, Figure 11.5), there is still a risk of inadvertent military conflict.[115] This risk is illustrated in the form of point X in Figure 11.5. In this case, North Korea calculates moves based on the solid lines indicating the average value of threat and threshold (Line 1/Line 2 and Red Line), but the actual value of the level of threat as perceived by the United States is higher than North Korea assumes it to be while the actual value of the applicable red line is a lower threshold than assumed.[116] Unexpectedly then, North Korea crosses a red line at point X (intersection between the upper boundary line parallel to Line 1/Line 2 and the lower boundary of Red Line) and *T1*, instead of at the expected point Y (intersection between Line 1 and Red Line) and *T2* that would give more time for policymakers to assess the situation and calibrate a proper response.

Figure 11.5: North Korea Escalation (Going Up to the Line or Crossing It)

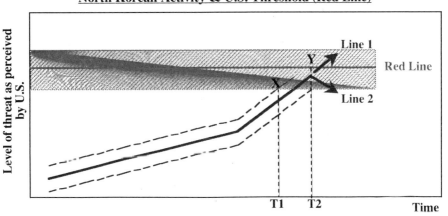

It is appropriate here to mention a consideration that is not often raised in policy circles and government, and one that complicates the use of coercive diplomacy, particularly in a high-stakes situation as with North Korea. It is the element of chance. To this point, we have assumed that both the United States and North Korea have the ability to maintain operational control over events; that they have the ability to calibrate the degree of tension that exists between the two with their actions. Some of this is true, but as Thomas Schelling points out,

233

general war can occur inadvertently, despite the intentions of the parties involved, "through some kind of accident, false alarm, or mechanical failure; through somebody's panic, madness, or mischief; through misapprehension of enemy intentions or a correct apprehension of the enemy's misapprehension of ours."[117] Therefore, as Figure 11.5 illustrates, we cannot forget that even a limited use of force increases the chances of a greater use of force and could lead to an unintended war, resulting from miscalculation.[118]

In the event that coercive diplomacy has no effect (Line 2, Figure 11.4), the outcome and concerns are the same as those when North Korea escalates in response to U.S. coercion. However, the trajectory of Line 1, reflecting the ongoing activity at Yongbyon, makes it inevitable that it will cross the $X + 1$ red line (See Figure 11.6).[119] The concerns about miscalculation as to when the red line will be crossed apply as well (see points X and Y, Figure 11.6). However, as mentioned earlier, unlike with other red lines, the United States has the ability to "move" the $X + 1$ red line, that is, to raise the number. If it decides to change the $X + 1$ number, then de facto the United States accepts the existence of a nuclear North Korea.

Figure 11.6: Crossing the Red Line (Continued Operation of Yongbyon and Other Nuclear Weapons Activity)

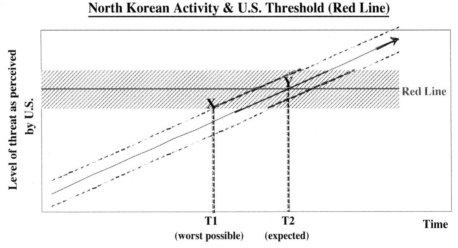

Conclusion

The status quo is inherently unstable—the continued operation of the 5 MW(e) reactor at Yongbyon steadily increases the level of threat to U.S. nonproliferation objectives and a number of regional goals. If North

Korea does nothing more than what it is known to be doing now, at some point in the future the steady stockpiling of fissile material would reach a level that is deemed a sufficient enough threat that it would required U.S. action—North Korea will have crossed the $X + 1$ red line. To address this increasing threat, a clear priority then is to freeze North Korea's plutonium-based activity at Yongbyon and to prevent other reactors from becoming operational. Admittedly, North Korean HEU efforts remain a difficult issue to counter.

If the six-party talks fail to produce results, then it appears likely that the Bush administration will pursue a policy of regime change through the use of pressure and coercion. Judging from its actions with regard to North Korea to date and with regard to Iraq and Iran, I would expect the Bush administration to be cautious—in an attempt to minimize the risk of escalation—and to pursue a course that involves a steady application of pressure. However, if the administration uses a coercive strategy, it should anticipate escalation. North Korea should be expected to react and react strongly, increasing the likelihood that it will come close to or actually cross one of the potential red lines examined in this chapter. It is important to note that the usefulness of red lines presupposes the United States has reliable intelligence to adequately anticipate that North Korea is about to cross such a line. But the recent report by the U.S. Commission on the Intelligence Capabilities of the United States regarding Weapons of Mass Destruction, indicating the United States knows surprising little about North Korea and its WMD programs, calls this assumption into question.[120]

Because of the known activity at Yongbyon and uncertainty surrounding the nature of the North's HEU program, time is not on the side of the United States The United States has sat by in effect doing nothing for the past four years, and it is unlikely that coercion employed by the Bush administration will now work. Further delay will allow North Korea the time to produce an operational nuclear weapon, perhaps several—if it has not already done so—and with it an established nuclear deterrent. In effect, by employing a policy of regime change, the United States is making a huge bet that collapse or compliance will come before the establishment of an operational North Korean nuclear weapons program.

We cannot discount the possibility that coercion misapplied may well indeed force North Korea into a corner, resulting in unimaginably bad consequences. We only need to look at what Imperial Japan did when it attacked the United States despite of its own calculations that the chance of victory was extremely slim.[121] In this regard, I am reminded of the fact that much of North Korea's leadership comes from Hamgyong, the northernmost of the country's provinces, where Korean kings once sent their "troublemakers." Just as the United States has its stereotypes of Texans and New Yorkers, so too does Korea have stereotypes about people from Hamgyong. When asked about people from Hamgyong and North Korea in general, most South Koreans reply that they are abrasive, stubborn, and emotional, underscored by an "if I am to die, I will take you with me" mentality. For this reason, many in South Korea are wary of an irrational North Korean response. However, initiating hostilities may indeed under certain circumstances be a rational thing to do.[122]

To increase the chances that coercive pressure would have the desired effect, the Bush administration may have to rethink its goal. Many point to the U.S. handling of the Soviet Union during the Cuban missile crisis as a successful example of coercive diplomacy. The key to defusing the crisis was Kennedy's decision to limit his objective—he was willing to settle for the removal of the missiles from Cuba; he did not seek to remove Castro or to end Soviet influence on the island.[123] Likewise, narrow U.S. aims in Somalia were deemed to be a major factor in judging the U.S. coercive strategy a borderline success.[124] In the case of North Korea, the Bush administration likewise may have to make it clear that regime change is no longer—or never really was—the desired end state.[125] However, the key is whether the North Korean leadership believes that this is in fact that case—and persuading the North Koreans of this policy change shift will not be easy. Still, if the Bush administration were willing to take its stated willingness to "peacefully exist" with North Korea, as set forth in last September's joint statement of general principles, and combine it with concrete economic and security incentives, it might find there is a path—albeit a long and arduous one—-to a final and sustainable agreement. Variations of this approach would turn the regime change objective into one of regime transformation, building on the North Korea's current push for economic reform.[126]

Finally, policymakers need to understand the nature of worst-case scenarios in order to do what they can to avoid them. It is only when one deliberates over the entire array of policy implications that one can then adequately calculate the risks and prepare for them. In contemplating past U.S. use of coercive diplomacy, Robert J. Art cautions "the United States should not start down the road of coercive diplomacy unless it is willing to resort to war, or unless it has devised a political strategy that will enable it to back down without too much loss of face should coercive diplomacy fail."[127] There are many instances in the past where the United States failed to re-examine long-held assumptions when formulating policy toward troubled areas of the world—to ill effect. This warning is particularly apropos with respect to North Korea.

Notes

This chapter was made possible by generous support provided by the Pantech Corporation. The author is grateful for the invaluable suggestions, criticism, and assistance of Soyoung Kwon, John Lewis, Robert Carlin, Jiyoon Lee, Gi-Wook Shin, Scott Snyder, Joon Suk Hong, Joon Nak Choi, Young Kwon Yoon, and John Yun.

[1] Robert Marquand, "Sharp Divisions over North Korea, *Christian Science Monitor,* June 24, 2003; Jay Solomon and David S. Cloud, "A Global Journal Report—Cold Front: A Split with Seoul Complicates Crisis over North Korea," *Wall Street Journal,* January 2, 2003; and Joel Brinkley, "China Balks at Pressing the North Koreans," *New York Times,* March 22, 2005.

[2] Though they are currently in a state of disrepair, if the Yongbyon 50MW(e) and Taechon 200 MW(e) reactors become operational, they would dramatically increase North Korea's capability to produce fissile material. The 50 MW(e) reactor could produce about 50 kg per year, the 200 MW(e), about 200 kg per year. For reference, Yongbyon's markedly smaller 5 MW(e) reactor is thought to be able to produce about 6 kg of fissile material per year.

[3] The media have reported widely on a split within the administration over North Korea policy between those that favor engagement and those that favor a harder line, including regime change. See David E. Sanger, "Administration Divided Over North Korea," *New York Times,* April 21, 2003; David Rennie, "Rumsfeld Calls for Regime Change in North Korea," *Daily Telegraph* (UK), April 22, 2003; Gerald F. Seib and Carla Anne Robbins, "Powell-Rumsfeld Feud Now Hard to Ignore: Bush Faces Decisions on North Korea, Israel, U.N. Role in Iraq—All Cabinet Battlegrounds," *Wall Street Journal,* April 25, 2003; Christopher Marquis, "Top U.S. Expert on North Korea Steps Down," *New York Times,* August 26 2003; and Bill Gertz, "State Confirms N. Korea Light-Water Reactor Talks," *Washington Times,* May 20, 2004.

[4] I have borrowed the term "superhawks" from Peter Hayes of the Nautilus Institute. In my opinion, any responsible U.S. policymaker is a hawk on North Korea—any policy toward North Korea cannot rely on trust or the goodwill of North Korea, but should be a blend of benefits and penalties.

[5] President Bush's references to Kim Jong-Il are well documented. For more recent statements see President Bush, press conference, April 28, 2005, at http://www.whitehouse.gov/news/release/2005/04/20050428-9.html.

[6] Ashton B. Carter, William J. Perry, and John M. Shalikashvili, "A Scary Thought: Loose Nukes in North Korea," *Wall Street Journal,* February 6, 2003.

[7] William J. Perry, "Review of United States Policy toward North Korea: Findings and Recommendations," October 12, 1999, pp. 6 7, at http://www.state.gov/www/regions/eap/99/991012_northkorea_rpt.html.

[8] Ibid. However, within a larger solution, a limited Nunn-Lugar type of arrangement could prove workable and helpful.

[9] Based on discussions I have had with various government officials familiar with the six-party talks.

[10] I cannot count how many times North Koreans made this point to me from 1998 to 2000 during the hundreds of hours of negotiations I participated in as a U.S. government official.

[11] Indeed, I have been sorry to find there are many in South Korea and elsewhere convinced that this is the primary motivation for U.S. action—pointing to U.S. action in Iraq as the most recent example.

[12] See Bruce Bennett and Nina Hachigian, "Don't Try Regime Change in North Korea," *International Herald Tribune,* January 31, 2004. A concrete example of this attitude is how the United States reacted to a personal letter from Kim Jong-Il to George Bush in November 2002—it was ignored. See Donald Gregg and Don Oberdorfer, "Seize the Moment," *Washington Post,* June 22, 2005.

[13] The purported tug-of-war within the Bush administration between the engagement and pressure factions over North Korea policy has resulted in a policy that in form allows for talks, but limits the substance of the discussion. See Gertz, "State Confirms N. Korea Light-Water Reactor Talk."

[14] See a DPRK Foreign Ministry statement, dated February 10, 2005 (KCNA, February 11, 2005, "DPRK FM on Its Stand to Suspend Its Participation in Six Party Talks for Indefinite Period," at http://www.kcna.co.jp), and a DPRK Foreign Ministry memorandum, dated March 2, 2005 (KCNA, March 2, 2005, "DPRK FM Memorandum: DPRK To Return to Talks 'Only When' 'Conditions,' 'Just Cause,' at http://www.kcna.co.jp/index-e.htm (title is given as it appears in English translation). While official DPRK statements do not necessarily reflect the true perceptions of the North Korean leadership, these particular pronouncements are relatively high level and should be given a great deal of weight when evaluating the North Korean leadership's thinking.

[15] The North Korean position has varied from requiring the United States go first to one that advances the notion of a simultaneous or reciprocal step-by-step format similar to the arrangements reached in past agreements between the DPRK and the United States in 1994 and 1999.

[16] DPRK Foreign Ministry Spokesman on Denuclearization of Korea, KCNA, March 31, 2005, at http://www.kcna.co.jp (see April 1, 2005 archive materials).

[17] Joseph Kahn and David E. Sanger, "U.S. Korean Deal on Arms Leaves Key Points Open," *New York Times,* September 20, 2005; and Steven R. Weisman, "U.S. Says North Korean Demand for Reactor Won't Derail Accord," *New York Times,* September 21, 2005.

[18] Anne Gearan, "Bush Diplomacy Means Settling for Less," Associated Press, November 7, 2005 (from http://www.washingtonpost.com), and Steven R. Weisman, "U.S. Says North Korean Demand for Reactor Won't Derail Accord, *New York Times,* September 21, 2005 (cites former Clinton and Bush administration official, Charles L. Pritchard). Some may dismiss this North Korean demand for light-water reactors as simple posturing, but this difference of views arguably indicates that there is a larger disconnect—and a lack of true understanding—between the United States and North Korea about next steps.

[19] See James Brooke, "South Korea Pushes to Engage the North, Rejecting U.S. Notion of a Quarantine," *New York Times,* May 15, 2005 (South Korea

does not support policy of pressure). There are a number of problems with promoting regime change or collapse. Most prominent is the issue of "loose nukes." Under a collapse scenario, it would be critical for the United States to locate and secure immediately all nuclear weapons–related material and facilities—a daunting task since we have little information. If fissile material were to fall into the wrong hands, then we will have created a circumstance that as a high-priority policy matter the United States has been trying to avoid. See also Kenneth Lieberthal, "The Folly of Regime Change," Nautilus website, PFO 05-25A, March 22, 2005, for other problems related to regime change. See http://www.nautilus.org/fora/security/0525A_Liberthal.html.

[20] See Chris Buckley, "Rice Warns N. Korea Standoff Can't Last," *International Herald Tribune*, March 22, 2005. Secretary of State Rice reportedly stated that "everyone is aware there are other options in the international system."

[21] See Scott Snyder, *Negotiating on the Edge: North Korean Negotiating Behavior* (Washington, DC: United States Institute of Peace, 1999). Snyder lays out numerous examples of North Korean response to U.S. negotiation tactics.

[22] See *The Report of the Commission on the Intelligence Capabilities of the United States Regarding Weapons of Mass Destruction*, Overview and chapter 5 (part 2), March 31, 2005.

[23] Sig Hecker, Testimony before the Senate Committee on Foreign Relations, "Visit to the Yongbyon Nuclear Scientific Research Center in North Korea," January 21, 2004. There is no electrical grid to which the Yongbyon reactor can be hooked. Therefore, this makes earlier claims that the experimental reactor was the first stage of a larger civilian energy program—consisting of a larger 50 MW(e) reactor also at Yongbyon and a 200 MW(e) reactor at Taechon—unconvincing.

[24] Ibid.

[25] While there is little reference to "red line" as a stand-alone concept in academic literature, Alexander L. George, in *Avoiding War: Problems of Crisis Management* (Boulder, CO: Westview, 1991), outlines a specific defensive and nonmilitary strategy called "drawing a line." George states that by "drawing a line" a party indicates what action by an opponent would generate a strong response (p. 389). A closely related, if not identical, concept is that of an ultimatum: in response to an opponent crossing a "red line" or threatening to cross a "red line," a party issues specific demands or terms of compliance within a specific period of time under threat of punishment. Paul Gordon Lauren, "Coercive Diplomacy and Ultimata: Theory and Practice in History," in Alexander L. George and William E. Simons, eds., *The Limits of Coercive Diplomacy* (Boulder, CO: Westview, 1994), pp. 23–45.

[26] Proliferation experts suspected that North Korea at that time already had in its possession one to two bombs' worth of fissile material, surreptitiously reprocessed from spent fuel rods unloaded some time between 1989 and 1992. See Don Oberdorfer, *The Two Koreas* (Reading, MA: Addison-Wesley, 1997), pp. 267–71. The view in 1994 was that, with one or two nuclear weapons, the risk to U.S. security was limited (one weapon would be needed as part of a test, leaving only one device for actual use); however, if the number went up to six to eight, the number of weapons available for actual use would grow significantly.

This line was passed in early 2003—North Korea removed the 8,000 fuel rods held in storage since 1994. On May 11, 2005, North Korea announced that it just completely the removal of an additional set of 8,000 fuel rods. See James Brooke, "North Korea Says It Has Pulled Nuclear Rods from Reactor," *New York Times*, May 11, 2005.

[27] Ashton Carter and William J. Perry, *Preventive Defense* (Washington, DC: Brookings Institution Press, 1999), pp. 123–33.

[28] There are conceivably other definitions of "red line." Indeed, in researching this chapter, I was struck by the differences held by policymakers in different countries as to the meaning of "red line"—both as a concept and operationally when applied to North Korea. For example, some view "red line" as a point where the party drawing the line will punish the transgressor; however, this did not necessarily mean the use of military force, but instead the use of political or economic tools to exact punishment. Thus, it was not at all clear that "red line" marked an interest so grave as to justify the possible use of military force.

[29] If North Korea decides to break its 1999 moratorium on long-range missile tests, the test firing would most likely send reverberations throughout Asia and the United States. Though difficult to predict, it is possible that a North Korean missile test would be a repeat of its Taepodong-1, a three-stage, liquid- and solid propelled rocket or possibly even more provocative, a test of the Taepodong-2, a three-stage, liquid-propelled rocket, which would approach the capabilities of an intercontinental ballistic missile. The key inquiry must be whether the test somehow increases the capability of North Korea to mate a nuclear device with a missile and deliver it. See Joseph S. Bermudez Jr., "*A History of Ballistic Missile Development in the DPRK*" (Center for Nonproliferation Studies, Monterey Institute of International Studies, 1999); and David S. Cloud and David E. Sanger, "U.S. Aide Sees Nuclear Advance by North Korea," *New York Times*, April 29, 2005.

[30] If the North Koreans tested a nuclear device, the primary purpose would be to make sure the device works. Though not absolutely necessary, North Korea's choice to produce plutonium requires that it test. This is because the techniques of building an implosion-type nuclear weapon are difficult to perfect, and there would always be a degree of uncertainty as to whether the weapon was reliable or not. Though technically more difficult, the implosion-type weapon uses less nuclear material and produces a greater explosive yield. See Richard L. Garwin and Georges Charpak, *Megawatts and Megatons* (Chicago: University of Chicago Press, 2002), pp. 58–61. However, if successful, the test would confirm the viability of the weapon's design and be a significant military advance.

[31] If we assume that North Korea obtained its technical know-how from the A. Q. Khan network, is basing its enrichment on the Pakistani model, and has built the needed machinery, North Korea would have the capability of building as many as two to three Nagasaki implosion-type or one Hiroshima gun-type weapon every two years. What is most significant about the North's alleged HEU activities is that they permit North Korea to construct a gun-type device, which requires no testing and relatively less engineering and technical know-how. Therefore, with a gun-type nuclear weapon, North Korea for all intents and purposes has a fully operational nuclear weapon. See Chaim Braun and Christopher F. Chyba, "Proliferation Rings: New Changes to the Nuclear

Nonproliferation Regime," *International Security* 29, no. 2 (Fall 2004): 13, and footnotes 24 and 25; Selig Harrison, "Did North Korea Cheat?" *Foreign Affairs* 84, no. 1 (January/February 2005); and Richard Garwin, "HEU Done It," *Foreign Affairs* 84, no. 2 (March/April 2005).

[32] In a post-9/11 world, a North Korean sale of fissile material or a nuclear device to a third party, directly or indirectly to a terrorist group, is the nightmare scenario. If this were to occur, many feel it would be just a matter of time before a crude nuclear device found its way to the United States and exploded. Therefore, any sale or transfer of such material outside of North Korea would be deemed to be a direct threat to the U.S. military's primary mission to protect the U.S. homeland. So, while many are confident that the material is secure for the time being in North Korea, given the extreme economic hardship in the country, this may not be the case at some point in the future. See Carter, Perry, and Shalikashvili,"A Scary Thought."

[33] North Korea is currently producing enough fissile material for one weapon every year. If North Korea reopens and refurbishes Yongbyon's 50 MW(e) reactor and resumes construction of the 200 MW(e) Taechon reactor, the production of plutonium would jump significantly. But at some point, whether the total number grows to 20, 30, or more, this buildup in nuclear material could be deemed a severe threat to our national security for the same reasons that the reprocessing of the 8,000 fuel rods in 1994 were. The problem is how to determine at what number the threat becomes unacceptable—and whether the United States has enough intelligence information to even calculate with reasonable certainty this future stockpile.

[34] Again, these upper and lower boundaries take into account the three kinds of uncertainty. The first adjusts for a different threshold levels among policymakers themselves; in this case, "superhawks" could justify a red line at a relatively lower threshold level to trigger a strong U.S. military response than someone else for the same action. The second accounts for the possibility that a future red line may have a slightly different threshold value as time goes on—an act that is provocative today may be deemed less or more of a threat tomorrow, and thus the actual value of the threshold would be higher or lower than the average value represented by the solid red line. The third allows for shifts in intelligence analysis.

[35] The studies by George and others are primarily descriptive analyses of past events. I found one paper that used the George framework to forecast events; however, the author appears to use earlier criteria. See Daniel J. Orcutt, "Carrot, Stock or Sledgehammer: U.S. Policy Options for North Korean Nuclear Weapons," Naval Post Graduate School thesis, June 2004. This piece notwithstanding, it still makes sense to take advantage of George's meticulous research and apply it to the ongoing dispute between the United States and North Korea. There are certainly a number of policy analysts who believe pressure in varying circumstances on the North Korean regime will never work; however, it would be useful to employ the qualitative analysis in this chapter within the established empirical framework developed by George.

[36] Alexander L. George, "Introduction: The Limits of Coercive Diplomacy," in George and Simons, eds., *The Limits of Coercive Diplomacy,* p. 8.

[37] Alexander L. George, "Strategies for Crisis Management," in George, ed., *Avoiding War,* p. 384. For a discussion about theoretical differences between deterrence, compellance, and coercion, see Robert J. Art, "Introduction" in Robert J. Art and Patrick M. Cronin, eds., *The United States and Coercive Diplomacy* (Washington, DC: United States Institute of Peace, 2003), pp. 6–10.

[38] George, "Strategies for Crisis Management," in *Avoiding War,* p. 384.

[39] These seven cases are U.S. efforts to stop Japanese expansion in the late 1930s, the Laos crisis of 1961–62, the Cuban missile crisis of 1962, the bombing of North Vietnam in 1965, the struggle between the Reagan administration and Nicaragua in the early 1980s, events leading to the U.S. bombing of Libya in 1985, and finally U.S. efforts to roll back Iraq's invasion of Kuwait in 1990–91.

[40] These eight bases are Somalia 1992–94, Haiti 1994, North Korea 1994, Bosnia 1995, China 1996, Iraq 1990–98, Kosovo 1999, and terrorism 1993, 1998, and 2001. See Art and Cronin, eds., *The United States and Coercive Diplomacy.* In some cases, the editors find a confrontation between the United States and a particular country results in separate instances of coercive diplomacy.

[41] Alexander L. George and William E. Simons, "Findings and Conclusions," in George and Simons, eds., *"The Limits of Coercive Diplomacy,* p. 269.

[42] See Robert J. Art, "Coercive Diplomacy: What Do We Know?" in Art and Cronin, eds., *The United States and Coercive Diplomacy,* pp. 361–70. Art gives four theoretical factors for why coercive diplomacy is difficult as well as two contextual factors that, if present, make coercion difficult.

[43] George and Simons, "Findings and Conclusions," pp. 279–87. See also, Art, "Coercive Diplomacy,"" pp. 359–420.

[44] Ibid., p. 287. Robert Art in essence reaffirms the aforementioned George and Simons findings. He says, "in sum, the successful exercise of coercive diplomacy is built upon eight ingredients. Six of these enhance the likelihood of success, but they alone cannot produce it. . . . The target's fear of unacceptable escalation and the coercer's stronger will to prevail are essential if the gambit [coercive diplomacy] is to have some chance of succeeding. If the last two ingredients are unfavorable to the coercer, the gambit will fail, no matter how favorable the other six are" (Art, "Coercive Diplomacy," p. 374).

[45] Jentleson looks at usable military options, asymmetry of motivation, ongoing diplomacy, international legitimacy, and domestic support. See Bruce Jentleson, "The Reagan Administration Versus Nicaragua: The Limits of Type C Coercive Diplomacy," in George and Simons, eds., *The Limits of Coercive Diplomacy* , p. 176.

[46] Jentleson's criterion of usable military options appears to be a variation of whether the coercer's threat is credible and potent, and thus I do not use this factor. International legitimacy and domestic political support are important factors and are particularly relevant in the case of North Korea.

[47] George and Simons, "Findings and Conclusions," pp. 287–90.

[48] Jentleson, "The Reagan Administration Versus Nicaragua," p. 177, citing Alexander L. George, David K. Hall, and William E. Simons, *The Limits of Coercive Diplomacy: Laos, Cuba, and Vietnam* (Boston: Little, Brown, 1971), p. 219.

[49] Jentleson, "The Reagan Administration Versus Nicaragua," p. 177.

[50] George and Simons, "Findings and Conclusions," p. 285.

[51] Jentleson, "The Reagan Administration Versus Nicaragua," p. 176.

[52] George, *Avoiding War,* pp. 384–85.

[53] George and Simons, "Findings and Conclusions," p. 284.

[54] See Jentleson, "The Reagan Administration Versus Nicaragua," p. 178.

[55] Bruce W. Jentleson, "The Pretty Prudent Public: Post Post-Vietnam American Opinion on the Use of Force," *International Studies Quarterly* 36 (March 1992).

[56] Jentleson, "The Reagan Administration Versus Nicaragua," p. 178.

[57] George and Simons, "Findings and Conclusions," pp. 282–83.

[58] Ibid.

[59] Ibid.

[60] This is very different from the kind of coercive diplomacy initiated by the administration in May 2005. In response to unusual North Korean activity suggesting preparations for a test of a nuclear device, U.S. National Security Advisor Stephen Hadley warned North Korea not to test a nuclear device or else it would suffer some untold punishment. Here, the United States was engaging in classic Type A coercive diplomacy—it was trying to prevent North Korea from taking a specific action, that is, the test of a nuclear weapon. It is unclear whether North Korea will or will not test, and, if it does not, whether U.S. threats had any impact at all since some believe North Korean activity is a ruse. However, in either case (test or no test), so long as the United States and North Korea remain at odds over the North's nuclear weapons program, U.S. pressure tactics will inevitably increase, and it is these circumstances that this chapter examines. Judging from Hadley's remarks, the United States is unlikely to initiate military action in the case of a North Korean nuclear test. Instead, it will again likely take a measured approach—either in the form of UN sanctions or quarantine—which is classic coercive diplomatic action. If North Korea does not test, then the United States will once again focus on the six-party talks and diplomacy, which I argue will likely fail—which then leads us again to the use of coercive diplomacy. See David E. Sanger, "U.S. Is Warning North Koreans on Nuclear Test," *New York Times,* May 16, 2005.

[61] See George and Simons, "Findings and Conclusions," p. 292. An entire paper taking many more pages than this chapter could be devoted to applying George's theoretical framework to the current North Korean nuclear situation; however, the truncated analysis here should suffice.

[62] Since we are using the George framework in a predictive manner, circumstances could change to make this analysis more or less relevant. Nonetheless, I focus on what I believe will be the foundation for any descriptive examination that may be done when the current standoff is resolved.

[63] George and Simons, "Findings and Conclusions," p. 292.

[64] See DPRK Foreign Ministry statement, dated February 10, 2005 (KCNA), February 11, 2005, "DPRK FM on Its Stand to Suspend its Participation in Six-Party Talks for Indefinite Period," at http://www.kcna.co.jp), which says, "As we clarified more than once, we justly urged the U.S. to renounce its hostile policy toward the DPRK whose aim was to seek the latter's 'regime change' and switch its policy to that of peaceful co-existence between the two countries."

[65] DPRK Foreign Ministry memorandum, section 1, dated March 2, 2005 (KCNA, March 2, 2005, "DPRK FM Memorandum: DPRK To Return to Talks 'Only When"Conditions,"Just Cause,'" at http://www.kcna.co.jp/index-e.htm. Title is as it appears in English translation.

[66] During my private discussions with DPRK officials in the summer and fall of 2000 as a member of the U.S. government negotiating team, I noticed that the conversation always came back to what a new Bush administration policy would be. Glenn Kessler reports on the significance that the phrase "no hostile intent" has with the North Koreans. See Kessler, "Three Little Words Matter to N. Korea," *Washington Post,* February 22, 2005.

[67] Donald Gregg and Don Oberdorfer, "Seize the Moment," *Washington Post,* June 22, 2005.

[68] In October 2004, the United States Congress passed the North Korean Human Rights Act of 2004, which focused on human rights and humanitarian concerns. It authorized, but did not appropriate, $24 million annually over four years to "promote human rights and democracy, freedom of information, and assistance to North Koreans outside of North Korea" as well as encourage the U.S. Department of State to expedite applications for asylum from North Korean citizens as refugees. See Karin Lee, "The North Korean Human Rights Act and Other Congressional Agenda," Nautilus Institute website at http://www.nautilus.org/fora/security/0439A_lee.html. With the passage and signing of the act, North Korean official condemnation was quick —accusing the United States of using the money allocated pursuant to the law to "take part in activities to bring down the system in the DPRK." KCNA, "U.S. 'North Korean Human Rights Act' Flailed," October 4, 2004, at http://www.kcna.jp/index-e.htm (posted on October 5, 2004). In private meetings I attended in 2004, the North Koreans' intense concern over the act was very clear. See also Richard Lugar, "A Korean Catastrophe," *Washington Post,* July 17, 2003. Lugar implies that regime change may be the product of what was an earlier iteration of the act.

[69] Kessler, "Three Little Words."

[70] On March 31, 2003, President Bush announced the establishment of the Proliferation Security Initiative (PSI), which created a multicountry partnership to search airplanes and ships for illicit cargo related to illegal weapons and missiles. On June 15, 2003, 11 nations joined the initiative. A key focus for PSI has been North Korea.

The National Endowment for Democracy (NED) is funded by the U.S. Congress and has provided grants to South Korean–based groups that seek to promote human rights in North Korea. Critics of these groups have alleged that they seek to overthrow the North Korean regime. Sung Lee, "Walking the Tightrope: NGOs and North Korean Refugees in China," senior thesis, Stanford University, Spring 2005.

[71] See Anne Gearan, "Bush Diplomacy Means Settling for Less," The Associated Press, November 7, 2005 (reports that despite her tough rhetoric, Secretary of State Rice appears to be focusing on diplomacy during the second Bush term), and Associated Press, "North Korea Distrustful of U.S. Overture," *Washington Post,* May 14, 2005. North Korea discounts Rice's statements regarding recognition of sovereignty.

[72] See Jim Lobe (Inter Press Service), "Hawks Push Regime Change In North Korea," *Asia Times*, November 24, 2004, at http://www.atimes.com/atimes/Korea/FK24dg01.html. This article identifies influential proponents of regime change. See also op-eds by R. James Woolsey and Thomas G. McInerny, "The Next Korean War: Using the Military is an Option—Here's How It Can Be Done," *Wall Street Journal*, August 4, 2003; and Nicholas Eberstadt, "Tear Down This Tyranny," *Weekly Standard* 010, issue 11 (November 29, 2004).

[73] John Bolton, "A Dictatorship at the Crossroads," remarks before the East Asia Institute, Seoul, Korea, July 31, 2003. See http://www.state.gov/t/us/rm/23028.htm.

[74] Sanger, "Administration Divided over North Korea"; and Rennie, "Rumsfeld Calls for Regime Change in North Korea."

[75] Warren P. Strobel, "Vice President's Objection Blocked Planned North Korean Nuclear Talks," *Knight Ridder News*, December 20, 2003.

[76] Kessler, "Three Little Words."

[77] Jentleson, "The Reagan Administration Versus Nicaragua," p. 190.

[78] George and Simons, "Findings and Conclusions," p. 289.

[79] Ibid.

[80] For a more detailed description of *juche*, see the following: Kongdan Oh and Ralph Hassig, *North Korea Through the Looking Glass* (Washington, DC: Brookings Institution Press, 2000), pp. 12–40; and Bradley K. Martin, *Under the Loving Care of the Fatherly Leader: North Korea and the Kim Dynasty* (New York: St. Martin's Press, 2004), pp. 111, 123, 176–77.

[81] Other examples are "President Bush and President Roh reaffirmed that they will not tolerate nuclear weapons in North Korea" in Joint Statement between the United States of America and the Republic of Korea, May 14, 2003, at http://www.whitehouse.gov/news/releases/2003/05/20030514-17.html; and "President Bush and President Roh reconfirmed the principles agreed upon in their summit meeting in May, that they will not tolerate nuclear weapons in North Korea and that they are committed to a peaceful resolution of the issue," in Joint Statement between the United States of America and the Republic of Korea, October 20, 2003, at http://www.whitehouse.gov./news/releases2003/10/20031020_2.html.

[82] Remarks by the president, "President Speaks to U.S. Troops in Seoul," Osan Air Base, http://www.whitehouse.gov/news/releases/2002/02/20020221-6.html.

[83] Nicholas D. Kristoff, "N. Korea, 6, and Bush, 0," *New York Times*, April 26, 2005.

[84] There are some who argue that North Korea is following the path of Pakistan. Pakistan announced that it had conducted six nuclear tests in 1998; it suffered international condemnation, but in the end it suffered little else. Even in the wake of recent revelations concerning the broad scope and depth of A. Q. Khan's nuclear proliferation activities, consequences for the Pakistani government have been relatively light.

[85] Anthony Faiola, "Despite U.S. Attempts, N. Korea Anything But Isolated," *Washington Post*, May 12, 2005.

[86] See David E. Sanger, "Nuclear Reality: America Loses Bite," *New York Times*, February 20, 2005. Sanger discusses how conflicting U.S. action toward

Iran and North Korea has created confusion as to what is acceptable and alludes to the blurring of once clear "red lines."

[87] For a description of the security apparatus and the reward-punishment system of Kim Jong-Il as a form of management style, see Martin, *Under the Loving Care of the Fatherly Leader,* pp. 262–69 (security apparatus) and pp. 282–87 (management style).

[88] Art, "Coercive Diplomacy: What Do We Know?" p. 362.

[89] Jon B. Alterman, "Coercive Diplomacy against Iraq, 1990–98" in Art and Cronin, eds., *The United States and Coercive Diplomacy,* pp. 296–97.

[90] South Korean and Chinese officials in the past have also made this argument to me. There may be parallels in the way the Kim Jong-Il treats and rewards his subordinates to the way Saddam Hussein did. However, given the lack of intelligence and information generally, reaching firm conclusions is difficult.

[91] See Donald Macintyre, "Kim's War Machine," *Time International,* February 24, 2003. Macintyre makes the point with its formidable fighting force—with a 1.2-million-man army, a large submarine force, large special forces, biological and chemical weapons, and 800 short-, medium-, and longer-range missiles—North Korea has a force that cannot be discounted. However, most of its equipment is "outmoded . . . , some of it going back to the Cold War." See also Michael O'Hanlon, "Stopping a North Korean Invasion: Why Defending South Korea Is Easier Than the Pentagon Thinks," *International Security.* 22, no. 4 (Spring 1998): 135–70; and the chapter by Taik-young Hamm in this volume.

[92] Paul K. Huth, "Extended Deterrence and the Outbreak of War," *American Political Science Review* 82, no. 2 (June 1988): 427.

[93] William J. Perry, "Review of United States Policy Toward North Korea: Findings and Recommendations," October 12, 1999, pp. 6–7, at http://www.state.gov/www/regions/eap/99/991012_northkorea_rpt.html.

[94] William M. Drennan, "Nuclear Weapons and North Korea: Who's Coercing Whom?" in Art and Cronin, eds., *The United States and Coercive Diplomacy,* p. 194.

[95] For example, when the United States informed the North that the Agreed Framework was dead unless the North admitted to the nuclear program's existence and undertook to eliminate it, North Korea acted and did so forcefully—it admitted having a program (which it subsequently tried to retract) and quickly expelled International Atomic Energy Agency (IAEA) inspectors, removed all monitoring equipment at the Yongbyon nuclear plant, and started up reactor operations, all in response to a U.S. action to halt regular shipments of heavy fuel oil. Another example is the North Korea's recent reaction to President Bush's April 28, 2005, press conference comments about Kim Jong-Il. The North Koreans severely criticized the U.S. position on April 29 and fired a short-range missile into the Sea of Japan on April 30, 2005.

[96] Art, "Coercive Diplomacy: What Do We Know?" p. 369.

[97] Ibid., p. 370.

[98] "Paying the Price: The Mounting Costs of the Iraq War," *Factsheet,* Institute for Policy Studies, revised March 23, 2005. The Congressional Budget Office has estimated the cost to be $141.5 billion through 2004; the number of

troops deployed will be over 100,000 for quite some time; casualties are about 2,000 deaths with approximately 11,000 wounded.

[99] William E. Simons, "U.S. Coercive Pressure on North Vietnam" in George and Simons, eds., *The Limits of Coercive Diplomacy,* p. 136.

[100] Robert Marquand, "Sharp Divisions over North Korea," *Christian Science Monitor,* June 24, 2003.

[101] Based on conversations and interviews with South Korean academics and former government officials. See also Jay Solomon and David S. Cloud, "A Global Journal Report—Cold Front: A Split with Seoul Complicates Crisis over North Korea," *Wall Street Journal,* January 2, 2003.

[102] See David Shambaugh, "China and the Korean Peninsula: Playing for the Long-Term," working paper prepared for the Task Force on U.S. Korea Policy, sponsored by the Center of International Policy and the Center for East Asian Studies of the University of Chicago, Washington, DC, January 9, 2003.

[103] Alexandre Y. Mansourov, "Mercantilism and Neo-Imperialism in Russian Foreign Policy during President Putin's 2nd Term," *Korean Journal of Defense Analysis* 17, no. 1 (Spring 2005): 178–82.

[104] See Ryu Jin, "Roh Rejects Calls for 'Regime Change' in North Korea," *Korea Times,* December 6, 2004. See also Shambaugh, "China and the Korean Peninsula"; and James Clay Moltz, "Russian Policy on the North Korea Nuclear Crisis," paper prepared for the 13th annual International Security Conference of Sandia National Laboratories, April 23–25, 2003, at http://cns.miis.edu/research/korea/ruspol.htm.

[105] See Paul Kerr, "U.S. Allies Split on North Korea; Talks Stalled as Pyongyang Waits," *Arms Control Today* (December 2004), at http://www.armscontrol.org/act/2004_12/nk.asp.

[106] A senior Chinese Foreign Ministry official, Yang Xiyu, publicly criticized the Bush administration for its "lack of cooperation" and cited Mr. Bush's references to Kim Jong-Il as a "tyrant." Sanger, "U.S. Is Warning North Koreans on Nuclear Test." However, Mr. Yang may have been misquoted.

[107] For example, China and Russia in July of 2003 blocked a U.S. bid to get a United Nations Security Council resolution condemning Pyongyang's nuclear activities. See also, Brooke, "South Korea Pushes to Engage the North, Rejecting U.S. Notion of a Quarantine," (South Korea does not support policy of pressure); Joseph Kahn and David E. Sanger, "China Rules Out Using Sanctions on North Korea," *New York Times,* May 11, 2005 (China rules out applying economic or political sanctions to pressure North Korea to abandon its nuclear weapons program); David Shambaugh, "China and the Korean Peninsula," (Shambaugh analyzes Chinese interest as to why it is unlikely to support sanctions-based punitive policy against North Korea); Moltz, "Russian Policy on the North Korea Nuclear Crisis," (Moltz specifically mentions that a strong push for sanctions by the United States could move Russia closer to North Korea, China, and possibly South Korea).

[108] Kim Ki-tae, "Can NK-China Comradeship Survive?" *Korea Times,* July 4, 2003. Estimates about Chinese inputs vary, and skepticism with respect to all numbers is recommended. For example, some put the percentage of total oil needs supplied by China close to 90 percent. See also John J. Tkacik, "Getting

China to Support a Denuclearized North Korea," *Backgrounder* No. 1678, Heritage Foundation (August 25, 2003) citing Jong Hoon Kim, "Overview of DPRK's Energy Industry," *International Market Insight,* December 18, 2000; and John R. Bolton, press conference on U.S.-China Security Dialogue, Beijing, China, July 28, 2003 at http://www.state.gov/t/us/rm/22917.htm.

[109] Based on ROK Ministry of Unification inter-Korean cooperation figures as of February 2005. Economic engagement between the North and South continues full steam ahead at this point on various fronts, despite U.S. concerns. See Norimitsu Onishi, "Two Koreas Forge Economic Ties to Ease Tensions on Their Own," *New York Times,* February 8, 2005.

[110] Faiola, "Despite U.S. Attempts, N. Korea Anything But Isolated."

[111] Tim Zimmerman, "Coercive Diplomacy and Libya" in George and Simons, eds., *The Limits of Coercive Diplomacy,* p. 208. However, a good argument can be made that U.S. force did change Qaddafi's behavior even if the threat of force did not. Contrast the result of international efforts 20 years later: through the use of quiet diplomacy and engagement, the international community's other concern—Libya's WMD activity—appears have been halted.

[112] Ibid, p. 219.

[113] Brinkley, "China Balks at Pressing the North Koreans."

[114] Jentleson, "The Reagan Administration Versus Nicaragua," pp. 175–200. Cf. U.S. efforts in 1994 to drive out the ruling military junta in Haiti—thereby paving the way for the return of properly elected Jean-Bertrand Aristide—were ultimately successful, although Art and Cronin consider this a "borderline" success. Robert J. Art, "Introduction" in Art and Cronin, eds., *The United States and Coercive Diplomacy,* p. 15. Nonetheless, Robert A. Pastor states that "Haiti is a superb case study, not of how to combine diplomacy with force, but why it is so difficult to do so, particularly for a democracy." Robert A. Pastor, "The Delicate Balance between Coercion and Diplomacy: The Case of Haiti, 1994" in Art and Cronin, eds., *The United States and Coercive Diplomacy,* p. 120.

[115] North Korea has a reputation of going "right to the edge" and is known for brinksmanship in the course of high-stakes negotiations. See Snyder, *Negotiating on the Edge.*

[116] Possible sources of miscalculation: superhawks may be in charge of policy; something happening in Iran may have heightened U.S. sensitivity; or simply U.S. decision makers get bad intelligence.

[117] Thomas C. Schelling, *The Strategy of Conflict* (Cambridge, MA: Harvard University Press, 1963), p. 188. See also Scott D. Sagan, "Perils of Proliferation: Organization Theory, Deterrence Theory, and the Spread of Nuclear Weapons, *International Security* 18, no. 4 (Spring 1994): 93–95. Though writing specifically about nuclear weapons and deterrence, Sagan points out the organizational problems of maintaining operational control.

[118] The United States, South Korea, and North Korea have had a long history without a breakdown, and this is certainly a good thing. However, war by accident might be possible when tensions have spiked and both sides are mobilized and on a war footing.

[119] At some point, the United States may very well decide that some unspecified amount of fissile material or number of nuclear devices is unacceptable. In this

circumstance, the United States may undertake to engage in coercive diplomacy to prevent North Korea from crossing this line. If it does so, it again increases the risk that it may have to use military force to enforce this.

[120] See *The Report of the Commission on the Intelligence Capabilities of the United States Regarding Weapons of Mass Destruction*, Overview and chap. 5 (part 2), March 31, 2005.

[121] Scott Sagan alludes to this problem in his analysis of events leading to the Japanese attack on Pearl Harbor. While an economic embargo is generally thought to be a less extreme form of pressure, it was a powerful lever against Japan because the country was so dependent on trade and oil. U.S. demands on Japan to withdraw its troops from China also became an issue of "face" to the Japanese leadership. Finally, U.S. hostility led Japan's leadership to fear the United States would not keep its commitment to sell oil to Japan even if it complied with Washington's demands. Scott Sagan, "From Deterrence to Coercion to War: The Road to Pear Harbor," in George and Simons, eds., *The Limits of Coercive Diplomacy*, p. 84.

[122] Many security experts allude to this circumstance—if North Korea is faced with a steady strangulation of its economic and therefore its military/deterrent capability to the point that it knows at some time in the future it will have no defensive capacity, it may decide the best chance for its survival is to attack sooner, when it has the most strength, rather than later. This is not so dissimilar to the situation faced by Japan in World War II. Journalist Bradley Martin also voices the same concerns. See Martin, *Under the Loving Care of the Fatherly Leader*, p. 635.

[123] Alexander George, "The Cuban Missile Crisis" in George and Simons, eds., *The Limits of Coercive Diplomacy*, p. 124.

[124] In the case of Somalia, the first phase was a success because it sought to compel faction leaders to "stop interfering with relief supplies and humanitarian assistance." The second phase failed because the objective was to establish political stability by getting rid of warlord Mohammed Farah Aideed. See Nora Bensahel, "Humanitarian Relief and Nation Building in Somalia" in Art and Cronin, eds., *The United States and Coercive Diplomacy*, p. 45.

[125] Arguably, this adjustment to U.S. policy may have taken place during the summer 2005 round of six-party talks, which led to the statement of general principles. See Anne Gearan, "Bush Diplomacy Means Settling for Less."

[126] It is not at all clear that the North Korean leadership is willing to give up its nuclear weapons program and that negotiations will succeed from an American policy perspective. However, at the very least, properly conducted negotiations under the right circumstances are a means to test the true nature of North Korea's intent—which to this point is still unknown. In the end, the United States may not like what it finds; strong measures may indeed be necessary. But to prejudge North Korea's intent and not test operating assumptions would amount to giving up the opportunity to resolve the nuclear impasse without confrontation.

[127] Art, "Coercive Diplomacy: What Do We Know?" pp. 408–9.

CONTRIBUTORS

William Brown is an economist and senior research analyst with CENTRA Technology, Inc. of Arlington, Virginia, where he specializes in East Asian economics. Brown manages a program of specialized seminars for the company's national security related sponsors and undertakes research on the Korean and Chinese economies. In addition, he is a member of the adjunct faculty of George Mason University's graduate School of Public Policy, where he teaches courses on Asian economic development and international trade and investment. Brown has extensive experience as an economic analyst in the U.S. government, having worked in the Chief Economist's Office of the Commerce Department, as Deputy National Intelligence Officer for Economics in the National Intelligence Council, and as an economic analyst in the CIA's Office of Economic Research, where he focused his research on the North Korean and Chinese economies. Brown served for two years in the U.S. Embassy in Seoul and has traveled extensively in the region, including a recent trip across the DMZ into North Korea.

Brown writes occasionally for the *Chosun Ilbo* in Seoul and speaks on Korean and Chinese issues to a number of Asian and U.S. audiences. He holds an M.A. in Economics from Washington University in St. Louis, with most of his Ph.D. coursework completed, and a B.A. in International Studies from Rhodes College in Memphis, Tennessee. Brown grew up in Kwangju, South Korea, as the son and grandson of Presbyterian missionaries in Korea, and in China. He speaks and reads some Korean and Chinese.

Robert Carlin has served as senior policy advisor at the Korean Peninsula Economic Development Organization (KEDO) since 2003. As chief of the Northeast Asia Division of the State Department's Bureau of Intelligence Research and senior advisor to the U.S. special ambassador on four-party talks, he attended virtually all significant U.S.-DPRK negotiations from 1993–2000. From 1971–1989, Carlin was an analyst in the Central Intelligence Agency.

Yong Sueng Dong is a senior researcher at Samsung Economic Research Institute (SERI) and a team leader in economic securities at SERI. Dong has been a member of the advisory committee of the National Security

Council and a member of policy advisory committee of the Ministry of Unification. His publications include *North Korea under Kim Jong-Il* (1997), and *Guidelines for Economic Cooperation between South Korea and North Korea* (2001).

Taik-young Hamm is a professor at Kyungnam University. Previously he was director, Institute for Far Eastern Studies, Kyungnam University. His research interests include international politics and North Korean politics. Hamm has published *Arming the Two Koreas: Stake, Capital and Military Power* (1999), and "North-South Korean Reconciliation and the Security on the Korean Peninsula," in *Asian Perspective* (2001). He received his Ph.D. from the University of Michigan, where he completed a dissertation on the state and armament of the two Koreas.

David Hawk is a prominent human rights investigator and advocate. Hawk worked for the United Nations directing the Cambodia Office of the UN High Commissioner for Human Rights in 1996 and 1997. In the early and middle 1980s, Hawk investigated and analyzed the genocide in Cambodia, publishing groundbreaking Khmer Rouge prisoner/execution photographs and original arrest and execution records, in association with the Columbia University Center for the Study of Human Rights. In the late 1980s and early 1990s, Hawk established and directed the Cambodia Documentation Commission (New York), which sought an international tribunal for the Khmer Rouge leadership, and human rights provisions and mechanisms in the 1991 Cambodia peace treaty and the UN transitional peacekeeping operation.

In August 1994 Hawk traveled to Rwanda for the U.S. Committee for Refugees to investigate that nation's massacres, and in 1995 returned to Kigali on a mission for Amnesty International. More recently, Hawk has consulted for the Landmine Survivors Network on U.S. landmine policy and humanitarian assistance projects for amputees in Cambodia and Vietnam. From 2001 to 2003, Hawk was a Brandeis University Fellow in Human Rights, Intervention, and International Law. A former executive director of Amnesty International/USA, he has served on the board of directors of AIUSA and Human Rights Watch/Asia.

In 2003, Hawk researched and authored a landmark study on the DPRK, *Hidden Gulag: Exposing North Korea's Prison Camps—Prisoners' Testimonies and Satellite Photographs for the U.S. Committee on Human Rights in North Korea. Hidden Gulag* has been translated into Korean and Japanese and published in Seoul and Tokyo. Hawk is presently directing a research project on freedom of thought, conscience, religion, and belief in the DPRK for the U.S. Commission on International Religious Freedom.

Kim Ki-Sik is the general secretary of People's Solidarity for Participatory Democracy (PSPD), which he founded in 1994. PSPD is a civil organization dedicated to promoting justice and human rights in Korean society through the participation of the people.

Haksoon Paik is currently the director of the Inter-Korean Relations Studies Program and the director of the Center for North Korean Studies at the Sejong Institute in Korea. He received his Ph.D. in political science from the University of Pennsylvania in 1993 and was a postdoctoral fellow at Harvard University from 1996 to 1997.

Paik has written extensively on North Korean politics, inter-Korean relations, Korean unification, and North Korea-U.S. relations, including the North Korean nuclear issue. He is co-author of *North Korea's National Strategy* (2003) (in Korean), *Survival Strategy of the Kim Jong-Il Regime* (2003) (in Korean), and *North Korean Party and State Institutions in the Kim Jong-Il Era* (2000) (in Korean), co-author and co-editor of *International Ramifications of the North Korean Problem* (1999) (in Korean), and co-author and editor of *The Structure and Strategy of North and South Korea's Unification Diplomacy* (1997) (in Korean).

Paik's published articles and book chapters include "Re-alignment of the ROK-U.S. Alliance and Overcoming Domestic Conflicts in South Korea" (2004); "Strategy of Korean Unification Diplomacy for 2020" (forthcoming) (in Korean); "Changing Dynamics of the North Korean System" (forthcoming); "Re-alignment of the ROK-U.S. Alliance and Overcoming Domestic Conflicts in South Korea" (2004) (in Korean),"Steering between Red Lines: A South Korean View" (2003); "The Future of the Korean Peninsula Energy Development Organization (KEDO)" (2003); "Changes in the U.S.-North Korean Relations during the Bush Administration and the North Korean Nuclear Problem" (2003) (in Korean); "The Vietnamese Experience of Reform and Opening and North Korea's Choice" (2003) (in Korean); "Assessment of the Sunshine Policy: A Korean Perspective" (2002); "North Korea's Opening and Reform and Prospects for De-socialization" (2001) (in Korean); "U.S. Policy toward North Korea and South Korea's Policy Options" (2001) (in Korean); "South Korea's Sunshine Policy: Achievements, Hurdles, and Prospects" (2000); "The Berlin Declaration and the Perry Report: Opening a New Era in North Korea-U.S. Relations" (1999); and "The Korean Peninsula Energy Development Organization (KEDO): Interests, Institutions, and Outcomes" (1999).

Paik is currently a policy advisor to South Korea's Ministry of Unification, while heading the Ministry's Policy Evaluation Committee. He serves as policy advisor to the Ministry of Foreign Affairs and Trade, and the Office of Inter-Korean Exchanges and Cooperation for the Korean Broadcasting System (KBS). He is also a news commentator for KBS, and chairman of the Special Committee on Promoting Korea-U.S. Academic Exchanges and Cooperation of Korean Political Science Association.

Henry S. Rowen is a senior fellow at the Hoover Institution, a professor of Public Policy and Management emeritus at the Stanford University's Graduate School of Business and a senior fellow emeritus of the Walter H. Shorenstein Asia-Pacific Research Center (Shorenstein APARC) at the Freeman Spogli Institute for International Studies at Stanford University. Rowen is an expert on international security, economic development, and high-tech industries in the United States and Asia. His current research focuses on the rise of Asia in high technologies.

In 2004–05, Rowen served on the Presidential Commission on the Intelligence of the United States Regarding Weapons of Mass Destruction. From 2001–04, he served on the Secretary of Defense Policy Advisory Board. Rowen was Assistant Secretary of Defense for International Security Affairs in the U.S. Department of Defense from 1989 to 1991. He was also chairman of the National Intelligence Council from 1981 to 1983. Rowen served as president of the RAND Corporation from 1967 to 1972 and was assistant director, U.S. Bureau of the Budget, from 1965 to 1966.

Rowen's most recent work is co-editing *Making IT: The Rise of Asia in High Tech* (forthcoming from Stanford University Press, 2006). He co-edited *The Silicon Valley Edge: A Habitat for Innovation and Entrepreneurship* (2000); *Behind East Asian Growth: The Political and Social Foundations of Prosperity* (1998); and *Defense Conversion, Economic Reform, and the Outlook for the Russian and Ukrainian Economies* (1994), which he co-edited with Hoover fellow Charles Wolf and Jeanne Zlotnick. Among his articles are "Kim Jong-Il Must Go," *Policy Review* (2003); "The Short March: China's Road to Democracy," *National Interest* (1996); "Inchon in the Desert: My Rejected Plan," *National Interest* (1995); "The Tide underneath the 'Third Wave,'" *Journal of Democracy* (1995); and "Vietnam Made Him," *National Interest* (1995/96).

Born in Boston, Massachusetts, in 1925, Rowen earned a bachelor's degree in industrial management from the Massachusetts Institute of Technology in 1949 and a master's in economics from Oxford University in 1955.

Gi-Wook Shin is senior fellow at the Freeman Spogli Institute for International Studies and associate professor of sociology at Stanford University. He also directs the Walter H. Shorenstein Asia-Pacific Research Center (Shorenstein APARC), and Stanford's Korean Studies Program. A historical-comparative sociologist, Shin's research has concentrated on areas of social movements, nationalism, and development.

Before coming to Stanford, Shin taught at the University of Iowa and the University of California, Los Angeles (UCLA). He served as acting director of the UCLA Center for Korean Studies, as a guest columnist for the U.S. edition of the *Korea Central Daily,* and on other councils and advisory boards in the United States and Korea. Shin received his B.A. from Yonsei University in Korea, and his M.A. and Ph.D. from the University of Washington.

Shin recently completed a book on the origins and politics of ethnic nationalism in Korea, forthcoming from Stanford University Press in 2006. His previous book dealt with the Kwangju uprising that occurred in South Korea in May 1980. Shin's other recent publications include, with Michael Robinson, *Colonial Modernity in Korea* (1999); "The Politics of Ethnic Nationalism in Divided Korea" (with Jim Freda and Gihong Yi) in *Nations and Nationalism* (1999); "Agrarian Conflict and the Origins of Korean Capitalism" in the *American Journal of Sociology* (1998); and "Social Crisis in Korea" (with Kyung Sup Chang) in *Korea Briefing 1997–1999,* edited by Katy Oh (1999). Shin lectures widely and gives seminars on various issues, ranging from Korean nationalism and politics to Korean-American relations.

Scott Snyder is a senior associate in the International Relations program of the Asia Foundation and Pacific Forum CSIS, and is based in Washington, DC. He spent four years in Seoul as Korea Representative of the Asia Foundation during 2000–04. Previously, he served as a program officer in the Research and Studies Program of the U.S. Institute of Peace, and as acting director of the Asia Society's Contemporary Affairs Program. He has recently edited, with L. Gordon Flake, a study titled *Paved With Good Intentions: The NGO Experience in North Korea* (2003), and is author of *Negotiating on the Edge: North Korean Negotiating Behavior* (1999).

Snyder received his B.A. from Rice University and an M.A. from the Regional Studies East Asia Program at Harvard University. He was the recipient of an Abe Fellowship, administered by the Social Sciences Research Council, in 1998–99, and was a Thomas G. Watson Fellow at Yonsei University in South Korea in 1987–88.

Philip W. Yun is currently vice president for Resource Development at The Asia Foundation, based in San Francisco. Prior to joining The Asia Foundation, Yun was a Pantech Scholar in Korean Studies at the Walter H. Shorenstein Asia-Pacific Research Center in the Freeman Spogli Institute for International Studies at Stanford University. At Stanford, his research focused on the economic and political future of Northeast Asia. From 2001 to 2004, Yun was vice president and assistant to the chairman of H&Q Asia Pacific, a premier U.S. private equity firm investing in Asia. From 1994 to 2001, Yun served as an official at the United States Department of State, serving as a senior advisor to two Assistant Secretaries of State, as a deputy to the head U.S. delegate to the four-party Korea peace talks and as a senior policy advisor to the U.S. Coordinator for North Korea Policy.

Prior to government service, Yun practiced law at the firms of Pillsbury Madison & Sutro in San Francisco and Garvey Schubert & Barer in Seattle, and was a foreign legal consultant in Seoul, Korea. Yun attended Brown University and the Columbia School of Law. He graduated with an A.B. in mathematical economics (magna cum laude and phi beta kappa) and was a Fulbright Scholar to Korea. He is on the board of directors of the Ploughshares Fund and a member of the Council on Foreign Relations and the Pacific Council on International Policy.

RECENT PUBLICATIONS OF THE WALTER H. SHORENSTEIN ASIA-PACIFIC RESEARCH CENTER

Monographs
(distributed by the Brookings Institution Press)

Jongryn Mo and Daniel I. Okimoto, eds. *From Crisis to Opportunity: Financial Globalization and East Asian Capitalism.* Stanford, Walter H. Shorenstein Asia-Pacific Research Center, 2006.

Michael H. Armacost and Daniel I. Okimoto, eds. *The Future of America's Alliances in Northeast Asia.* Stanford, Walter H. Shorenstein Asia-Pacific Research Center, 2004.

Henry S. Rowen and Sangmok Suh, eds. *To the Brink of Peace: New Challenges in Inter-Korean Economic Cooperation and Integration.* Stanford, Walter H. Shorenstein Asia-Pacific Research Center, 2001.

Studies of the Walter H. Shorenstein Asia-Pacific Research Center
(published with Stanford University Press)

Rafiq Dossani and Henry S. Rowen, eds. *Prospects for Peace in South Asia.* Stanford, Stanford University Press, 2005.

Henry S. Rowen, Marguerite Gong Hancock, and William F. Miller, eds. *Making IT: The Rise of Asia in High Tech.* Stanford, Stanford University Press, forthcoming Spring 2006.

Gi-Wook Shin. *Ethnic Nationalism in Korea: Genealogy, Politics, and Legacy.* Stanford, Stanford University Press, forthcoming Spring 2006.

Andrew Walder, Joseph Esherick, and Paul Pickowicz, eds. *The Chinese Cultural Revolution as History.* Stanford, Stanford University Press, forthcoming Spring 2006.